A Tour in Chuong
Thien Province

A Tour in Chuong Thien Province

A U.S. Army Lieutenant with MACV Advisory Team 73 in the Mekong Delta, 1969–1970

John S. Raschke
Colonel US Army Retired

McFarland & Company, Inc., Publishers
Jefferson, North Carolina

LIBRARY OF CONGRESS CATALOGUING-IN-PUBLICATION DATA

Names: Raschke, John S., 1947– author.
Title: A tour in Chuong Thien Province : a U.S. Army lieutenant with MACV Advisory Team 73 in the Mekong Delta, 1969-1970 / John S. Raschke, Colonel US Army Retired.
Description: Jefferson, North Carolina : McFarland & Company, Inc., Publishers, 2022 | Includes bibliographical references and index.
Identifiers: LCCN 2022042818 | ISBN 9781476689081 (paperback : acid free paper) ∞ ISBN 9781476646817 (ebook)
Subjects: LCSH: Raschke, John S., 1947- | United States. Military Assistance Command, Vietnam. Advisory Team 73. | Vietnam War, 1961-1975—Personal narratives, American. | Military assistance, American—Vietnam (Republic)—Vị Thanh. | Vietnam War, 1961-1975—Campaigns—Vietnam (Republic)—Vị Thanh. | United States. Army—Officers—Biography. | BISAC: HISTORY / Wars & Conflicts / Vietnam War
Classification: LCC DS559.5 R366 2022 | DDC 959.704/38 [B]—dc23/eng/20220907
LC record available at https://lccn.loc.gov/2022042818

BRITISH LIBRARY CATALOGUING DATA ARE AVAILABLE

ISBN (print) 978-1-4766-8908-1
ISBN (ebook) 978-1-4766-4681-7

© 2022 John S. Raschke. All rights reserved

No part of this book may be reproduced or transmitted in any form or by any means, electronic or mechanical, including photocopying or recording, or by any information storage and retrieval system, without permission in writing from the publisher.

Front cover: Second Lieutenant John S. Raschke, patches and medals (author's collection)

Printed in the United States of America

*McFarland & Company, Inc., Publishers
Box 611, Jefferson, North Carolina 28640
www.mcfarlandpub.com*

This book is dedicated to people close to my heart:
My family, all my military and civilian brothers who served
in Chuong Thien province, and my Vietnamese comrades.

Acknowledgments

I first want to thank my wife, Jane, for her patience during the time I took to write this book. She, too, spent many hours in working on this project. I especially applaud her mastery in editing my memories and in helping to portray them in a coherent manner. Without her help the contents of this book would probably be little more than military gibberish.

Then, too, I would like to thank George "Jug" Eastman, Dave Nickinovich, Bob Noonan, and Harvey Weiner for their encouragement and their help in refreshing my memory of certain events.

A special thanks to George "Jug" Eastman, Gene Griffiths, Dave Nickinovich, Bob Noonan, Larry Hickey, Frank Perra, Harvey Weiner, Chauvin Wilkinson, and Mal Zellefrow for allowing me the use of their pictures contained in this book.

Table of Contents

Acknowledgments — vi
Preface — 1
Introduction — 3

Chapter 1. Getting Ready — 5
Chapter 2. On My Way — 13
Chapter 3. A Place Called Vi Thanh — 19
Chapter 4. New Guy with 362 and a Wake-up — 31
Chapter 5. Men Like Me in Jungle Fatigues — 36
Chapter 6. Fumbling Around in the Dark — 43
Chapter 7. Slogging Around in the Rice Paddies — 48
Chapter 8. The First Weekend in September — 55
Chapter 9. Routine, Money, and Morale — 68
Chapter 10. Mostly Blowing Stuff Up — 84
Chapter 11. Soldiers, Units, and Friends — 95
Chapter 12. Command and Control (C&C) and Radios — 103
Chapter 13. Holidays 1969 — 106
Chapter 14. An, Saigon, and Shopping — 109
Chapter 15. The Dry Season — 114
Chapter 16. Grenades and Airplanes — 117

Chapter 17.	Tet and Rest and Relaxation	123
Chapter 18.	Pride, Volunteering, and Annoyances	127
Chapter 19.	Food and Customs	135
Chapter 20.	Night Flight into Sickness	140
Chapter 21.	Something Funny or Frustrating Just Happened	146
Chapter 22.	Getting Close	152
Chapter 23.	The End and a Beginning	158

Epilogue	165
Those in This Book	177
Glossary	185
Chapter Notes	207
Works Cited	225
Index	229

Preface

On September 14, 2017, I was sitting on the stage of the Abraham Lincoln Presidential Museum as a member of a five-person panel. The panel consisted of people affected by the Vietnam War. This panel included a former army nurse who served in Vietnam, a Vietnamese "boat person" who left Vietnam at age seven and was now an American citizen and medical doctor, a Vietnam war protester, the moderator, and me. The panel and audience of several hundred were gathered in anticipation of Ken Burns's documentary on the Vietnam War, which was premiering the following Sunday—a preview of the film was shown to set the stage for our discussions.

It was during the question and answer period of the evening that it occurred to me that many people knew so little about this time in our nation's history. It was not that I could fill in the details for why and how the war was fought at a strategic level, for I saw little of that. What I could do was relate my experiences, hopefully in a way to let others see what life was like for me and others who served as military advisors. My story is one shared by countless other advisors of all branches of the services. We had a noble mission but somehow that was not enough. Today as I write this story I cannot accept that we advisors failed.

My recollections in this book are based on notes I took at the time and events as I remember them. All events and interactions described are real. Sadly though, after 50+ years, I lost contact with some past teammates whose portrayals are significant to my story. These lost teammates, whether they have passed on or may still be living, I have given fictitious names out of respect for their privacy. Where I have used a pseudonym for these lost teammates, I indicate the fictitious name with an asterisk at its first use. All others mentioned herein are real and have consented to use of their name.

I especially hope my family will better understand my simple contribution to this country and the country of Vietnam. Though I was young, idealistic, and perhaps sometimes naïve, I am proud of my Vietnam service and consider it to have been one of the more enriching periods of my life.

Introduction

It was 1968, a year that was to be the deadliest one for U.S. forces fighting in Vietnam, as I, a 20-year-old boy, was thrust into a man's world. On August 31 I received a commission as an army second lieutenant and was to embark on a three-year tour of duty that would include, beginning a year later, 10½ months serving as an advisor in Vietnam. This book is a narrative of a portion of that journey—my preparation for and service in Chuong Thien province.

I learned early on in my military career that the adage of "don't volunteer for nothin'" was guidance I could not follow. I volunteered for Officer Candidate School, for service in Vietnam with a prior stop at the army's Advisor's and Vietnamese Language School, and for many other duties during my time in Vietnam. In-country, I voluntarily went on numerous combat missions, acted as a demolition specialist, served as a funds custodian, and accompanied medical evacuation helicopters, serving as an interpreter between the aircrew and the Vietnamese ground forces. Volunteering for these duties became my way of coping with the boredom I sometimes encountered in army life.

As a young officer I had a close relationship with those I was advising as well as the small group of American military and civilian advisors who lived and served in one of the least pacified of Vietnam's 44 provinces. My story captures the thoughts and events as seen through the eyes of a young army lieutenant. It deals with a range of emotions and experiences, from the mundane to the inquisitive, the hilarious to the deadly. I have purposely gone into great detail to portray people, places, and things so the reader can better understand what advisors really did in Vietnam. In total, this book offers a unique perspective of service not previously seen in other books written about the Vietnam conflict. This is my story.

Chapter 1

Getting Ready

It was a hot, sunny afternoon in late June 1970 at the Moline, Illinois, airport. As one of the last to exit my seat, I found myself at the top of the stairs that had been pushed up to the airplane. I stood there at the landing wearing my khaki uniform adorned with a Combat Infantryman's Badge. Squinting in the bright sunshine, I was transfixed by the color and beauty of the Midwest as I was taking in the sounds and smells of everything around me. Slowly, I descended the stairs in a near hypnotic trance, not believing I was finally home. Then, as soon as I stepped on the tarmac, my legs felt like Jell-O and I was overwhelmed with emotions. Simultaneously, I felt confused, incredibly weak, and torn between wanting to shout for joy, cry, or collapse into a fetal ball. My world was in slow motion and everything seemed surreal. Struggling to put one foot in front of the other as I headed to the baggage claim area, I wondered, how did I ever come to this point?

It began like this:

At slightly after 10:30 a.m. on a muggy Friday, August 30, 1968, at Fort Belvoir, Virginia, I, a 20-year-old kid, and 52 other men, mostly in their mid-twenties, were squirming in our seats in Wallace Theater. We had reached the end of our 23-week ordeal called Engineer Officer Candidate School (OCS)[1] and we could hardly contain our excitement. As I was half listening to our guest speaker (Major General Patrick F. Cassidy, chief of army personnel operations) my thoughts were of what I had just been through, my family members in attendance, and how did I end up here? On this last matter, I reflected.

In 1966, like most other 18-year-olds, I was keenly aware that both the draft and Vietnam were gobbling up men at an alarming rate. I would surely receive my personalized "greetings" from Uncle Sam in the form of a draft notice any day. As I thought about this reality, I assessed myself. As a kid I had been raised on John Wayne movies and the TV show *Combat*, becoming fascinated with history and the military. Adding to my patriotic bent, the 100th anniversary of the Civil War had been widely celebrated during my impressionable teenage years. Then, too, I did not see much of a future as a decal applicator in the paint department at International Harvester's Farmall Plant in Rock Island, Illinois, where I had worked for the last year. In October 1966, I decided to cut the best deal I could with the Department of Defense. Motivated to make the most of my time in the military, I went to an army recruiter and told him I wanted to be trained in something that would help me get a good job once I reentered the civilian world. I enlisted in the army, believing I was going to become an X-ray technician.

During my February–April 1967 basic training at Fort Campbell, Kentucky, I was told I was among a handful of trainees in my company whose test scores qualified them for OCS. As such, I was required to interview with the company commander. On the appointed date I listened to my commander's mandatory spiel, but in the end told him I was not interested in OCS, since I had enlisted in the army to become an X-ray tech. In late April I graduated from basic training and eagerly looked forward to my Advanced Individual Training (AIT) at Fort Sam Houston in San Antonio, Texas.

Upon arrival at "Fort Sam" (as it was called in military jargon), I was stunned when the in-processing personnel specialist showed and explained my enlistment contract to me. He told me my recruiter had misled me and I was "coded" to become a combat medic, not an X-ray technician. Against my protestations, I entered medical specialist training. It happened that my recruiter, like other recruiters at the time, had sought to fill his quota without regard to my own preference. Although I learned a lot, enjoyed the 10-week combat medic training course, and received training that was to be of lifelong benefit, I wanted a marketable skill or something from the army to prepare me for my post–army civilian life. Thus far, it looked like I had failed.

It was toward the end of my medical specialist training that I decided to pursue the OCS option mentioned to me in basic training. As required, I submitted the necessary forms in triplicate, got the necessary recommendations from my chain of command, and was interviewed by a board of officers. Deemed qualified to attend OCS, I spent an additional six months at Fort Sam in leadership roles as an acting corporal and later sergeant. In late February 1968 I finally received orders to report to Fort Belvoir to attend Engineer OCS.

When I reported in at Fort Belvoir in early March 1968, I had absolutely no idea the most difficult and self-revealing six months of my life were about to begin. As I was to find out, the upcoming 23 weeks were to be punctuated by food and sleep deprivation, near constant "attention" by TAC[2] officers and upperclassmen, running everywhere, more push-ups than one can imagine, stress galore, very basic engineering classes, and constantly being chided by my fellow candidates for being the youngest member of my class. This all said, OCS allowed me to see my strengths and limitations while recognizing my unlimited potential. Contrary to what I was led to believe by my father, I proved to myself I had worth!

As my mind brought me back to Wallace Theater, I realized I had made it. Now, I just wished those words of congratulation and inspiration from the general would end—and soon! Seconds were hours and I could hardly stand it. Mercifully, the general's speech was finally over and the Regimental S-1 (personnel officer) said, "Officer Candidates of Class 516-A, please stand, raise your right hands, and repeat after me." In unison, we repeated the words we had struggled so long and hard to hear and recite:

> I [state your full name] having been appointed an officer in the Army of the United States in the grade of Second Lieutenant do solemnly swear or affirm that I will support and defend the Constitution of the United States against all enemies, foreign and domestic; that I will bear true faith and allegiance to the same; that I take this obligation freely without any mental reservation of purpose of evasion; and that I will well and faithfully discharge the duties of the office upon which I am about to enter, so help me God.[3]

There, about 40 seconds after beginning the oath, I became one of the newest Corps of Engineers second lieutenants in the United States Army. Despite our new exalted status in life, my classmates and I had to remain standing at our seats for the benediction. With the words "Class 516 Alpha, you are dismissed" there arose the hardy shouts of joy rising from 53 throats and the customary tossing of caps in the air. It seemed like we nearly trampled one another as we rushed toward the theater exits to have loved ones pin on our new shiny gold bars.

As I entered a brand-new world, I was overcome with emotion as I saw my mother, teary-eyed while beaming with pride and joy. She, my fiancée, and my older sister and her husband were there to celebrate this day with me. Composing myself, my thoughts were of collecting my gear from the barracks, getting off Fort Belvoir as fast as I could, and heading to nearby Washington, D.C., to relax in the city. The next day I began a 15-day leave back in the Quad Cities[4] by way of Washington National and O'Hare airports to Moline. The army would have to wait for my services as I was simply too consumed with seeing family, having fun, and recovering from OCS to care about anything else.

My leave was refreshing, as I was able to sleep beyond 5:00 a.m. and I thoroughly enjoyed my unstructured days. While on leave I realized I hadn't kept up with current events, nor had I heard any of the new popular songs during my time in OCS.[5] I was shocked at the former and tried to catch up with the latter. But as with all military leaves, time sped by and it ended far too soon. My father, with whom I had always had a strained relationship, helped me negotiate the purchase of a new 1968 Camaro a day or two before my leave ended. My leave over, with a new car and new adventure in front of me, I felt on top of the world as I drove nonstop the 800+ miles from Geneseo, Illinois, to Fort Belvoir. I was back at Fort Belvoir to attend an advanced engineer school. My ultimate assignment after that course was Fort Hood, Texas.

It was during this six-week Engineer Equipment

Newly commissioned Second Lieutenant John S. Raschke and his proud mother, Betty Raschke, August 31, 1968, at Washington National Airport, as it was then known (author's collection).

Officer course that my former OCS classmate and now current roommate, Lieutenant Ralph Diaz, and I got to better know one another. We also "mingled" with our OCS TAC officers, Lieutenants Knute Dietze and Travis Lee.[6] Having seen the pair as our personal tormentors since early March, Ralph and I soon found Knute and Travis to be smart, congenial, and dedicated officers. It was good to see them in this light, and from my time with them I learned the attribute of separating personal from professional roles.

Ralph and I had plenty of time off during this "gentleman's course" and we spent it exploring Washington, D.C., watching *Laugh-In* and the 1968 Summer Olympics, enjoying songs like "Harper Valley PTA," "Ode to Billy Joe" and "Born to Be Wild," and just relaxing. Gradually, we were getting used to being officers, including the saluting thing and having enlisted men call us "sir." Our course concluded the last week of October and I drove to New Orleans, Louisiana, for an overnight stay at Ralph's home. That evening, Ralph and I enjoyed a great meal at the Top of the Mart restaurant. Following this tremendous meal, he took me to Pat O'Brien's in the French Quarter, where he introduced me to the famous Hurricane. I awoke early the next day, had a cup of Ralph's chicory coffee, and departed New Orleans on the final leg of my journey. En route to Fort Hood, I made a slight detour off Interstate 10 to Fort Sam Houston. At Fort Sam I showed off my new gold bars to my former cadre members, receiving their salutes and congratulations in the process. With a slightly inflated ego, I made the relatively short drive from Fort Sam to Fort Hood, arriving there before dark. As my orders instructed, I reported to the 501st Replacement company for assignment.

Fort Hood had changed little since I had attended the Fourth U.S. Army NCO (Non-Commissioned Officer) Academy there in November–December 1967. At the time, I was a private first class (although an acting sergeant) stationed at Fort Sam Houston waiting for orders to go to OCS. My attendance at the NCO Academy was a great precursor to OCS and filled voids in my previously scant tactical and weapons training. Fort Hood was a sprawling post, home to both the First and Second Armored Divisions, III Corps Headquarters, and many other tenant and garrison units. Since I now had a car, I was able to see a much greater part of the fort. It was hard to grasp the enormity of the installation and the beehive-like activities going on around me. Maybe, this was going to be a good assignment.

Like most new lieutenants, I eagerly set out to use the knowledge the army had given me. Unlike some other young officers I met or observed, I certainly understood I still had a lot to learn. With another year in the army under my belt, second lieutenant bars on my shoulders and turning old enough to legally drink (21) on my second day on post, I felt much more confident reporting in at Fort Hood in November 1968. It was also nice to have Ralph stationed there as well. Ralph was in the same battalion as me, just in a different company.

My first memory upon assignment as a platoon leader in Company C, 16th Engineer Battalion of the 1st Armored Division, was qualifying with the .45 caliber pistol. I qualified on the same day Richard M. Nixon was elected the 37th President of the United States. While 1968 was an election year, during OCS we were mostly isolated from the news and knew little of what was going on in the world. This was because our primary concern was making it through the grueling course, and sitting around reading the newspaper or listening to the radio were time luxuries we were not afforded. Having just turned 21, I had not registered to vote, and for that matter, had not really thought about it. Now on the pistol range I thought of the lyrics in Barry McGuire's 1965 hit song, "Eve of Destruction": "you're old enough to kill, but not for votin'," as I fired my pistol. I qualified with my assigned weapon that day but could probably have done better if I could have thrown the pistol at the targets.[7]

My world at Fort Hood was one of doing those tasks normally assigned to new lieutenants such as giving classes on mandatory general subjects and riot control procedures (code name—Garden Plot); pulling officer of the day; supervising motor stables; serving such important tasks as vector control officer, mess officer, motor officer, etc. I easily fell into the routine of being an officer in the army. For the first time in my life, even with some of these menial duties, I was in charge of something and I was able to make a difference, albeit small.

My mechanized combat engineer platoon had about half the number of soldiers authorized for a full-strength platoon. The platoon sergeant (authorized to be a sergeant first class) was a staff sergeant named Bish*. Specialists were mostly occupying the position of squad leader (authorized a sergeant), and their average experience level in the army hovered at about two years. What was also strange was that as an engineer platoon we did very little engineer-related training or work. As a unit we stood morning formations, performed post-support duties, and, on one memorable occasion, supported a live-fire demonstration for visiting dignitaries. My platoon spent most of its time either in the motor pool maintaining vehicles and equipment or in the classroom covering all of those mandatory training subjects. Strangely, I never spent a night in the field at Fort Hood.

This rather boring schedule was OK with me, since foremost in my mind was the thought of my upcoming wedding at the end of December. During my off-duty time, I took instructions in the Catholic religion, and this was a great diversion from the hum-drum daily routine. My impending wedding subjected me to considerable harassment from the other four Company C officers, all of whom were unmarried. These lieutenants seemed sworn to permanent bachelorhood. They made me feel like I was almost betraying them, and perhaps all men, by getting married. I found their supposed playful ribbing actually got old fast!

Friday, December 20, finally arrived, and at the end of the duty day and week, I went on leave. Being young and foolish (a recurrent theme during this part of my life) I jumped in my Camaro and proceeded to drive nonstop the almost 1,100 miles to Geneseo, Illinois. There, I stayed with my grandparents the week prior to my wedding and had a memorable time with them. During our time together my grandmother reminded me of what a great cook she was. My grandfather, who I absolutely worshiped and adored, still had his dry sense of humor on display. On Saturday, December 28, Sue and I were married at Saint Malachy's Catholic Church in Geneseo. (I distinctly remember the song "Different Drum" by the Stone Poneys playing as I drove to the church.) The next day, pulling a small U-Haul trailer filled with our meager possessions, we began a much more leisurely drive to Fort Hood.

As the weeks passed at Fort Hood, with me not having to think about an upcoming wedding, the reality of the place began to sink in. As I more closely looked around it became apparent to me there were two types of soldiers serving at the post. There were those who had recently returned from Vietnam and who were waiting to get out of the army, and those, like myself, who were in the queue to go to Vietnam. Regardless of which category a soldier fell into, judging from their actions and appearances, attitudes were not the best. These attitudes, the command's inability to conduct effective training or maintain mission readiness due to low troop strength numbers,[8] and the grayness of the Texas winter, contributed to my general sense of malaise. Before long, I reluctantly admitted to myself that with this gloomy cloud hanging over the post my morale was beginning to suffer. I had to do something!

It was sometime during this funk that I learned one could volunteer to serve as an advisor in Vietnam. In doing so, I could also attend advisor's school at Fort Bragg, North Carolina, and follow-on Vietnamese language training at Fort Bliss, Texas. Advisor duty sounded like a good assignment. With my belief in the government, patriotism, and knowledge I would most likely end up in Vietnam anyway; I jumped at the opportunity. I called my branch assignments officer in the Pentagon and asked for assignment to Vietnam as an advisor. By volunteering I figured this would free me from what appeared to be random assignments meted out by the Pentagon and also get me out of this now godforsaken place called Fort Hood.

In early March 1969, I received orders for Vietnam to become an Operations Officer[9] with a required top-secret clearance. First, however, I had to attend the Military Assistance Training Advisors (MATA) course. We packed the Camaro, said goodbye to Fort Hood, and traveled through the heartland of the South to Fort Bragg.

MATA was a great school. There, I learned Vietnamese history and culture, Military Assistance Command Vietnam (MACV) command structure, advisor traits and duties, pacification reporting, counterinsurgency operations, basic demolitions training, map reading, and the operation and firing of ARVN (Army of the Republic of Vietnam)–issued weapons.[10] The weapons we fired were M-1 Garands, M-1 carbines, Thompson submachine guns,[11] .30 and .50 caliber machine guns, BARs (Browning automatic rifles), M-3 "Grease" guns, 60-mm mortars, and the 57-mm recoilless rifle. For me, an avid hunter as a teenager, the highlights of this course were the time we spent on the range firing those World War II– and Korean War–vintage weapons and the demolitions training by Special Forces (Green Beret) soldiers. Each day at MATA, we received four hours of Vietnamese language training from native Vietnamese instructors and frequently ran the infamous cross-country MATA mile, which was actually 2⅜ miles. The beauty of North Carolina in the spring, the fragrant smell of flowers blooming, paratroopers from units of the 82nd Airborne conducting parachute jumps, and the loud noises from the ranges were my lasting memories of Fort Bragg. The downside to MATA was the need to study my workbooks and listen to language tapes during the evenings and on weekends.

At Fort Bragg I remember that training was canceled when President Eisenhower died and that I took the day to go see the movie *2001: A Space Odyssey* in a downtown Fayetteville theater. On the less happy scale, during our training all students received the necessary and often painful shots required for Vietnam. The plague shot was the absolute worst of the lot. I really believed my arm was going to fall off. Six weeks after arriving at Fort Bragg we were in the Camaro again, this time heading west to Fort Bliss, Texas.

My time at Fort Bliss (actually the school was at the adjacent Biggs Field) was idyllic. Vietnamese instructors taught the eight-week course of more advanced language training. Students attended classes six hours per day, during which time we listened to tapes, studied our textbooks, and recited lessons before our instructors. When not studying, I spent time hanging around the swimming pool at our studio apartment, did a trip or two into Juarez, Mexico, and just enjoyed my remaining days of normality. At the end of this course, I attained a language proficiency rating of R2 S2 in the Vietnamese language. This meant I read (R) and spoke (S) at a higher level than required for course graduation—R1 S1. In late June 1969, with a Vietnamese language course diploma and orders in hand to report to Travis Air Force Base, California, we drove the packed Camaro to Geneseo for a 30-day leave.

My pre-deployment 30-day leave was mostly a blur. Foremost in my memory of my leave time was watching the Apollo 11 landing on the moon on Sunday, July 20. I also spent my time seeing family and friends and visiting the farm where I grew up. There, on the family farm (in Edford Township, Henry County, Illinois), I showed my 16-year-old brother, Ed, the place where I would like to be buried if that were to be my Vietnam fate. In what seemed like the blink of an eye, my leave ended as my departure date arrived. After saying goodbye to my relatives and friends, July 25 found me at the Moline airport climbing the stairs of an awaiting Ozark Airlines flight bound for Chicago. After a long last glance I entered the aircraft and began the most dramatic and transformative year of my life.

Chapter 2

On My Way

On the flight from Chicago to San Francisco, a flight attendant, seeing me in my khaki uniform, approached me and asked me my final destination.[1] When I told her I was en route to Vietnam, she invited me to sit in an available seat in the first-class section of the plane. My memory of the flight to and arrival in San Francisco was clouded as the flight attendants proceeded to ply me with the complimentary champagne available to first class passengers. The champagne lightened my otherwise depressed mood and, I think, made the flight go faster. In retrospect, I only hoped that when I departed the plane, I thanked the flight crew for their graciousness during the flight.

On the ground in San Francisco, I made it to the military desk at the airport. There, the military liaison NCO looked at my orders and told me where to sit and wait. He told me a bus would soon arrive to take me and a group of sad-looking men in uniforms to Travis Air Force Base. The bus ride to Travis was solemn, though I was impressed at the size and majesty of the Golden Gate Bridge. The bus pulled up to the terminal area of the air base, where about 40 dejected souls got off the bus and plodded into the terminal departure area. Upon showing an airman at the departure desk my orders, I was told the flight departure time and gate and it was suggested that I get something to eat. I followed his advice, grabbed a bite to eat, and then changed from my khakis into a set of jungle fatigues and boots I had privately purchased at a military surplus store in Fayetteville, North Carolina.

Soon, a chartered commercial airplane pulled up at the designated gate and a throng of sullen-looking men in uniform slowly proceeded up the stairs into the plane. As we boarded and filled the seats on the plane, the flight attendants asked for all O-6s (colonels or civilian equivalents) and above to move into the first class section of the plane. This brief announcement reminded me of my lowly status and dampened my already bad mood. Doors shut, taxiing complete, our commercial charter plane was soon gaining airspeed and altitude as we headed west over the Pacific Ocean.

Like others on the plane, I was too keyed up to sleep, and since I neither had anything to read nor was ever a talkative person, I looked out the plane window and lost myself in my thoughts. I wondered if I would be killed or injured in Vietnam; if I knew enough to do a credible job in my assignment—whatever that was to be; if everyone back home would be OK while I was gone; and what, really, was Vietnam going to be like? Despite these concerns, I did feel I was doing the right thing in supporting my country, and I was of the opinion that Vietnam was a "just" war. Time will tell, I thought.

Hours had passed when the pilot came over the intercom and said we would be making a scheduled refueling stop in Honolulu, Hawaii. In Hawaii, we all deplaned, stretched our legs, and sought out restrooms and food. An hour and a half or so later, we reboarded the plane, which soon climbed to around 30,000 feet en route to Clark Air Force Base in the Philippines, where we were to make another refueling stop. It was dark when we landed in the Philippines and sleep was overwhelming me, but again we had to get off the plane. The plane was quickly refueled, and soon we were back in the air. Once airborne, the pilot announced that our next stop would be Tan Son Nhut airport, Saigon, Vietnam. I slowly drifted off to sleep.

It was July 27, 1969, when I landed at Tan Son Nhut airport, which was slightly northwest of Saigon. As my five-nine, 180-pound frame began to descend the stairs that had been pulled up to the airplane, a hot blast of acrid air greeted me.[2] Though it was right around noontime and in the middle of the rainy season, I guessed it had to be at least a humid 95 degrees outside. I wondered if I could survive these climatic conditions for the next year, as I was soon drenched in sweat as I followed the crowd toward the terminal building.

Moving with the crowd, I could not believe the primitive appearance of the terminal in this international capital city. It was a plain concrete open-air structure filled with a mixture of joyfully departing U.S. military members, stoic ARVN military personnel, and frantic-looking Vietnamese civilians. Cheap-looking Vietnamese posters seemed to cover all the walls, and around the terminal building and airport grounds were Vietnamese security guards in what I thought were ridiculous numbers.

Like other MACV arrivals, I went through a maze at the airport, got my duffel bag, and was directed to a waiting military bus. I was startled to see the bus had a Vietnamese civilian driver. On the bus I immediately became aware of (but was not surprised by) the wire mesh covering the bus's side windows. This protective barrier was to ward off hand grenades thrown at the bus and reminded me I was not back in the U.S. It was time to get serious. Leaving the airport and making the short drive in a traffic system that I was sure was totally out of control, we came to the massive expanse of MACV headquarters—affectionately known as Pentagon East.[3] After clearing the checkpoint at the main gate the bus rolled to a stop in front of a huge two-story building that served as our orientation and in-processing point.

We piled off the bus and into a medium-sized air-conditioned classroom where a senior officer in an immaculate medal-adorned khaki uniform welcomed us to Vietnam. He soon turned the podium over to a junior officer for our orientation. The orientation was a condensed version of the Vietnamese history and cultural lectures I had heard at Fort Bragg, though we also got an update on the current situation in-country. Probably like others in the room, I surreptitiously looked around wondering who in this room would not make it back home. I was sure the briefings were interesting, but after my long, mostly sleepless and foodless journey, I was only concerned with sleep and food in that order. Following the welcome and orientation, we newly arrived officers received a checklist of actions we had to accomplish at the headquarters. Checklist in hand, I was shown to a Bachelor Officer Quarters (BOQ), which, although newer, was reminiscent of my basic training barracks at Fort Campbell, Kentucky. Food would have to wait as I sought out a bunk in a corner of the room, and within minutes, I was fast asleep.

The next morning I ate in the mess hall and then went to the administrative center, where I was efficiently in-processed. Processing consisted of surrendering the records I had been carrying to the personnel specialist and then completing a number of forms. These forms were the next of kin notification, the Servicemen's Group Life Insurance beneficiary designation, allotment forms for the disposition of my monthly pay, and mail locator cards. Next, I was sent to the medical station, where they thoroughly reviewed my shot record. I was glad to hear that I was current on all my shots. At another station, I received an MACV ration card and a Geneva Convention card, and, at another, a military driver's license.

At one of my stops I had to convert my American greenbacks into the Monopoly-like money called military payment certificates, or MPC. MPC looked absolutely worthless, but I was to find it worked just like real money. With all other stations cleared, my last stop was at the assignments desk. At that desk, the Specialist Five told me my assignment was to Advisory Team 73,[4] located in the distant Mekong Delta in Chuong Thien[5] province. With a new set of orders in hand I was told by the clerk to be at a certain place the next morning, where a bus would take me back to Tan Son Nhut airport. However, today my next stop was to be the central issue facility (CIF), where I needed to draw a weapon and all other necessary field gear. At the CIF I was issued about 80 pounds of everything I would need for my tour in Vietnam except a porter to carry my two overstuffed duffel bags, weapon, and necessary paperwork.

Later that day and back at the BOQ, I had two memorable experiences. One was a conversation with a lieutenant who was passing through Pentagon East on his way home after completing his one-year tour of duty. This lieutenant regaled me with his exploits of the past year as an advisor in I Corps (northern part of South Vietnam) and told me what a terrible place Vietnam was. With a wry smile, he also reminded me I had 360 days remaining in-country. Successful at deflating my spirits, he was kind enough to give me his pair of worn red clay-encrusted jungle boots.

The second event of the late afternoon was more traumatic. As I was using the urinal in the BOQ latrine, I heard a noise behind me. Out of the corner of my eye, I was shocked to see a black-pajama-clad figure with a conical Vietnamese hat moving behind me. Just knowing the figure was a Viet Cong (VC) by his appearance, I quickly finished my business, felt for my Colt .25 automatic, and turned to confront my assassin. I was surprised to see the VC was just a middle-aged woman cleaning the latrine, totally unbothered by my presence or activity. Knowing the truth, I was relieved the person lurking behind me was not a VC but was mortified there was a woman in the men's latrine. With a deep breath, I reminded myself that my conservative Midwestern roots were showing. Day two in Vietnam was coming to a close as I had a good meal and restful sleep.

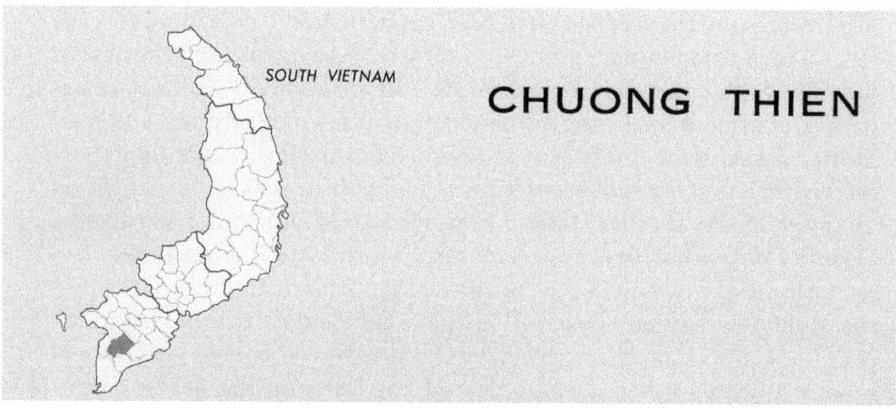

Above and facing page: maps showing Chuong Thien province. The map above shows the province's location within South Vietnam. The facing-page map shows the province's boundaries in relation to surrounding provinces and identifies the province capital of Vi Thanh as well as the five military districts within Chuong Thien and their district headquarters towns (22290110001, Edgar R. McCoin Collection, Vietnam Center and Sam Johnson Vietnam Archive, Texas Tech University).

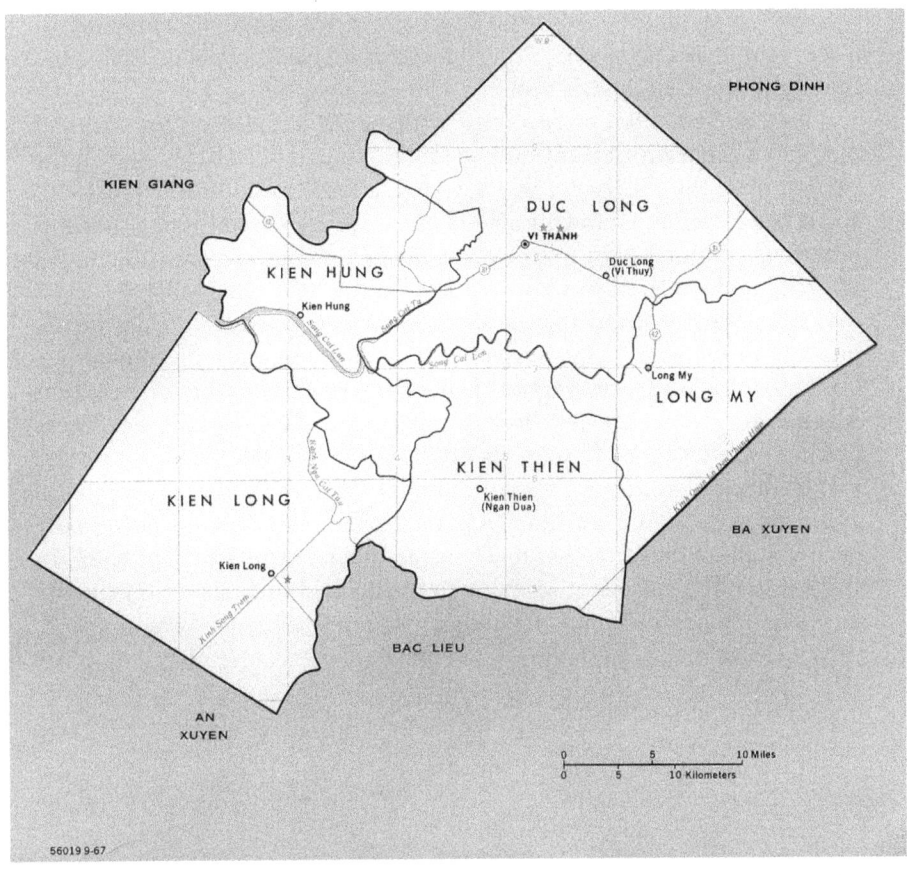

I spent the next morning eating breakfast, checking my gear, and taking a bus ride to, and waiting for a plane at, Tan Son Nhut Airport. I was scheduled for and given a boarding pass for a late-morning flight. I finally boarded a C-123 Provider aircraft heading to Can Tho in the midafternoon. Despite my long wait at Tan Son Nhut, I was impressed with the transportation system in place to process and get people to where they were supposed to be. Within an hour after takeoff, the plane landed at Can Tho airfield in the heart of the Mekong Delta region.

IV Corps was headquarters for DMAC (Delta Military Assistance Command) and was located in Can Tho. It provided command and control, administrative, and logistic support to American activities in the Delta. In July 1969, there were no divisional American ground combat units in the lower portion of the Delta. There, the American effort was primarily advisory (military and civilian) and providing support to ARVN forces. Non-combat American units in the Delta consisted of helicopter lift and medical evacuation (MEDEVAC),[6] hospitals, engineers, military intelligence detachments, other combat service support, army and air force reconnaissance and transport, Naval Riverine forces and SEALs, and smaller specialized detachments.

In Can Tho, a young specialist with a MACV patch on his shoulder met me in the terminal and took me to Eakin compound, located on the perimeter of the air base. I was assigned a BOQ and told the mess hall hours and location. Following a good meal, I retired to my bunk. The most notable event during the evening was seeing little geckos crawling on the screened and louvered windows of my BOQ.

Early the next morning the specialist who greeted me the day before took me to the MACV IV Corps headquarters compound in downtown Can Tho. This in-processing was just a cursory check of my orders, after which I was given some neat little round subdued IV Corps patches. These patches were designed to be sewn onto one's jungle fatigue jacket pocket and featured a prominent roman numeral IV in the center with "Delta" at the top and "MAC" (Military Assistance Command) at the bottom. By my estimation, these patches made me an official member of the team. In short order, the specialist took me to the airfield to catch a flight to my final destination, Vi Thanh,[7] Chuong Thien province.

CHAPTER 3

A Place Called Vi Thanh

It was late morning on a cloudy, dreary day when the C-7 Caribou landed with a thud followed by an intense rattling vibration. This rattling was from the steel planking[1] that served as the airfield runway. Once off the plane in this drab place, I looked around and saw several soldiers near the terminal building. I suddenly felt out of place with my recently issued clean, shiny jungle fatigues. I came to learn that shiny, clean uniforms made one recognizable as a "newbie" in-country. Lugging what felt like at least 200 pounds of gear, I trudged over to a shell of a building. The open-air structure had a sign that said "Vi Thanh." This sad-looking building's only resemblance to an airport terminal was the windsock hanging limply at its side and several radio antennae mounted on top. I thought this place made Tan Son Nhut airport look ultramodern by comparison. The airfield NCO saw and welcomed me and then called the MACV compound, requesting a driver to pick me up. A driver quickly showed up and helped me cram my duffel bags into the beat-up jeep.

The approximate two-kilometer drive from the airfield to the compound was interesting, not for the small talk exchanged between the driver and me, but rather for the condition of the road. In comparison, I had traveled over cow paths on our 212-acre family farm in northwestern Illinois that were in better condition. The driver explained it was the rainy season and the deep water-filled ruts had resulted from the heavy military traffic (2½-ton trucks and jeeps) going to and from the airfield with supplies and troops. Soon, our jeep pulled into the MACV compound, where the gate sign proclaimed, "Welcome Chào to Mừng Adv Tm 73." This would be my home sweet home for the next 12 months.

Finally at the end of my journey, I hoped to finally unpack my gear and get myself cleaned up. But, first things first, so I reported to the orderly room[2] and was welcomed to Advisory Team 73 by a young personnel specialist. I gave him the packet that contained my assignment orders and other necessary documents. After in-processing the specialist told me the mess hall hours, gave me a brief tour of the compound, and

My first view of Chuong Thien province: the "terminal" building at the Vi Thanh airfield (courtesy Malvin R. Zellefrow).

most importantly, assigned me a room (hooch). At the hooch, the specialist told me I could take either of the two open bunks in the room and once I decided, I could stow my gear in the nearby locker. Before leaving, my escort told me the province senior advisor (PSA) would want to meet me later that evening. After stowing my clothing and equipment, I sat on my bunk wondering just where in the world I was.

The Mekong Delta in the southern portion of Vietnam was known as the country's breadbasket for its ability to produce enough rice to sustain the country, and in pre-war years, to enable rice exports. The Delta, with the exception of a small area located near the southeastern corner border area with Cambodia, was as flat as a pancake, with most of its land mass less than two meters above sea level. The French, during their decades of occupation of Vietnam, built the numerous canals that crisscrossed the Delta. These canals and the many natural rivers and streams served as

Chapter 3. A Place Called Vi Thanh

Aerial view of the MACV compound from the northeast. Note tennis court at lower left, and volleyball court (formerly the compound parking lot) at lower right. The orderly room is directly at the top center off the volleyball court and the PX is to the right of the court. The long building at the top left of the volleyball court is the mess hall (courtesy Malvin R. Zellefrow).

the highways over which people, food, and materials (both friendly and enemy) traveled. Mangrove trees, nipa palm, and other species of palm trees (including coconuts) lined the banks of these man-made and natural waterways. Over the centuries, most arable land was cleared for cultivation to support the growing of rice and other commodities such as bananas, pineapples, watermelons, coconuts, etc. Rice paddies, with their diminutive rice paddy dikes, were everywhere.

One particularly foreboding terrain feature in the Delta was the U-Minh forest,[3] the reputed birthplace of the Viet Minh and currently an impenetrable Viet Cong stronghold. The U-Minh was located in the southwestern corner of Chuong Thien province and into the adjacent[4] Kien

Giang province. The U-Minh forest, in reality, was much more a mangrove swamp than a forest, and was a frequent target of U.S. and Vietnamese air and artillery bombardment and ARVN ground operations. This forest of darkness was massive and was reputed to hold VC base, supply, and POW camp(s).[5] Despite the bombings, defoliation, and multiple forays into it by the ARVN forces, the U-Minh forest was never wrested from the control of the Viet Cong, or later the NVA (North Vietnamese Army).

Chuong Thien province is about 240 kilometers (150 air miles) southwest of Saigon and located in the heart of the Mekong Delta region. It was one of 17 southern Vietnamese provinces[6] assigned to IV Corps. Chuong Thien province was formed by the Diem regime of South Vietnam on December 24, 1961, from parts of An Xuyen, Ba Xuyen, Kien Giang, and Phuong Dinh provinces. It was created to provide a more manageable tactical and administrative area.[7] Chuong Thien contained about 890 square miles (around 2,300 square kilometers, with farm fields measured in hectares), which made its land area roughly three-quarters the size of the U.S. state of Rhode Island. Chuong Thien province was really flat, with the highest elevation in the province (per the U.S. Army–issued topographical maps) at one meter above sea level. Most of the land within the province was used for rice cultivation.

The weather conditions in Vietnam were seasonal and predictable. There were two seasons, the wet or monsoon season and the dry season. The monsoon season was May through October, and during these months an average of about 11 inches of rain fell each month. The dry season was November through April, though it did rain during the six months of the dry season. However, rain averaged less than two inches per month—with January to April having about an inch or less of rain. The average temperature in November and December was 87 degrees Fahrenheit, with the average in the remaining months being in the low to mid-90s. Adding to the sauna-like weather, the humidity was in the range of 60–80 percent throughout the year. These topographical and weather conditions were ideal to me when I considered the terrible conditions our soldiers suffered through during World War II's frigid Battle of the Bulge in December 1944, or during the Korean War.

Security-wise, Chuong Thien was shaky. The former Secretary of Defense Robert McNamara, with his proclivity for measurable results, instituted the Hamlet Evaluation System (HES). This statistics-based program was developed to demonstrate America was winning the civilian peace and the military war.[8] Based on HES analysis, in July 1969 Chuong Thien had the dubious honor of being the 43rd least pacified of Vietnam's 44 provinces. I consider myself fortunate to not have known this statistic prior to and during my time in Chuong Thien.

Chapter 3. A Place Called Vi Thanh   23

There were about 290,000 people living in Chuong Thien province in 1971.[9] They were mostly ethnic Vietnamese (about 85 percent), with about 11 percent being of Cambodian descent and a smattering of Chinese, at roughly 4 percent. Most civilians were peasant farmers (about 70 percent) whose principal objective was to survive the omnipresent war and its effects. Peasant farmers were caught between the Viet Cong and the ARVN. The VC moved through their hamlets/villages at night, levying taxes and "drafting" military-age men. Though remote villagers had infrequent contact with the ARVN in the form of patrols and combat operations, they were still subject to a compulsory draft. All men between the ages of 20 and 45 were subject to being drafted into the ARVN forces. As a result of those competing influences, the population living in the rural areas seemed to be wary, distrustful, and apathetic.

The dominant religions in the province were Buddhism (69 percent), Catholicism (16 percent), *Hòa Hảo* (7 percent), *Cao Đài* (4 percent), with other religions making up 4 percent. A formal elementary and secondary school education was available in the Vi Thanh and the larger villages. However, the education of children living in the rural areas was mostly learning the skills of their mothers and fathers. As such, most rural children, their parents, and grandparents received little formal education. Rural Vietnamese homes (we Americans also called these hooches) were mostly made of thatched materials with mud floors and were scarcely more than 20' × 20'. These hooches had a very small cooking area and rolled-up mats for beds. Many of the hooches had a log-reinforced mud bunker large enough to accommodate the family in times of danger.

In Chuong Thien province, to preserve the maximum amount of land for cultivation, most peasants' homes were located on the banks of waterways or on otherwise untillable sections of their meager farms. In 1971 within the province there were about 120,000 hectares (approximately 296,000 acres, or 460 square miles) under cultivation. Where farmers lived close together, the groupings were called hamlets, or in Vietnamese, *Xóm*. Hamlets were roughly equivalent to an American small town of the 18–19th centuries. Several hamlets located together were called *Làng* or *Ấp*, or villages. In the early 1970s, Chuong Thien province had 168 hamlets and 32 villages. As a political subdivision, a village was similar to an American township, though much smaller. All Chuong Thien province subsector (district) team locations were considered villages. Vi Thanh, with civilian and military members included, numbered around 25,000 and was considered a city.

Whether supporting the Saigon government[10] or the VC, each strata of civil organization had leaders and militias. In government-controlled areas civil governance was through democratically elected village and hamlet chiefs and councils. Some "government controlled" villages had shadow VC leaders.[11] Then there were villages under total VC control that had VC civil leaders and often military elements, usually from squad- (6–10 men) to platoon-sized (15–30 men) units. Our mission as advisors was to train and assist the ARVN troops in rooting out the VC military and the covert cells, the VC infrastructure (VCI); assist civil authorities in establishing democratic and responsive government; and improve the overall living standards of the Vietnamese people. All of these actions were under the aegis of winning the hearts and minds of the populace. Our ultimate goal was to turn over all former American-conducted military functions to the ARVN—a process called "Vietnamization."

Vi Thanh, located in the northeastern portion of the province, was the largest population center in Chuong Thien province and was about 30 kilometers (20 air miles) southwest of Can Tho. Vi Thanh was a bustling city with local merchants and farmers selling their wares and produce, shoppers, children going to and from school, and large numbers of uniformed police and military members providing security to the crowds. The Kinh Xa No canal ran through Vi Thanh adjacent to the airfield and on to Can Tho. The city was home to the Advisory Team 73 MACV compound, which was located about two blocks from the town center and served as the headquarters for staff personnel and subordinate advisory elements assigned to Team 73.[12]

Chuong Thien province had five district (also called subsector) teams, each situated near a Vietnamese military and civilian headquarters subordinate to province headquarters. Eight kilometers southeast of Vi Thanh was the district team at Duc Long (pronounced "Duke Long"), which was easily accessible by road. Long My (pronounced "Long ME") was further down the road from Duc Long and was about 16 kilometers southeast of Vi Thanh as the crow flies. While it was possible to drive the approximately 25-kilometer gravel road to Long My, a certain portion of the road, as I discovered, was unsecure and known to have an occasional sniper harassing vehicular traffic.

The rest of the district teams were more remote than Duc Long and Long My. Kien Hung (pronounced "Ken Hung") was about 21 kilometers west-southwest of Vi Thanh. Kien Hung was located on the formidable *Sông Cai Lǒn* river. To reach Kien Hung from Vi Thanh, one had to cross the nearly 150-meter-wide *Sông Cai Tu* river using a civilian ferry[13] and drive south about 15 kilometers. Kien Thien (pronounced "Ken Tin") and Kien Long (pronounced "Ken Long") had the two remaining district teams. Due to inaccessible roads and the security situation, both of these subsector teams were only accessible by helicopter. Kien Thien was 22 kilometers southwest of Vi Thanh. Situated at the junction of two canals, Kien Long was about 38 kilometers south-southwest of Vi Thanh. Notably, Kien Long was the only team location other than Vi Thanh to have an airstrip.[14] Kien Long was a mere and perilous 14 kilometers from the eastern edge of the U-Minh forest.

I spent most of my first day in Vi Thanh putting gear away and marveling at the fixtures in my hooch. I was amazed we had electricity with overhead lights and outlets. My hooch was on the end of a single long building that contained four separate officer living spaces. Physically, the room was probably 16' × 16' and contained three sets of bunks, dressers, and metal lockers. Additionally, each bunk had two small wall shelves at its head and a desk lamp for reading in bed. Lastly, we had a small table centered in the room, a military-issue safe in the corner, a TA-312 military telephone, and a refrigerator. Adding elegance and ambience to the room were two Golden Nugget Casino posters on the wall plus a makeshift curtain. The curtain was a liberated VC propaganda sign that had been suspended over a canal warning the locals to reject the "Puppet Government" and the American Imperialists. I had no idea of what to expect for quarters in Vietnam, but to me, while Spartan in appearance, my hooch was beyond plush. Maybe this next year was not going to be too bad after all.

After his duty hours, I met my roommate, First Lieutenant Harvey Weiner.[15] Commissioned through the ROTC[16] program, Harvey was a Columbia Law School graduate and had been in-country since May. Lieutenant Weiner was my first exposure to someone of the Jewish faith. Like most everyone in his hometown, he had a thick Boston accent, which took me a while to get used to. Harvey was incredibly smart, and although he wore Infantry brass[17] on his collar, appropriately he was a military intelligence (MI) officer.[18] Initially Harvey was assigned as the province assistant Phoenix program advisor. Later he became *the* province Phoenix advisor. I consider myself very fortunate to have had Harvey as a roommate, and as time progressed we became friends. I learned a lot from him and consider him like a two-semester full-time live-in college professor. When I first arrived, the third bunk in our room was unoccupied, though officers passing through Vi Thanh often used it.

I knew what the Phoenix program was, as it was introduced to me at the MATA course at Fort Bragg. Harvey told me the "nuts and bolts" of the Phoenix program was to develop VC targets for capture (if possible) or elimination if necessary. The American and Vietnamese personnel in the Phoenix program worked closely with the province S-2 Intelligence (Intel) section. Together, these organizations used information gleaned from numerous sources to identify VC and Viet Cong infrastructure for action. These sources included captured VC, *hồi chánh*s (the name for former VC who rallied to the government under the *Chiêu hồi*[19] program), local villagers, and/or captured VC documents or signals intercepts.

Lieutenant Colonel Thomas LeVasseur, province senior advisor (left), at the "Hail and Farewell" for Captain Harvey Weiner (right) in May 1970. The photo was taken inside the club on the MACV compound (courtesy Harvey Weiner).

After dinner on my first night with Advisory Team 73, I met the province senior advisor, Lieutenant Colonel Tom LeVasseur. Colonel[20] LeVasseur was an armor officer on his second tour to Vietnam.[21] After initial pleasantries, he confirmed that I was to be the province engineer advisor but suggested there were few engineer activities in the province. He did mention that Vi Thanh was short of tactical advisors to accompany the Regional Forces (RF) and Popular Forces (PF) on operations. As events unfolded, I must have looked or sounded receptive to his last statement. Colonel LeVasseur listened as I gave him my background, and he later gave me the lay of the land and the team's mission. During our discussion, I sensed he was sizing me up. He encouraged me to learn the province geography and team locations and to familiarize myself with the facilities on

Chapter 3. A Place Called Vi Thanh

the MACV compound. He ended our meeting by saying I should take it easy the next week to get acclimated to Vietnam. In all, I found Colonel LeVasseur to be welcoming, gracious, energetic, and professional. While he exuded the presence of a senior officer, I found it easy to talk with him. As we ended our meeting, my day one in Vi Thanh was coming to a close.

The next morning, following the most restful night I had in a week followed by a great breakfast, I took inventory of the compound. It was an irregularly shaped facility that I guessed to be about three acres in size. The perimeter had an eight-foot-high chain-link fence with concertina wire on the top and extensive barbed wire barriers at ground level. Fighting bunkers with firing ports and constructed of timbers and sandbags were at each corner and midpoint along the perimeter. Other strictly protective bunkers were located on the interior of the compound. In the event of ground or indirect fire[22] attacks, team members would run to assigned bunkers located near their hooch. Each bunker had a bunker commander and a TA-312 telephone to communicate status and events with those in the command bunker. Perimeter fighting bunkers had grenades and extra ammunition. My assigned bunker was conveniently located about four feet from the door of my hooch, with Harvey my bunker commander.

In addition to bunkers, outside each building were rows of double-stacked 55-gallon oil drums filled with sand. The purpose of these drums was to absorb shrapnel from mortar or artillery rounds exploding near the buildings and to provide a measure of protection to occupants. As effective as this barrier was, it did not work too well if a building suffered a direct hit. Such was the case with my hooch in May 1969, two months before I arrived. During an indirect fire attack, a 75-mm recoilless rifle (likely a Type 52/56 Chinese copy of the U.S. M-20 recoilless rifle) round crashed through the roof of my hooch directly over my eventual bunk and exited just to the left of the door.[23] No one was injured in this attack, since, having taken shelter at the first sound of the alert siren, all hooch occupants were safely ensconced in the bunker when the round impacted. Miraculously, the spent remnants of the round landed just feet from the entrance of the bunker. This event explained the patched roof, the Golden Nugget poster covering the wall patch job, and an unpainted section of the exterior wall of my hooch.

I was told navy Seabees built the MACV compound in Vi Thanh sometime in the early 1960s, with follow-on MACV personnel making compound improvements. Concrete sidewalks had been laid and an approximate 100' × 20' PSP strip had been put down adjacent to the exterior wall of the mess hall. These walkways prevented the compound from turning into a sea of mud during the rainy season. The buildings were of wood construction, painted olive drab (OD) green with tin roofs. There

Interior of MACV compound in Vi Thanh looking toward the aid station. The PX is in the left foreground and the province senior advisor hooch is in the right foreground (courtesy George M. Eastman).

were no windows in any of the buildings, as all had screen mesh and louvers in place of them. Interiors were plain, with a very light pea-green paint adorning the walls and ceiling. As far as I was concerned, this beautiful array of buildings beat a canvas tent, foxhole, or bunker any day.

As for facilities, the compound had a small club that was located directly outside my hooch door. After duty hours the club served as a bar, a place to purchase snacks, a location for promotion and award events, and a place to get together for welcoming new members and saying goodbye[24] to teammates. An exterior wall of the club served as the movie screen, below which was a small stage. The open-air theater area had an overhead tin canopy and enough wooden seats to accommodate about 50 people. In addition to the showing of movies in the evening, this area was used for an occasional USO (United Service Organizations) show, awards ceremony, religious service, or somber remembrance ceremony for our fallen teammates.

Close to the theater area was the mess hall. The mess hall was of typical army layout with a kitchen area comprising about one-third of the approximately 20' × 60' building, with the dining area taking up the rest of the building. Army mess sergeants supervised female Vietnamese cooks who always prepared excellent meals, with one exception—roast beef. The roast beef never tasted bad. It was just the frequency of having it as a main course that made it bad.[25] Helicopter crews and transiting personnel were present at many noon meals, and as I came to understood from talking to them, our mess hall had a reputation as being one of the best in the Delta.

The majority of compound buildings were barracks for junior enlisted soldiers, NCOs quarters, and officer BOQs. Near these hooches was a community latrine for enlisted soldiers and one for officers, both of which had hot showers and flush toilets. Additional buildings were the orderly room, a mailroom, a small PX (post exchange) open at limited hours of the day, a communications/command bunker manned by a small detachment of soldiers from Company D, 52nd Signal Battalion, a one-man aid station, and a shed housing compound mechanicals. In addition to the many other compound defensive bunkers, there was also a small ammo bunker on the compound from which we drew our ammo, smoke and hand grenades, and explosives. Outside the perimeter of our compound and abutting the eastern fence was a French- or Japanese-built tennis court that got frequent use.

The army contracted Pacific Architects and Engineers (PA&E) to serve as the compound's public works crew. These unsung heroes kept the compound humming and lived in the mechanicals part of the compound. This area housed the generators, a water purification unit, and a small carpenter shop. Above their area sat a small (probably 1,000-gallon) water tower. PA&E personnel were a mixture of Filipinos and Vietnamese supervised by a U.S. civilian. This small crew managed the facilities that added most to our morale. They operated 24 hours a day, seven days a week, and they generated the compound's electricity, purified the water, unplugged the flush toilets, and maintained the buildings and infrastructure on the compound. Of this long list of duties, to me, providing hot showers was most important. We, at the MACV compound, took these amenities for granted. Our district and mobile advisory team (MAT) advisors and many U.S. soldiers and Marines serving in Vietnam were living a much more primitive existence, except perhaps at their base camps.

Finishing my initial tour of the compound, I was startled to see two rather feeble-looking, middle-aged Vietnamese men armed with M-1 carbines guarding the entry gate of the compound. These men were obviously too old for regular military service, and while they always had pleasant smiles, they did not look like they could stop the Easter Bunny. With civilian roads on three sides and Vietnamese civilian houses on my side of the compound, I was naturally concerned about security. To my surprise and great satisfaction, these guards served well during my time on Team 73, fending off but a single security incident at the compound.[26] Just as important, they did an excellent job of cleaning my M-16.

I have several memories of my first days in Vi Thanh. I met two departing lieutenants, Rick Burg* and Jim Jaegers. Rick, a red-headed

Irishman, was the man I was replacing as province engineer advisor. Rick spent more time on operations than performing any engineer duties. During his time in Chuong Thien he earned the Bronze Star for valor and a Combat Infantryman's Badge (CIB). He briefed me on his duties and activities of the past year, and within days, he disappeared, or DEROSed.[27] Jim was on his way home to Missouri. An infantry officer, he had served as the deputy district advisor in Long My and was spending his last days in Chuong Thien lounging on our room's vacant bunk. In both Rick and Jim, I sensed a pride in what they had accomplished, surpassed only by their eagerness to get home.

The night before Lieutenant Jaegers departed Vi Thanh he had the customary going-away party in the club, followed by a smaller get together at the Civil Operations and Revolutionary Development Support (CORDS) compound.[28] Why it was at the CORDS compound escapes me, but Harvey, Jaegers, Lieutenant Al Miller (the Phoenix advisor from Kien Long and the other person of Jewish faith in the province), Bernie Merritt*, several enlisted men, and I were there. I did not remember most of that evening but only know about it because Harvey gave me a photo of all of us arrayed in the midst of many empty beer cans. The large number of empties in the picture indicated we had a good time. The next day, lucky Jim Jaegers was homeward bound.

Arriving in Vi Thanh during the rainy season, I could not get over the torrential rains that occurred every day, mostly in the afternoons. These afternoon showers came on suddenly, violently raining buckets of water, and ended as suddenly as they started. Once the rains departed for the day, the sun shone brightly. These downpours were annoying while I was on the compound, but as I was later to experience, downright nasty in the field.

CHAPTER 4

New Guy with 362 and a Wake-up

As I took initial stock of myself and looked around at my teammates, one of the things that stood out to me were the cameras hanging around many of my teammates' necks. I found this strange, since, before arriving in-country, I had decided Vietnam was not going to be a pleasant experience. Choosing in advance to forget my experiences in Vietnam, I did not want to take pictures while there.[1] I think, too, growing up without taking many photos, this picture-taking pastime was irrelevant to me. Instead of carrying a camera, I focused on constantly wearing my Colt .25 automatic under my jungle fatigue shirt. For me, this made more sense.

One of my early concerns upon being settled at the compound was to do something about a nagging ingrown toenail I had managed to cause myself. Harvey told me I needed to see the compound's medical NCO, Sergeant First Class Ruffino Ramirez*, which I promptly did. Though also a new arrival on Team 73, Sergeant Ramirez was nearing the end of his army career, with many years of experience. His recommended treatment was to wedge a small rolled-up piece of a cotton ball beneath the nail as it grew. This was such an easy remedy, but I took a valuable lesson from it. During my 10-week Medical Specialist course I had never learned the "trick" Sergeant Ramirez just taught me.[2] My takeaway from this brief interaction with Sergeant Ramirez was that army senior NCOs possess incredible "book" and practical knowledge gained through their many years of experience. This revelation, because of an ingrown toenail, was a lesson I often witnessed over my entire 33 years of army service. I followed Sergeant Ramirez's advice, and within two months my ingrown toenail problem was well on its way to being solved.

Sergeant Ramirez also instructed me to take the weekly malaria pill (chloroquine-primaquine) and told me they would be available in the mess hall. Each Sunday we were supposed to take this "horse pill," as many of us referred to it. I religiously took this pill for my first several months in-country. After a while I gradually took the malaria pill less often and eventually not at all. As it turned out, I never heard of any Americans in Chuong Thien province contracting malaria.[3]

One day during my first weeks in Vietnam, I went to the Vi Thanh airfield for the express purpose of firing the M-16[4] I received at CIF in Saigon. The truth of the matter was that before arriving in Vietnam, I had never so much as touched an M-16.[5] There the airfield NCO gave me permission to go to the east end of the landing strip and familiarize myself with my rifle. As I was walking in that direction the NCO, with a strange-looking dog at his side, reminded me to cease fire if I saw any approaching aircraft. Obviously, he had been around second lieutenants before.

During basic training, I learned the army had strict procedures for achieving a battlefield zero,[6] after which, a soldier would then fire his weapon for qualification. The appropriate zero and qualification ranges were not available in Chuong Thien, so it was time to improvise. I fired into the pond that had been excavated during the construction of the airfield, just to get a feel for my weapon. Then I picked out imaginary targets to engage and fired on those in full automatic mode. My thought during firing, contrary to army training doctrine, was that a high rate of fire would trump the accuracy gained from achieving a battlefield zero. Soon out of ammo, I considered myself "qualified."

The initial advisory effort in Vietnam was the responsibility of the Military Assistance Advisory Group (MAAG) that had first arrived in Vietnam in 1950. MAAG and its mission continued until May 1964, when it was absorbed into the newly created organization called MACV. Advisory Team 73 had its lineage through MAAG, and then Advisory Team 58. It was redesignated from Advisory Team 58 to Advisory Team 73 in August 1968. As the war effort increased, MACV and its advisory effort in Vietnam expanded. To meet that expansion, MACV demanded increased manpower, equipment, and aid. The road to escalation had become a superhighway.

A Table of Distribution and Allowances (TDA) was the document that prescribed staffing levels for administrative headquarters,[7] while a Table of Organization and Equipment (TO&E) did the same for corps and divisional units. Like a TO&E, a TDA authorized personnel, ranks, and military occupational specialties for these staffed positions and equipment. Advisory Team 73 was a TDA unit, and it was organized as follows.

Colonel LeVasseur was the province senior advisor. He was responsible for American military and civil efforts within the province. Mr. Norm Olsen, a civilian, was the deputy province senior advisor and the second in command on the province team. The team TDA resembled a battalion staff, providing the S-1, S-2, S-3, S-4 ,and S-5 functions.[8] Each of these staffs worked closely with and advised their respective Vietnamese staff counterparts. The TDA also included the specialty positions of Phoenix advisor, RF/PF advisor, province engineer advisor (me), river boat advisor, communications security advisor, province agriculture advisor, as well as a cadre of civilian personnel working for CORDS.

In addition to these battalion staff-like positions, there was a 10-man section whose responsibility was to perform activities directly supporting team members. This support included preparing the morning reports, scheduling and preparing officer and enlisted efficiency reports as required, typing award recommendations, ordering necessary supplies, maintaining team vehicles and equipment, scheduling transportation as required, and ensuring great meals were prepared in the mess hall.

Also on the TDA were the soldiers assigned to the various district advisory teams. In 1969, six members were assigned to each of these teams: a district senior advisor (usually a combat arms[9] major or captain); a Phoenix program advisor (a military intelligence first lieutenant or captain who also served as the *de facto* deputy district senior advisor); a medical, operations/intelligence, and weapons NCO (usually a sergeants first class); and a radio telephone operator (RTO, a private first class or specialist fourth class).

The last group of personnel on the TDA were those who served on the MATs. The MATs were technically a IV Corps asset and subject to assignment by them, though they received their support from the province in which they were located. During my tour, Chuong Thien province had five MATs (54, 55, 56, 104, and 110). Each mobile advisory team had a captain or first lieutenant officer in charge (OIC), assistant OIC (a first or second lieutenant), and NCOs (sergeant through sergeant first class) serving as a heavy weapons advisor, a light weapons advisor, and a medical advisor. MAT members lived with the Vietnamese units they were advising. This meant they were living in remote locations far from any other Americans. Accordingly, life on a MAT was very primitive and dangerous.[10]

Some soldiers in the province were attached to Advisory Team 73. In military terms, attachment means the unit to which the personnel are attached is responsible for the day-to-day needs of the soldier. Most of these attached personnel were physically located on the MACV compound in Vi Thanh. There was a 21-soldier detachment from Company D, 52nd Signal Battalion. With their NCOs, these junior enlisted soldiers ensured the team had continuous communications with higher headquarters, subordinate advisory team elements, adjacent provinces' advisory teams, transiting aircraft, and "dustoff" helicopters. There was also a four-man team from the 221st Reconnaissance Airplane company, call sign "Shotguns." This team flew the army's O-1[11] observation aircraft and had two pilots (commissioned and/or warrant officers) and two aircraft maintenance/armament enlisted soldiers. The last element attached to Advisory Team 73 was a four-man U.S. Air Force detachment from the 22nd Tactical Air Support squadron, call sign "David." In formal military parlance, the air force "Davids" were called forward air controllers, or FACs. Like the army "Shotguns," the two "David" pilots flew the O-1 aircraft and had a two-man aircraft support crew with them. Though not on the TDA, navy SEALs (Sea, Air, Land) frequently made appearances in the province. In total, there were about 125 military personnel assigned (or attached) to the advisory effort in the province with about 70 being stationed in Vi Thanh, the balance in the hinterlands. Manpower in Chuong Thien province was at its peak in early 1970; thereafter, numbers were gradually reduced as Vietnamization progressed. In March 1973, all military and civilian personnel were removed from Chuong Thien province.

In a parallel structure within the province and working in concert with the mission objectives of the PSA were those civilians assigned to CORDS. CORDS civilians were a much unheralded part of the Vietnam conflict. While sharing the dangers inherent with military service, these civil servants worked tirelessly with their Vietnamese civilian counterparts on improving the civil, political, security, and economic conditions affecting the everyday life of Vietnamese civilians. Norm Olsen, a 28-year-old career State Department official and deputy province senior advisor, oversaw the efforts of about a dozen civilian and several military personnel within the province. Another State Department career professional, Frank Gillis*, was Mr. Olsen's deputy within CORDS.

Separate from the CORDS efforts were several "Agency" personnel who lived in a hardened compound in downtown Vi Thanh. Bernie Merritt was the agent-in-charge of the Vi Thanh "office," and he had another American civilian working with him as well as several navy SEALs. These Americans lived in an ultra-secure compound guarded by a cadre of the biggest Cambodians[12] I ever saw in Vietnam.

I spent my "acclimatization" weeks catching up on my letter writing, decompressing, and meeting others who served on the compound and those from subordinate team elements passing through. I also went to the TOC (Tactical Operation Center)[13] to get a sense of what was going on in the province and to the airfield to pick up new arrivals and to observe activities there. My last major accomplishment was in studying a province map, paying particular attention to the locations of the five district headquarters and the formidable U-Minh forest. On the map, since I heard others talking about them, I asked to be shown "Mickey's Ears" and the "Snake" River. In reality (either on a map or from the air) these two features were easily discernible rivers; one had a feature resembling Mickey

Mouse's ears, the other, a river that looked like a squiggly slithering snake. As I was to learn during my time in Chuong Thien, both of these areas were very much pro–VC and would be the object of many military operations.

My time on Advisory Team 73 was anything but routine. I did not have to report to an office each day or accomplish specific tasks. The fact that there were few engineer activities in the province made it difficult to keep busy. I did not have anyone to supervise, and I did not have an assigned vehicle. This last fact limited my ability to get around mostly to bumming rides. These factors led me to volunteer for many things, thinking that staying busy would make the days go faster in Vietnam. This last belief proved true; however, it makes my ability to present my year in a logical, chronological manner somewhat difficult.

CHAPTER 5

Men Like Me in Jungle Fatigues

Vietnam introduced me to a number of individuals who forevermore would be my brothers. Judging only from my limited time with troops at Fort Hood, my brothers on Team 73 (both officers and NCOs) were more educated, experienced, and dedicated to their mission. Our junior enlisted soldiers, most of whom were Signal Corps soldiers from the 52nd Signal Battalion, were young, full of energy, and very competent. My interaction with junior enlisted men was limited to the mess hall, the club, the movie "theater," and TOC duty. This was not because I was status conscious—that's just the way it worked out. In fact, with people coming and going in different directions, my group of close associates was only about 20 or fewer people.

Two enlisted soldiers I got to know better than others were Staff Sergeant Dave Paulson and Specialist Fourth Class Mal Zellefrow, both highly trained intelligence analysts. Prior to operations, I received my map(s) from them, and I was always impressed with their helpfulness. Dave Paulson was a young 20-something who often smoked a pipe. Mal, who looked like he was closer to 14 rather than 18 years old, ran the PX during its limited noon-time open hours. Always talkative and with boundless energy, in addition to his Intel work Mal also served two incredibly important functions: obtaining new movies and running the movie projector each evening.

Another member of the Intel section I came to know was the section's Vietnamese interpreter, *Trung sĩ* An Phung Tho. An was born in Cho Lon, near Saigon, and was around 23 years old. He was a frequent visitor to the MACV compound and had a good mastery of English and a talent for analyzing raw intelligence.

In addition to Colonel LeVasseur, I worked with many others during my time in-country.

Major James Martinson* was the province S-3 (operations') advisor and an infantry officer. He was definitely "old army," stern in character,

Chapter 5. Men Like Me in Jungle Fatigues

and had a difficult time relating to junior, non–RA[1] officers like myself. Major Martinson was easily recognizable by his army-issue baseball cap[2] and the map case seemingly always slung over his shoulder. It seemed like he was constantly scurrying around. He spent a lot of time in the command and control (C&C) helicopters flying 1,500 feet over the operations area, tracking and coordinating ground activities. During my tour, Major Martinson earned the moniker of "Pop Smoke" Martinson because from the air he was often unable to locate friendly ground elements. As a result, he would tell us to "pop smoke."[3] Behind his back, Major Martinson quickly became a magnet for lieutenants' jokes. Thankfully, Major Martinson was neither the rater nor senior rater for my officer efficiency report (OER). Nonetheless, I was his subordinate and had to do as he directed—especially when it related to combat operations.

Captain Howard McCullough was an air defense artillery officer from New England, commissioned through the ROTC program at the University of Vermont. Captain McCullough was the province senior operations/training advisor, and was a competent, tactically proficient officer. He took me on my first combat operation, and he taught me a lot. Captain McCullough's strongest trait was his ability to rapidly assess a situation and quickly determine the proper action/response. Cool under fire, Captain McCullough was instrumental in training and mentoring me and other lieutenants. Accordingly, I always enjoyed being in his presence.

Captain Dave Andrews* was an Adjutant General Corps officer and was the team's administrative/executive officer in charge of the support section. As such, he technically was not an advisor and had little interaction with the Vietnamese. In his assigned administrative duties he was competent; however, Captain Andrews came across as aloof and indifferent. During my time in Vietnam, Second and first lieutenants considered ourselves on the same level. We received similar assignments and did not salute one another. We lieutenants, however, did salute captains and above on the compound, and per military protocol, called them "sir." If we were ever to fail in this matter of military courtesy, Captain Andrews, more than any other superior, was quick to point out our transgression. This trait soon landed Captain Andrews into the category as Major Martinson—deserving the brunt of lieutenant ridicule. Captain Andrews always carried a fish filleting knife on his web gear. Besides their looking ridiculous, we could never figure out why he needed a knife, or web gear, for that matter.

Captain Dick Childress was a field artillery officer commissioned through ROTC. Captain Childress had received both PSYOPs (psychological warfare) and Vietnamese-language training prior to arriving in-country. He was initially assigned as the civil affairs officer at the province level before he was later assigned as the district senior advisor of Duc Long district. As it was the closest district to Vi Thanh and easily accessible by road, I spent more time in Duc Long than with any other district team. I often visited Duc Long due to a growing friendship with the lieutenants assigned there—Noonan and later Nickinovich. I came to know and respect Captain Childress, as he was another captain who treated lieutenants as near equals. I saw him as a quiet, thoughtful, and intellectual professional who was totally dedicated to his district and the Vietnamese people.

Captain George "Buddy" Shieldes was the district senior advisor in Kien Hung district. Captain Shieldes was an armor officer and a Texas A&M (Aggie) graduate who had a very deliberate way about himself. Captain Shieldes easily could have been the "poster boy" for the army due to his always "squared away uniform," square jaw, trim build, and crew cut. My interactions with Captain Shieldes were limited to his visits to Vi Thanh, my visits to Kien Hung a time or two, and talking with him over the radio during combat operations. Captain Shieldes was another "good guy" captain.

Frank Gillis was a no-nonsense civilian assigned to CORDS. Frank was an experienced career State Department employee and was the rater on my OER. I always thought Frank was at least 15 years older than me. I believe this may have been due to his knowledge, authoritative presence, and his premature balding. In fact, Frank was only about 10 years older, but he had twice the amount of energy of any 20-year-old I had ever seen. Frank was the bravest civilian in the province, and he encouraged me to spend time with the Vietnamese public works chief to assist him with civilian projects.

During my time in Vi Thanh, I became close with the two U.S. Air Force FACs. Captain Howard Taylor was a gregarious and skilled O-1 pilot. Like his roommate, Lieutenant George "Jug" Eastman, he was incredibly competent, brave, and totally dependable. These skilled professionals were the eyes and ears in the sky for those on the ground. Like their army "Shotgun" counterparts, the FACs would loiter overhead during the most intense fights, spotting targets, providing tactical information to those on the ground, and passing radio traffic—leaving the area only to refuel and rearm. In the case of Captain Taylor and Lieutenant Eastman, their primary task was to mark ground targets by firing smoke rockets for engagement by U.S. Air Force jets, and later in my tour, VNAF (Vietnamese Air Force) propeller-driven A-1E Skyraiders. On my slow days, Captain Taylor or Lieutenant Eastman would allow me to accompany them in their O-1 as a backseat observer. This experience gave me a greater appreciation for the type of information pilots needed from the ground element and allowed me to see just how beautiful Vietnam really was.

Chapter 5. Men Like Me in Jungle Fatigues

Captain Howard Taylor (left) and First Lieutenant George "Jug" Eastman, our forward air controllers (FAC), in front of their "David" hooch (courtesy George M. Eastman).

A source of constant banter between the army and air force teammates was the better accommodations the air force pilots had. Though Captain Taylor and Lieutenant Eastman were on the far end of the same long building in which my hooch was located, theirs was luxurious by comparison. Instead of three, the air force hooch had just two occupants (obviously giving them more space) and a dartboard featuring Ho Chi Minh's picture. They also painted their hooch with a much better color scheme than ours. In reality, I thought they were always painting something. Lastly and most importantly, they had the louvered and screen windows of their hooch covered in clear vinyl. This reduced bugs and critters entering their hooch and made the operation of their portable fans much more efficient. In all, they had a great set-up and some interesting reading materials. Banter aside, I really liked spending time with them.

Lieutenant Bob Olderson* was another field artillery officer who received an OCS commission at Fort Sill. Lieutenant Olderson was the province assistant RF/PF[4] advisor. The Regional Forces were employed as a company of approximately 60–80 soldiers. PF soldiers were assigned to village areas as platoons of about 25–30 soldiers. During my tour, Lieutenant Olderson extended for an additional six months' service in Vietnam and, per the then-army promotion policy, he was promoted to captain on the second anniversary of his commissioning. Bob was a prototypical

Scandinavian with a tall slim build, blond hair, blue eyes, and a wry smile. I went on several operations with Lieutenant Olderson and saw just how cool and focused he was under pressure. Bob was a good soldier and a skilled and competent tactician whom the Vietnamese greatly respected.

In October 1969, Harvey and I welcomed our new roommate, Lieutenant Gene Griffiths. Gene was a graduate of Lehigh University and, before coming into the army, had worked for the U.S. State Department. He was a graduate of Infantry OCS at Fort Benning and was the province S-5 advisor.[5] Gene was an ideal fit for our hooch. He was smart, had a quick wit, was somewhat reserved, and quickly complimented the prevailing loose mood of the room. For his fastidiousness, Harvey and I soon dubbed Lieutenant Griffiths "Clean Gene."

Sergeant First Class William "Wild Bill" Haley was an incredible soldier! Bill was trained as a medic. However, to me, he was the most proficient field soldier and bravest individual on the compound. Prior to my arrival, Bill had been awarded the Silver Star[6] during his time on Advisory Team 73. Standing about 5'4", Sergeant Haley always wore a camouflage uniform and a U.S. Marine Corps camouflage "bush" or "boonie" hat. Given his stature, he easily blended in with Vietnamese troops. Though I was his superior in rank, I readily followed Sergeant Haley's lead while on operations with him. Sergeant Haley patiently trained me, sharing with me his wealth of combat experience. I had the utmost respect for Bill Haley and was thankful to have served with him. In great part, I credit him with my survival in Vietnam.

Bernie Merritt (one of two "Agency" officers in Chuong Thien province) worked with several Navy SEALs, the MACV Phoenix Program advisors, and the Vietnamese Provincial Reconnaissance Unit (PRUs).[7] Bernie grew up in Springfield, Massachusetts, but with his 20 years' service as an explosive ordnance disposal sergeant in the air force, he had completely lost his northeastern accent. Secretive about his mission and duties, Bernie was very intelligent, fun to be around, and always had some great stories to tell of his earlier tour of duty in Vietnam while he was in the air force.

Lieutenant Bob Noonan was the Phoenix advisor at Duc Long. A graduate of Notre Dame, one could not get much more Irish than Bob unless you were born on the Emerald Isle itself. Following graduation from Notre Dame, Bob attended the U.S. Army Infantry School at Fort Benning and later the Military Intelligence School at Fort Holabird. Bob was smart, witty, and a true warrior. He could have spent his time behind a desk collecting, analyzing, and passing on intelligence concerning the VC and VCI. In addition to his Intel duties, Bob went on a number of combat operations with district RF and PF units. I was fortunate to accompany him on several operations. The Vietnamese soldiers seemed to love

Chapter 5. Men Like Me in Jungle Fatigues

Bob, since he was brave, tactically proficient, and always cool under fire. In the field or not, Bob could always find the best of every situation, had an incredibly dry sense of humor, and possessed a throaty, infectious laugh. I thoroughly enjoyed Bob's company and tried my best to emulate this solid soldier.

Dave Nickinovich was another Duc Long lieutenant. Dave arrived in Chuong Thien in December 1969 and was a third officer on the Duc Long team, a replacement for Lieutenant Carlile. Dave graduated from Infantry OCS at Fort Benning. He and Bob were similar from the standpoint that they both got along well with, and were highly respected by, the Vietnamese soldiers. Dave missed his calling as a model. At the very least, he could have been on the cover of *Infantry Magazine*. He was tall, lean and focused. Though he had a genial smile, Dave exuded an air of self-confidence and determination seldom seen in lieutenants. A consummate warrior, Dave received the Silver Star and several Bronze Stars for valor during his tour of duty.

As the assistant officer in charge of MAT 54, Lieutenant Frank Perra was the replacement for Lieutenant Steve Young. MAT 54 was a hard-luck team that in the course of three weeks of August and September 1969, had three of its team members killed in action (KIA). Frank was a graduate of the University of Rhode Island ROTC program and was an airborne qualified infantry officer. I got to know Frank when he initially stayed in Vi Thanh en route to join MAT 54. Thereafter, he would also occasionally stop by for a visit during his supply runs to the MACV compound. He was an absolute free spirit who saw every circumstance in the most positive of ways. Notable about Frank was his pre–army life; he was a danseur (male ballet dancer). During one visit, after Harvey, Gene, and I encouraged him, Frank performed several ballet moves for us. While he was talented, pirouettes just seemed out of place at this remote corner of the world, especially given our circumstances. Collectively, we kidded Frank about earning his airborne wings, saying they were a natural extension of his dancing career.

Ralph Howard was a 20-year-old warrant officer. (Army warrant officers were called "Mister.") Ralph, a Mormon from Utah, arrived in Vietnam in July. Assigned to the 221st Reconnaissance Airplane company and attached to our team as a pilot, his call sign was "Shotgun." He received his warrant commission through the army's Warrant Officer Candidate Program, which trained both fixed-wing and helicopter pilots for Vietnam. He lived in the same long block of hooches as I and flew the low and slow O-1 "Bird Dog" aircraft. Mr. Howard occasionally allowed me to fly backseat with him on reconnaissance missions. As with my flights with the FACs, this gave me a much better appreciation of the lay of the land and sharpened my map-reading skills. Ralph was a competent pilot. He was also probably the most taciturn person on the compound.

Captain Jim Bugansky, a Field Artillery OCS graduate, was the other "Shotgun" pilot and he shared the hooch with Ralph Howard. Jim was a quiet, very methodical, courageous, and skilled pilot. Just like the air force O-1 pilots, both "Shotgun" pilots spent many long hours in the sky supporting ground operations. Unlike the USAF pilots, whose primary mission was to guide in high-performance aircraft, the "Shotgun" pilots often had Vietnamese artillery spotters as "backseaters" who adjusted artillery onto enemy locations. The "Shotguns" preformed aerial reconnaissance, provided enemy assessments to the ground element, and provided radio relay as required. They could also attack targets with their wing-mounted 2.75" rockets.

Chapter 6

Fumbling Around in the Dark

My initial days in Vietnam soon turned into weeks. With little to do, I felt like I was fumbling around in the dark. Not only was I a new lieutenant, but I did not have a readily identifiable job. I knew I could not keep my sanity if I didn't find something to keep me busy. Contrary to the established soldier's dictum and practice of never volunteering for anything, I made it known I was willing to do any task that would get me off the compound. I just needed something meaningful to do.

My first volunteer assignments were as a ground-based radio relay. The purpose of the ground radio relay was to keep track of an operation's progress by following it on the map and ensuring the maneuver elements had constant contact with the TOC, the overhead O-1 pilots or the ground relay.[1] Accordingly, the ground relay was located in the near vicinity of the operation area. The first time I performed this role, I set up my base station adjacent to a small Vietnamese café[2] on a canal bank about 12 kilometers northeast of Vi Thanh. An accompanying NCO and I erected an RC-292 antenna, which extended the range of the PRC-25 radio[3] I used to monitor and report on the ground operation. My assignment that day, like the ground operation I was supporting, was quiet and rather boring, although I did get my first introduction to Vietnamese iced tea and dried squid. This being my first experience with it, I found the iced tea seemed watered down as compared to the American version. Later, I discovered this was the way all Vietnamese iced tea was served. The dried squid was actually pretty good and resembled and tasted like beef jerky. In the late afternoon, the troops were airlifted back to the airfield and the TOC ordered me to return to the compound. Though nothing of note occurred, I was glad to get off the compound and finally felt like I was contributing something to the war effort.

My next assignment as a radio relay was a week later near Long My. This was to be my first solo assignment and required a longer trip. In addition to getting directions, I went over my route on the map. It was a long drive, and being inexperienced, I failed to ask about security conditions along the route. I arrived in Long My early that morning without incident and, with the help of district team members, quickly set up the antenna. I then settled in to monitor and track the progress of the operation. This operation, in my role as radio relay, was as uneventful as that of the previous week. It validated the elusiveness of the VC, or perhaps the faultiness of our intelligence. In the late afternoon, I received permission from the TOC to take down the antenna and return to Vi Thanh. I quickly disassembled and packed the antenna and departed Long My. Getting on my way, I realized daylight was quickly slipping away.

As I drove back in my jeep the well-rutted gravel road made a sharp turn to the northwest about 10 kilometers north of Long My. With the roughest part of the road behind me, I figured I was home free. I was now on a more well-traveled, mostly gravel road, and it was just a straight shot past Duc Long to Vi Thanh. However, about a kilometer or two after my exit from the Long My road, I heard something I had never heard before—the sound of bullets slicing through the air and passing close to my jeep. It suddenly occurred to me that someone was trying to kill me! Instinctively, I hit the gas as I reached for the radio to report I was under fire.

It was just a minute or two after the TOC acknowledged my situation when, out of nowhere, I heard a high-pitched screaming noise and a giant swoosh coming from the rear of the jeep. Already at a heightened state of alert, I imagined the sudden and loud noise to have been a mortar or rocket propelled grenade (RPG)[4] being fired at my jeep. Those cumulative events sent me into a state of near panic. Just then in my front windshield I caught the sight of the underbelly of a small plane just feet off the ground and climbing for altitude. I was so startled by all of this that I nearly drove my now speeding jeep into the canal that was just feet away from the edge of the gravel road. I'm sure I put Craig Breedlove's recent land speed record[5] in jeopardy as I zoomed past Duc Long en route to Vi Thanh. Though unscathed, my breathing and heart rate were barely restored to normal before I was safely inside the MACV compound walls.

It was near dark as I got back onto the compound. I reported my arrival to the TOC, ate dinner, and told Harvey of the sniper and "strafing" events on my way back from Long My. Rather matter-of-factly, he told me that the area I traveled through was well known for having a VC sniper. He said the VC often flew a VC flag from a crude flagpole several hundred meters from the bend in the road in the distant tree line. The VC flag not only marked their territory but also served as bait for souvenir hunters. The good news was that the sniper was a notoriously bad shot so no one

Chapter 6. Fumbling Around in the Dark

worried about him. This information earlier in the day could have spared this 21-year-old a potential heart attack.

Seeking justice and some sort of revenge, I questioned the pilots on the compound to find out which one "buzzed" me, though I never did find out who it was. With the fading light and my adrenaline overload caused by the sniper, I had failed to see whether the offending O-1 was army green or air force gray. Apparently, the mob code of *omerta* had been taught to army and air force pilots during flight school, as none of the pilots confessed. Nonetheless, I suspected it was one of the air force FACs as this would be in keeping with their sense of humor, and they both had a smirk on their faces when I asked them. My investigation concluded, I finally realized this was just another day in Vietnam.

Long My was the last time I performed radio relay duty. As I thought about it later in my tour, my time as a radio relay was an invaluable training experience. It introduced me to many things I would later use on my own ground operations: The lingo used between the different parties during combat operations, the need to always know where you were on the map, the interaction between ground troops and air assets, and the frequency and types of reports required. Just as important as learning all of these concepts, I was becoming acclimated to Vietnam.

Colonel LeVasseur gave me my next assignment. He said the previous night the VC mortared Kien Long district headquarters. One of the rounds left a gaping hole right in the middle of the airfield, making it unusable for fixed-wing aircraft to land. As an Engineer officer who was supposed to know how to fix such things, my mission was to go to Kien Long, get the hole filled, and repair the PSP so aircraft could use the airstrip. With my assignment in mind and *Field Manual* (FM) *5–34 Engineer Field Data*[6] in hand, the next morning I went to the Vi Thanh airfield and awaited the "swing ship."[7] I carried several canteens for my mission to Kien Long, C-rations for three days, and my M-16 as I boarded the swing ship. In reality, I had no idea of what was in store for me or how to make the repairs needed.

At nearly 23 air miles from Vi Thanh, Kien Long was the most remote of our districts. It had been the site of a huge battle April 12–20, 1964.[8] It was during this battle that the VC assaulted the district headquarters, executed the district chief, and occupied the village and district headquarters. After a brutal eight-day pitched battle, the VC finally slipped back into the U-Minh forest under the cover of darkness. This temporary but symbolic VC victory resulted in the loss of 55 ARVN KIA, 175 ARVN wounded in action (WIA) and 17 Missing in action (MIA). One American advisor was KIA and 25 other Americans, mostly aviation personnel, were WIA.[9] The Vietnamese captured one prisoner and estimated 175 VC were killed. This battle was similar to the Battle of Ap Bac in January 1963. At the Battle of Kien Long, the VC demonstrated a willingness to engage in a large-scale fight with the ARVN and their supporting American air power. Now, five years later, Kien Long had a permanent American advisory team presence and was relatively quiet but certainly not safe.

While I had no expectations on the conditions at Kien Long, I was shocked to see how Spartan they really were. The wooden five-man team house was about 50 meters from the pockmarked district headquarters building and had evidence of multiple shrapnel hits of its own. Surrounding the district headquarters building and team house were strands of barbed wire entanglements, and beyond the barbed wire was an expansive minefield. The last notable feature on this mini-compound was a huge bunker the team used for protection against indirect fire like the airfield mortaring that brought me to this forsaken place.[10] Captain Al Bundons, the district senior advisor, introduced himself and told me the bunker was to be my quarters for the duration of my time in Kien Long. Lieutenant Al Miller, whom, I met earlier in Vi Thanh, was the district Phoenix program advisor and Captain Bundon's deputy. Al was gregarious, tall, and solidly built. He looked like he should have been a professional football middle linebacker rather than an advisor. After stowing my gear, Lieutenant Miller walked me back to the airfield and showed me my assigned task.

About all I could do when I saw the hole in the airfield PSP was to verify that it was, indeed, a hole. An 82-mm mortar most probably caused the crater, which measured about three feet in diameter and two feet deep. I had no idea how to fix the hole, but as happened frequently throughout my tour, the Vietnamese saved the day. My saviors were the Kien Long interpreter and several Vietnamese *Binh nhì* (equivalent to privates in the U.S. Army) who were assigned to help me. With enough bodies but lacking the proper equipment, we hired some local Vietnamese civilians to assist in this project.

It took us several days to get organized and then make this repair. After cutting out several mangled sheets of PSP with a Vietnamese civilian's torch, we purchased some scarce imported gravel from a local merchant. This precious gravel was used to fill the hole. Then, with my Vietnamese labor crew, we removed several sheets of PSP from the far end of the landing strip and welded this PSP over the gravel-filled and compacted hole. The project's most difficult task was transporting a bulky portable welder and an electric generator over a rickety canal bridge that separated the airfield from the small village of Kien Long. In the end, I accomplished the task Colonel LeVasseur had given me, but knew in my mind it was the Vietnamese alone who deserved all the credit for this feat.

As an interesting side note during my short stay at Kien Long,

Chapter 6. Fumbling Around in the Dark 47

helicopters brought in new M-16 rifles as replacements for the World War II–era M-1 Garands that the RF and PF soldiers currently carried. It was amusing to see the reaction of the soldiers upon receiving these weapons. Their broad smiles and obvious glee reminded me of kids opening presents at Christmas with evident joy and excitement. Thinking about it now, those joyous displays over instruments of war and death were really sad indeed.

Another memory of my short stay in Kien Long was watching a young Vietnamese girl fishing in what appeared to be a crater just outside the team house. Growing up, I enjoyed fishing in a creek that ran through our farm. Back home I caught mostly shiners, bullheads, and occasionally pan fish like blue gill and sunfish. What this girl was catching (and keeping) were fish the likes of which I had never seen before. Not only were these fish unrecognizable, they were so small I would not have used them for bait, let alone food; however, in Vietnam they were a necessary source of sustenance.

As I was waiting to get out of Kien Long, I reflected on the lessons I learned. Foremost on the list was the helpfulness of the Vietnamese and their ingenuity. Other remembrances were the remoteness of Kien Long, the dreariness of living in a bunker, and the potency of a rice whiskey that tasted somewhat like gasoline.[11] Thankfully, I completed my mission four days after arriving in Kien Long and eagerly boarded the "swing ship" heading back to Vi Thanh.

Even though I had just begun to get to know a few of the many soldiers present, at breakfast on the morning of August 19 I sensed a somber mood among my teammates. I joined Harvey and asked him what was going on. He told me he had just received word that two advisors from MAT 54 were killed several kilometers north of Vi Thanh yesterday. Lieutenant Bob Donaway was the team OIC of MAT 54 and was with team medic Sergeant First Class Howard Ard. They were in a sampan heading to Vi Thanh when they were ambushed and killed in the middle of a canal. The initial thought among the Intel officers was that either the advisors had established a predictable pattern or a VC double agent told his comrades of the advisors' intended movement. I had never met either Donaway or Ard but heard they were both good soldiers. Their deaths reminded me Vietnam was a dangerous place where things can change in an instant. Several days later, I attended a memorial service for Lieutenant Donaway and Sergeant Ard that was held on the MACV compound's movie theater stage.

CHAPTER 7

Slogging Around in the Rice Paddies

On August 22, I went on my very first combat operation. It was an airmobile (a helicopter insertion) operation into Kien Thien district, and Captain McCullough was the lead of our two-man advisory effort. This being my first operation, I had no idea what to expect or what to carry with me. In this last regard, I took four Mark-2 (World War II– and Korean War–vintage "pineapple" grenade) grenades, two smoke grenades, two ammo pouches loaded with three magazines each, a canteen, a giant Bowie knife I had purchased at Fort Bliss, the contents of a C-ration pack in my cargo pockets, my M-16, my web gear with compass, first-aid pack, and steel helmet. As I painfully learned later in the day, I packed a little bit on the heavy side.

Very early that morning Captain McCullough, our interpreter, and I met the Vietnamese command group at the Vi Thanh airfield. We advisors were to accompany an *ad hoc* command element[1] that was to coordinate the actions of several company-sized units on that day's operation. As the soldiers loaded onto the helicopters, we advisors and the command group briefly went over the concept of the operation. While I was unable to contribute anything at the briefing, I did try to absorb as much information as I could. The briefing completed, Captain McCullough carried the radio[2] as he, our interpreter, the Vietnamese captain with his small command element, and I boarded the waiting UH-1 "Huey" transport helicopter ("slick"). Captain McCullough told me to sit in one of the helicopter's seats. Since we never closed the aircraft's doors, he sat on the floor of the helicopter with his legs dangling outside. From my seat I curiously watched the actions of the helicopter crew chiefs.

The crew chief and machine gunner performed basic preflight checks on the aircraft, refueled it, operated the M-60 machine guns on each side of the helicopter, and told the pilots what was going on behind them. Prior to takeoff, they ensured the safe loading of personnel and equipment. As

Chapter 7. Slogging Around in the Rice Paddies

Captains Howard McCullough (left) and Howard Taylor (FAC) holding a captured VC flag outside the FAC hooch (courtesy George M. Eastman).

I was to see from that day forward, the crew chiefs made the Vietnamese soldiers, but not the Americans, remove their magazines and clear their weapons before they boarded. I was told this was a safety issue to prevent accidental weapon discharges. This policy, though understandable, worried me. I was afraid if we landed in a hot LZ, loading magazines would only slow our response to the enemy; but at this stage, what did I know? On this inaugural flight I also noticed all M-16s were placed muzzle down on the helicopter floor. This, I learned, was another safety procedure to prevent an errant round from hitting the engine or vital hydraulics of the aircraft.

I was both "pumped up" and a little apprehensive as the pilots of the 10 "slicks" throttled up, hovered about 20 feet above the airfield, dipped the noses of their aircraft to gain lift and speed, and rapidly headed to a distant LZ. About 15 minutes later, I heard what was to become a very familiar and comforting sound: the distinctive whop, whop, whop of a "Huey" helicopter as it came in for a landing. The "slicks" landed in a linear formation and were scarcely on the ground when everyone on board jumped off, half to the left of the helicopter and half to the right into a flooded rice paddy. I watched as everyone went 10–15 meters away from their helicopter and took a knee to avoid both enemy fire and spinning rotor blades.

With gunships swirling around the LZ providing suppressive rocket and machine gun fire, I was on an adrenaline rush as I jumped from the helicopter into the paddy. Apparently, the accompanying gunships had done their job[3] well that morning, since we landed in a cold LZ (no enemy activity or fire). As I knelt in the paddy, the helicopter that delivered me was picking up RPMs prior to lifting off, filling the air with the strong smell of the JP-4 (helicopter fuel) exhaust. At full throttle, the helicopter rotor wash was splashing the hot paddy water into my face. I was pushed to sensory overload at the sight of the gunships juking around, the smells, the sounds of exploding rockets and machine gun fire, and the Vietnamese commander and NCOs yelling for their men to move toward the tree line surrounding the rice paddy while they reconned by fire.[4] The feeling of exhilaration that swept over me during this chaotic time was indescribable. It took a while to come down from this high, but when I did, I saw Captain McCullough motioning for me to join him and the rest of the command group. My feeling of being somewhat important by this summoning didn't last long. My spirits were dashed when Captain McCullough unceremoniously handed me the radio and told me to carry it for a while.

Once it was determined the LZ was secure, we scanned the map overlay that had our predetermined checkpoints along the way, took a compass reading to determine an azimuth, and moved out to our objective. It was during this movement that Captain McCullough took on the role of instructor as he explained to me the advisor's role during operations. He said our primary mission was to assist the Vietnamese commander in accomplishing the tactical plan. This required the advisor to walk the delicate line of advising versus commanding the unit. Command, he emphasized, was the responsibility of the Vietnamese officers. Captain McCullough told me the key to success was to establish a good working relationship with the commander. Trust, tactical competence, and courage were the building blocks for this relationship. I never forgot this advice and tried my best to embody these traits during my tour.

Captain McCullough also told me that an advisor would have to "prove" himself when dealing with a new unit or commander. That meant establishing those components of rapport: being tactically competent and brave while being willing to share in the same hardships the Vietnamese faced. He said there could be times when the advisor may have to cajole a commander into taking the right action. He explained some commanders might be reluctant to employ the more aggressive actions we Americans had drilled into our heads. He said the proper thing to do was to seek help through advisors' channels and keep the senior American advisor (typically in the C&C helicopter) informed of any tactical concerns. The senior

Chapter 7. Slogging Around in the Rice Paddies

American advisor could, in turn, pass these concerns to his Vietnamese counterpart who was also in the C&C. Most of the time it was not necessary to use this process; though when used, it often worked.

An important role for advisors was to coordinate U.S. assets in support of the operation. These assets included MEDEVAC; helicopter lift into LZs and out of pickup zones (PZs), gunship support, rocket fire from the "Shotgun" or FAC pilots, and high-performance aircraft bombing. In Chuong Thien we did not have to worry about field artillery fire support, since no American artillery was present. For the RF and PF operations I participated in, a Vietnamese gun section (two guns) from a 105-mm artillery battery provided fire support. Typically, artillery was positioned to support the operation and, when needed, it was adjusted by either a Vietnamese artillery spotter flying backseat in the "Shotgun" O-1 aircraft or by the Vietnamese ground element. Fort Bragg taught me about these types of support; however, my on-the-job training was just beginning.

On that first operation we probably walked 8–10 kilometers (5–6 miles) but found no VC. However, there were two remarkable events on this operation. The first occurred early on when we had to cross a canal. Captain McCullough was carrying the radio at the time and was in a villager's sampan[5] crossing to the other side of the canal. For some reason, Captain McCullough chose to stand in the sampan (à la the painting of George Washington crossing the Delaware) as he traversed the approximately 15-meter-wide canal. About two-thirds of the way across, the sampan (which had been taking on water, as it was overloaded) began to sink. At that moment, Captain McCullough reminded me of a cartoon character I had seen as a child. He remained standing as the Vietnamese soldiers scrambled out of the sampan as it sank. He then literally walked to the far bank with the radio and his weapon—but not with his dignity intact. I joined the Vietnamese soldiers in having a great laugh at Captain McCullough's expense.

The second matter was not funny to me at all. We were toward the end of our all-day trek, and the water-filled rice paddies with their quicksand-like muck (this being the rainy season) had sapped every ounce of energy out of my unconditioned body. I was reminded of my pathetic physical condition as I had watched a 90-pound Vietnamese soldier covering the same distance as I while effortlessly carrying a 45-pound 57-mm recoilless rifle on his shoulder. In the early afternoon, I began shedding the extraneous gear I had carried with me. The Vietnamese commander recognized my plight and instructed his soldiers to carry my extra equipment. In the end, Vietnamese soldiers carried all of my gear except my M-16. Although I was totally exhausted, out of a small sense of dignity, I refused to give up my weapon. I began to think I would not be able to complete the operation, but the thought of further embarrassment carried me onward.

Thankfully, Captain McCullough saw me struggling and mercifully radioed the driver who would be picking us up later in the afternoon to bring something for me to drink. While the ARVN had to walk back to Vi Thanh, I barely had the strength to climb into the back of the jeep. At that moment, the sergeant gave me the best-tasting warm beer I ever had in my life. As I later thought about this day, I was disgusted with myself for being in such terrible physical condition. On the plus side, I learned some important lessons on this, my initial excursion against communism. Of those lessons, I vowed that carrying excess gear and running out of water and energy early in the afternoon were actions I would never repeat. My field education was just beginning.

During the first week of September, I went on three uneventful air-mobile operations. Those operations improved my physical conditioning and tactical awareness but were otherwise without results. On one of those operations, I accompanied an RF company that supported the provincial reconnaissance unit. The PRU was composed of a rough-looking bunch of men who appeared far older than RF or PF troops. The PRU were accompanied by navy SEALs and "Agency" personnel. It was rumored that some individuals in the PRU had been criminals before they were recruited into this deadly business. Their rewards for joining the PRU were commuted sentences and the prospect of cash bonuses for their efforts. Their mission that day was to neutralize VC or VC infrastructure targets in the operation's area who had been identified by Phoenix Program officials. This day was not a payday for the PRU, since they did not encounter any bad guys. Back in my hooch that night I talked to Harvey about the PRU, since he dealt with them on a frequent basis. I told him in all seriousness that I did not know who I was more afraid of, the PRU or the VC. Laughingly, he agreed.

On my next early-September operation, I accompanied Sergeant First Class Bill Haley. The operation was a bust but was the first of several I was to go on with "Wild Bill." Fortunately for me, Bill taught me a great deal about tactical operations. He had also apparently heard of my overpacking incident on my first operation with Captain McCullough. Being the extraordinary NCO that he was, he fixed that. After he had finished with me, I established my combat ensemble for the rest of my time in Vietnam. Following Sergeant Haley's guidance, on future operations I carried two canteens. The evening before an operation I would place these canteens in the freezer compartment of our refrigerator. These canteens would be frozen solid the next morning and remain cold for a couple of hours. As for food, I carried one entrée from a C-ration pack. However, most of the time I relied on eating with the Vietnamese soldiers in the field.

Chapter 7. Slogging Around in the Rice Paddies

From left to right: Lieutenant Jim Jaegers, Captain Jim Bugansky, Warrant Officer Ralph Howard, Sergeant First Class Bill Haley, and Major George Speck (FAC). Jaegers and Haley appear to be ready to go on an operation. The photo was taken on the Vi Thanh MACV compound near the FAC hooch (courtesy George M. Eastman).

For firepower, I took a standard seven-pocket 5.56-mm bandolier and cut the strap in half. I removed the 20-round cardboard cartons from the bandolier and replaced them with seven fully loaded 20-round M-16 magazines. I then took a 10-round stripper clip from the 20-round cardboard cartons and placed it with the magazine in each pocket of the bandolier. All totaled, I carried 210 M-16 rounds in the bandolier that I tied around my waist and a 20-round magazine in my M-16. I carried the magazine clip charging guide safety-pinned to the first buttonhole of my jungle fatigue shirt. This guide enabled rapid loading of a magazine with the 10 rounds held in each stripper clip.

Like the ARVNs I served with, I modified the sling on my M-16 to carry my weapon in a nonstandard way. I removed the ringed clips of my sling and adjusted the slide to fit tightly around the small of the butt stock. I then took the loose end of the sling and ran it through the rear portion of the front sight and clamped it to allow a generous loop. This easy modification allowed me to carry my M-16 slung horizontally in a quickly accessible near-firing position. This was the first of many "tricks" I was to learn from these diminutive soldiers.

On my web gear suspenders attached to my pistol belt, I carried my first-aid dressing clipped upside down to the ring near my shoulder, a smoke grenade[6] on the other suspenders ring, and, near the clasp of my pistol belt, one M-61 egg-shaped hand grenade. My final accouterment was an M-7 bayonet for the M-16. I never anticipated having to engage in close-quarter combat with the enemy, but this bayonet was handy for carving open coconuts for their milk. Unnoticed by most, I always carried my Colt .25 automatic pistol in its holster attached to my jungle fatigues trouser belt underneath my jungle fatigue shirt. Finally, I always wore my wristwatch with the watch face on the inside of my wrist. This was primarily so the watch dial would not reflect in the sun and more easily give my position away. I guess it worked!

After my promotion I wore the Vietnamese equivalent of a first lieutenant (*Trung úy*) rank on my left breast pocket[7]; a compass with its lanyard tied to my jungle fatigue shirt lapel buttonhole so I could quickly access it and would not drop or loose it, a grease pencil, and a 1:50,000 map with overlay of the operation area only covered in a plastic bag. In my breast pocket, I always carried a small green army notebook. With the help of my various interpreters, I added Vietnamese words and phrases to my vocabulary and other information in this notebook. I also carried an SOI (Signal Operating Instructions) extract in my pocket[8] that gave the radio call signs, frequencies, and passwords we were to use on an operation. Like some others who operated in the Delta, I wore neither a T-shirt nor underwear as this helped avoid rashes and sped up the process of ridding oneself of the leeches[9] picked up while crossing streams or canals. We got rid of these nasty little critters by removing our uniforms and checking one another for leeches. If found—and they were often found—we burned them off with a cigarette. Lastly, I wore a single dog tag tied into the lace of my boot and, during my first couple of operations, a "boonie" hat. After September 6, I wore a steel pot (helmet).

Lieutenant Raschke ready to go on an operation with the 987th RF company, as indicated by the red scarf I'm wearing. This picture was taken from the steps of the hooch I shared with Gene Griffiths and Harvey Weiner. The club door is to my left (author's collection).

Chapter 8

The First Weekend in September

Friday, September 5, 1969, was (I thought) the last of my three long operations for the week. During those operations I accompanied the 987th RF company, a unit that was to become one of my favorites during the year. I had gained confidence and stamina over the past couple weeks, and my Vietnamese was improving each day. That evening after dinner I attended the pre-operation briefing in Colonel LeVasseur's hooch, since I had volunteered to participate in the next day's operation. Throughout my tour of duty, pre-operation briefings were held the evening before every planned operation. The purpose of these briefings was to read participants into the mission, enemy situation, support requirements, and other relevant information.

The Vietnamese planned operations in concert with the Intel (S-2) and Operations (S-3) advisors who arranged U.S. support assets. These pre-operation briefings were conducted in a ritualistic manner. That evening Captain McCullough discussed the concept of Saturday's operation following the army's standard operation's order format. This format included information pertaining to the operation's situation, mission, execution, administrative and logistical aspects, and command and signal. The order's format was dry but all-inclusive. It ensured we received the necessary, if not always accurate, information for the upcoming operation. As he read through the operations order, Captain McCullough used a huge map of the province on Colonel LeVasseur's hooch wall to point out specific objectives, LZs, and routes of approach.

An interesting but most often inaccurate part of the briefing was the intelligence assessment of the enemy. Invariably, the S-2 advisor (Captain Ken Johnson* or Lieutenant Tim Gere*) would announce the operation was going after this or that VC unit, which was often an element of the 303rd VC Main Force Battalion believed to be at a specific location. They would give an alphabetic (A–D), designation as to the source of the information on the enemy (U.S., ARVN, or civilian) and a numeric value (1–4) as to the reliability of the information.[1] As I was listening to this segment of the briefing, I thought about the several "walks in the sun" I had thus far been on. Based on my limited observation, I certainly believed they needed to get better sources of information. The key points of the briefing for me were the map and overlay we were to use, the unit I was to accompany, the American advisors on the operation, any special communications instructions, and the departure location and time. Little did I know as I sat comfortably in Colonel LeVasseur's hooch that evening that I was about to embark on the worst 40 hours I would spend in Vietnam.

Occasionally, such as for the next day's operation, district or MAT advisors would be involved. The army "Shotgun" pilots or air force FACs had the unenviable task of getting up very early in the morning and dropping the operations order from their aircraft to the near vicinity of a waiting advisor. In addition to this early-morning requirement, September 6 would prove to be a trying day for our pilots.

Ho Chi Minh, president of North Vietnam, died on September 2, 1969.[2] "Uncle Ho's" passing was announced by Hanoi on September 3. When I heard this, I naively and incorrectly thought Ho's passing would lead to a shortening of the war. In the early-morning hours of Saturday, September 6, I was to learn the truth. As was happening at other locations throughout Vietnam, Vi Thanh, the Advisory Team 73 compound, and I were rudely awakened by a piercing siren announcing an incoming mortar attack.[3] Like others on the compound, I scrambled out of bed, grabbed my M-16,[4] flak jacket, and steel pot and headed for the bunker. Safely in the bunker, I could hear mortar rounds impacting in Vi Thanh near the province Headquarters and within the MACV compound itself. I guessed about 6–8 rounds landed in the compound, leaving shrapnel flying into protective barriers, in the PSP near the mess hall, and taking out telephone and electrical wires near the PA&E building. Fortunately, on the compound this night, there were no casualties. As a precaution, however, we stayed in the bunkers for about a half hour after the last round had landed. I later learned the VC initiated this attack to commemorate the passing of "Uncle Ho."

I was already dragging as I wolfed down my breakfast that Saturday morning. In addition to getting up before dawn for today's operation, I was still tired from yesterday's operation and having my sleep interrupted by "Uncle Ho's" celebration. My sleep deprivation mattered little, for today was to be my first mission as the most experienced of the two American advisors[5] (boy, that was a dreadful thought) to accompany the 120th RF company. Sergeant First Class Van Blarcum was the other advisor on my team. I was concerned about him for several reasons. First, Sergeant

Chapter 8. The First Weekend in September

Van Blarcum probably stood about 6'3" and outweighed me by about 70 pounds. Though Van Blarcum was an experienced 11 Bravo (infantryman),[6] he was in his mid-40s and had only recently arrived in Vietnam. Today would be his first operation in the Delta, and I thought back to my lack of physical conditioning on my first operation. I silently prayed Sergeant Van Blarcum would neither be hit nor be unable to complete the mission. I doubted I could move him.

It was just at sunrise as Sergeant Van Blarcum and I climbed into a jeep driven by a young sergeant. Per our orders, we drove westward through the town of Vi Thanh and proceeded about five kilometers along the canal road to meet our assigned company—my breakfast bouncing all the way. As we arrived at the designated location, I saw the soldiers of the 120th RF company milling around and an artillery section of two 105-mm howitzers setting up right in the middle of the road. The site of these howitzers was reassuring as we were going into the Snake River area and it had a very nasty reputation.

Dismounting from the jeep, Sergeant Van Blarcum and I met our interpreter and my counterpart, the Vietnamese company commander. The four of us briefly went over the plans for the operation. The 120th RF company would be ferried across the canal and move to a blocking position[7] south and west of the Snake River. Another element, with Lieutenant Rick Carlile[8] as the lead advisor, would be helicoptered to an LZ about four "klicks"[9] north of our blocking position. Carlile's unit was to proceed from west to east, guiding on the prominent dense vegetation jutting from the banks of the Snake River. Lieutenant Stephen Young advised the third element, which was to be inserted by helicopter about three "klicks" east of my blocking position. This company would approach the Snake River area from the southeast, heading northwest. This was Lieutenant Young's first operation as he had just arrived in-country (on August 7) to replace Lieutenant Donaway on MAT 54.

The collective mission of all units that day was the destruction of an expected company-sized VC unit located in the area of the Snake River. Notable for this operation were the facts that this was a well-known VC-controlled area, none of the American advisors had ever worked with one another or had ever accompanied any of the Vietnamese units they were advising, and the approach to the objective was across open rice paddies. As events unfolded, each of these negatives would prove consequential.

As I had observed when with Captain McCullough, and as Sergeant Haley had pounded into me, I carried the advisor radio that morning. The purpose of this was twofold. First, I wanted to ensure that if something went wrong I could immediately call for help. And second, I did not want to overburden Sergeant Van Blarcum.[10] That somewhat hazy but serene Saturday morning we easily crossed the canal by sampan. Once across, I provided a situation report (SITREP)[11] to the TOC, giving them my location and reporting that we had "negative contact" with the enemy. Soon, the 120th RF company commander ordered his troops forward as we headed north toward our blocking position.

Radio traffic picked up as Lieutenant Carlile's and Lieutenant Young's companies landed in their designated LZs. Both units reported arriving in their landing zone with no enemy contact. Major Martinson (flying in the C&C) instructed them to advance to their objectives. In an hour or so, my unit reached our designated blocking position as the companies Carlile and Young advised moved more slowly toward their objectives. The commander of the 120th RF company ordered his troops to deploy into a defensive posture as he, his command element, and two advisors set up a command post in a nearby hooch. Once settled in, I radioed another SITREP to the TOC and then proceeded to get to know and establish rapport with the 120th RF company commander.

This commander, like most of his company, was *Hòa Hảo*. This offshoot Buddhist sect was fiercely independent. Since their founding in 1939, *Hòa Hảo* adherents had fought the Japanese, French, Viet Minh, and the Diem regime. Fortunately for this operation and throughout the Vietnam conflict, the *Hòa Hảo*s were on our side.[12] The commander was a *Chuẩn úy*, the equivalent of a U.S. Army officer cadet (also called an aspirant), who was about 50 years old. He had been fighting his religion's enemies for the last nearly 30 years and had no problem kicking, hitting, screaming at, or otherwise motivating his soldiers to get them to do what he wanted. Despite his background and habits, I felt comfortable being with him as we sat in a farmer's hooch listening to our respective radios' command frequency chatter.

I tracked the progress of the two converging units as they proceeded toward their objectives. The morning was mostly quiet and routine. It was before noon when the proverbial all hell broke loose! Initially, I had a hard time figuring out what was going on as both Lieutenants Carlile's and Young's units were reporting heavy contact. As I was to repeatedly experience during my year's tour, when a unit came under fire, radio traffic picked up and everyone seemed to be talking—but few were listening. Confusion reigned as Major Martinson in the C&C could not seem to get a handle on the ground situation. Contributing to this confusion was the fact that the American advisors were providing their situation reports while at the same time the Vietnamese were sending theirs. Reconciling the sometimes conflicting ground reports was difficult because at the very same time the VC were shooting at and killing or wounding friendly forces.

Chapter 8. The First Weekend in September

Listening to the radio traffic led me to believe Lieutenant Young's unit was being shot to pieces. Gunships were currently unavailable, and there were extended radio discussions on the feasibility of using aerial-delivered smoke in front of Lieutenant Young's company. The thought was to employ the smoke between the tree line and the RF company. The smoke would obscure the VC's ability to fire on the soldiers in the rice paddy and would thereby allow the RF company to withdraw. For reasons I was never told, smoke was not employed, and the continued heavy firing prevented friendly reinforcements. The result was a terrible fate for those soldiers pinned down in the rice paddy.

At some point I heard a Vietnamese voice come across the American advisor radio frequency. My immediate (though incorrect) thought was the VC had compromised our radio net and were providing false information. I sent out a radio alert to "friendlies" of my suspicion. I soon learned the Vietnamese voice I heard was the interpreter who accompanied Lieutenant Young. That brave Vietnamese soldier reported Lieutenant Young had been hit and heavy VC fire from the wood lines had the company pinned down. The unit was several hundred meters from the tree line adjacent the Snake River. As I listened to the radio, I felt helpless and guilty, since I was not under fire and felt relatively safe.

I had radio contact with Lieutenant Carlile when the shooting first started, but now he was eerily quiet, though I could hear gunfire from his unit's general direction. This was starting to get spooky for me and I knew I had to do something. I implored the commander of the 120th RF company to move toward the Snake River with the hope of relieving pressure on the two elements, which, by the sound of things, were in very serious trouble. Through my interpreter, the Vietnamese commander repeatedly told me he could not move unless his higher headquarters directed him to do so. I called Major Martinson, requesting that he prod his Vietnamese counterpart to allow us to move to help the beleaguered units. Major Martinson curtly told me to stand by, since a plan was being formulated.

Due to our inactivity I became extremely frustrated with the situation, my condition exacerbated by an exhaustion that had accumulated over the last several days. Despite the battle going on around me, my exhaustion was now trying to take control of me. I addressed this problem by taking one of the anti-drowsiness tablets[13] the army placed in my issued survival pack. In short order, the pill perked me up. Unable to eat because of the situation swirling around me, I decided to walk around and check on the disposition of the 120th RF company soldiers. The soldiers had taken up proper defensive positions, but while they could hear distant gunfire, they looked relaxed and unconcerned about what was going on around them. I estimated probably half the company was alert while the other half was taking their post-lunch siesta.[14] I had a hard time accepting that the company was not at full alert and went back to discuss the situation with the commander. Politely, the *Chuẩn úy* told me to relax. Following Captain McCullough's advice I deferred to the commander, but I could not relax!

Flying 1,500 feet above the two besieged RF companies lying in the rice paddies were Lieutenant Eastman and Mr. Howard. Ralph had a Vietnamese aerial observer with him, and this observer was adjusting rounds from the two 105-mm howitzers that I had seen setting up earlier that morning. I could hear the rounds whistling overhead en route to the VC positions adjacent to the Snake River. I later learned it was the artillery that caused the majority of casualties to the VC force.

By looking at my map and having an understanding of a defensive position, I guessed the VC were arrayed in the tree lines abutting the banks of the river. The river at that point took a dramatic bend. Since the VC were able to simultaneously engage both Carlile's and Young's units, I surmised the VC troops were placed in two legs forming a nearly 90-degree angle, with each leg extending several hundred meters. One leg of this angle directly faced Lieutenant Carlile's element; the other leg was oriented toward Lieutenant Young's company. The vee (junction of the two legs) pointed toward us (the blocking force) several "klicks" away.

Except for refueling and rearming his 2.75" rockets, "Jug" Eastman spent the day assessing the ongoing, though one-sided, fight. He provided time-sensitive situation reports and directed fighter aircraft on bombing runs against the well-entrenched VC. Lieutenant Eastman's actions and the Vietnamese artillery fire prevented the VC from overrunning the RF companies trapped in the rice paddies, but only temporarily slackened enemy fire. For his coolness and courageous actions over that extended day,[15] Lieutenant George "Jug" Eastman was awarded the Silver Star.

After several hours of my company sitting on the sidelines, Major Martinson contacted me and told me to get ready to move out. He told me the 120th RF company would be picked up near our current location and we would be airlifted into the vicinity of Lieutenant Carlile's company. My expressed mission was to relieve pressure on Carlile's unit to prevent it from being overrun and to evacuate the wounded.

Through my interpreter, I confirmed the *Chuẩn úy* had received the same instructions, and I told Sergeant Van Blarcum the plan. As a unit, we immediately proceeded to the designated PZ in a nearby rice paddy. Not too long after receiving the mission orders, the helicopter flight leader came onto my frequency, telling me he was inbound and several minutes[16] from my location. I waited for a while and then, at the pilot's command, "popped" and threw a smoke grenade into the paddy. The

Chapter 8. The First Weekend in September

flight leader verified the color of my smoke, and soon there were about a dozen helicopters landing to pick up our stacked troops. Carrying the radio, I boarded the lead helicopter with the company commander, Sergeant Van Blarcum, and our interpreter. We were soon airborne,[17] and the flight to the LZ took only a few minutes. During this short flight, I was neither apprehensive nor afraid; instead, I was incredibly at peace with myself.

My peace, however, was soon shattered as we approached the LZ. This LZ was probably 600–800 meters away from the tree line where the VC were located. It was nearing dusk, with the artillery intermittently firing on the VC locations, as the relief force and I jumped off the helicopters. Without prodding we ran through the flooded rice paddies in the direction of the tree lines and VC positions.

Knowing Lieutenant Carlile's unit was nearby, with the radio on my back and my M-16 in my hand I swiftly moved toward the faintly smoking tree line. Incredibly, it took me a while to realize there were enemy bullets whizzing by and splashing up paddy water around me. This was my first time under serious enemy fire. I heard and distinguished, for the first time, the distinctive sound of an AK-47[18] rifle. When it dawned on me I was being shot at, I ran faster, being thankful the VC were poor shots. During my sprint I crouched low, as I had once done in my days on the farm when my brothers and I were engaged in dirt clod or corn cob fights. At that moment I did not think about Sergeant Van Blarcum, my interpreter, the 120th RF company, or anyone else for that matter.

Though I was thus far unharmed, the bullets zinging by and impacting near me spurred me to increase my already fast pace across the rice paddy. A solitary hooch that was several hundred meters to my right front became the focus for my safety. Moving as fast as one can run through a flooded paddy while laden with gear, I suddenly fell into a water-filled bomb crater. The 20-pound radio on my back caused me to fall face-first into the hole. Initially fully submerged and loaded down with the radio, my weapon, and gear, I struggled to get out of the hole. I finally got up, spit out a mouthful of muddy water, and laughed at myself until I realized the seriousness of my situation. (Strangely, I could not remember seeing any of my movie or TV heroes doing anything like what I had just done.) Back to reality, I continued toward the hooch.

As I got closer to the hooch, enemy fire seemed to ease up. I attributed this to impacting artillery rounds the combined small-arms fire from the remaining elements of Lieutenant Carlile's company and the ARVN who landed with me. These factors seemed to keep the VC pinned down. In minutes that seemed like hours, I finally got to the hooch, where I briefly caught my breath before seeking out Lieutenant Carlile.

As I left the hooch that was about 200–300 meters from the enemy-occupied tree line, I saw a scene forever etched into my memory. About 10–15 meters from the hooch, there, in the rice paddy, was a very young Vietnamese soldier lying on his back, his limbs articulated in a strange way. He wore the traditional ARVN fatigue uniform with the white circle, red-lettered IV Corps patch sewn onto his breast pocket, and, as Vietnamese soldiers sometimes did, no boots. This was the first combat death I saw in-country, and years later, the sight of this soldier remains permanently burned into my memory. Shot through the lung, this young man had aspirated a frothy blood from his mouth and at the site of his entry wound. I was transfixed as I momentarily stared at this soldier's face. Despite his violent death and now ashen pallor, he appeared peacefully asleep.

Snapping out of my trance, I knew I had to find Lieutenant Carlile. I soon located Sergeant Lewis Henderson, the NCO who accompanied Lieutenant Carlile. Henderson was uninjured and he had managed to drag Lieutenant Carlile toward the hooch once the VC fire abated. Henderson took me to Carlile, who had suffered numerous gunshot wounds.[19] Carlile was barely conscious and was fighting for his life. In the fast-dimming light, we dragged Carlile to the side of the hooch away from the tree line and laid him on the ground. Falling back on my medical corpsman training, I assessed his wounds. I was impressed with the care the Vietnamese medic had given him. Though this medic had his hands full that afternoon, under fire he had skillfully bandaged Carlile's wounds—likely saving his life. I called the TOC to report finding Lieutenant Carlile and gave them his medical status and the general situation on the ground. The TOC said they would request an immediate MEDEVAC for Carlile and several badly wounded RF soldiers. As darkness fell, I awaited the MEDEVAC.

The TOC officer informed me a Vietnamese command element had landed with me in the LZ. This was news to me. The TOC told me to find the Vietnamese captain, who was the overall ground commander, and to coordinate efforts with him. I found the Đai úy, who told me his mission was to hold the area, take care of the wounded, police up the dead, and send periodic updates to the Vietnamese TOC. It later occurred to me that I had not seen the Chuẩn úy (commander of the 120th RF company) after I had jumped off the helicopter at the LZ. I did not know if this was lack of focus, tunnel vision, or preoccupation with events.

Reminiscent of my late-morning and early-afternoon experience, time moved slowly as I awaited the MEDEVAC. I checked on Lieutenant Carlile several times while I waited. He remained stable, but with his labored breathing, I knew he was in serious condition. I wanted to get him and the other wounded out of there as soon as possible. I made repeated pleading inquiries to the TOC on the status of the MEDEVAC. Finally, "dustoff" came on my frequency and asked for my grid location. Looking at my map through the dimly lit hooch, I gave my location to the pilot. The pilot asked if I had a strobe light or flashlight to mark the pickup site. I told him I had neither, which made this serious situation critical, as the "dustoff" helicopter had to locate and to land exactly at my location in now pitch-darkness.

In my slowly numbing mind, I told Van Blarcum and Henderson to begin taking thatch from the sidewall of the hooch to use for a fire to mark our location. Getting a fire started in the rainy season was no easy task. As the helicopter circled at a distance, we used kindling from the hooch's cooking fire to get a fire started. Once the "dustoff" pilot identified our fire, I told him the azimuth of approach he should use to avoid flying over or near enemy positions. He acknowledged my instructions. While I was talking the pilot into an approach landing, the two NCOs found a makeshift litter and loaded Lieutenant Carlile onto it.

As the "dustoff" neared my location they turned on their landing lights. I stood by the fire with the radio on my back and directed the helicopter in for the pickup using hand and arm signals. The pilot saw me and skillfully landed the aircraft. In doing so, the rotor wash scattered the flame and ashes of the fire as well as my "boonie" hat. Most importantly, however, Lieutenant Carlile and several wounded Vietnamese were loaded onto the "dustoff," which then flew directly to Can Tho. I later learned the "dustoff" crew was concerned about enemy fire near my location. This explained their arrival delay and insistence on a visible landing site. Their concern about enemy fire was valid, for after they picked up the wounded, they received several hits on their aircraft from the VC-controlled tree line.

The TOC had followed the radio traffic between the "dustoff" crew and me. After the MEDEVAC departed, the TOC instructed me to remain in place for the evening, which I had fully expected. Following this conversation was the first lull for me in hours after assaulting into the area, assessing the situation, and working through the frustration of getting the MEDEVAC. It occurred to me that I had not eaten since breakfast, and I was famished! Additionally, my pep pill had completely worn off and I was about to physically crash.

I again talked with the *Dai úy* and he reconfirmed his orders to maintain a perimeter but not to go into the tree line. Once I was satisfied that everything was done that could be done, the command element, we Americans, and a very frightened peasant family (who had spent the day in their hooch's bunker while a fierce battle raged outside) settled down for an uneasy evening in the crowded hooch. Outside the hooch, the VC fire had totally ceased, though friendly harassment and interdiction (H&I)

artillery fires would continue throughout the night. The purpose for the intermittent artillery H&I fires was to impede the VC escaping from the area.

Exhausted and ready to catch some sleep, I decided I would keep the radio with me during the night, since it was my lifeline to the TOC for periodic updates and/or in the event of VC activity. In the dimly lit hooch I crawled on top of the family bunker, placed my M-16 by my side, Colt .25 caliber automatic pistol on my chest, and radio handset near my head. Soon I began a fitful sleep. Every now and then I was jolted awake by the occasional static of a radio transmission or an exploding artillery shell. In my semi-awake state the sound of H&I fire coupled with the absence of enemy small-arms fire was reassuring. As I intermittently slept, the VC adeptly collected their casualties; and despite the artillery fire, exfiltrated the area.

Early mornings in Vietnam were generally serene and quite beautiful. As I awoke very early, I went outside the hooch to relieve myself and found that this September 7 was no exception. That morning, however, there was a slight ground fog, which dulled the rising sun. The stillness outside was surreal, given what the area around the hooch had experienced a day earlier. The Vietnamese command group was stirring and there was some muted radio chatter inside the hooch, but the chaos from yesterday was absent.

Soon I heard the familiar voice of "Jug" Eastman on my radio. "Jug" said he had just lifted off from Vi Thanh and was en route to assess the enemy and friendly ground situation. The hum of the single engine O-1 was soon overhead, and after a recon of the area, "Jug" reported to the TOC. On my radio I heard him say he saw no signs of enemy activity. As I surveyed activities around me, I saw Vietnamese soldiers moving through the rice paddy, recovering the bodies of their comrades and collecting equipment scattered about. Soldiers brought the KIAs to the vicinity of the lone hooch and laid them out in a neat row wrapped in ponchos or those flimsy plastic rain sheets the Vietnamese often carried.

A little later, I received a call from the Duty NCO at the TOC, who said the plan was to send several helicopters to my location with food and ammunition for the Vietnamese and several advisors to replace Van Blarcum, Henderson, and me. Those helicopters would also pick up any remaining wounded and the KIAs. It was around 9:00 a.m. when I received a radio transmission from the inbound helicopters. The flight lead requested I pop smoke, which I did and which he quickly identified.

The helicopters were a welcome sight as they came into the LZ near the hooch, sat down, and throttled back their engines. Without hesitation, the crew chiefs and the onboard American advisors threw off ammo and supplies. Once this was complete, the Vietnamese and advisors carefully

Chapter 8. The First Weekend in September

USAF lieutenant George "Jug" Eastman, one of our forward air controllers (FAC), standing next to his O-1 "Birddog" airplane. The photo was taken with the plane in its revetment at the Vi Thanh airfield. Note the PSP landing surface and the 2.75 rocket pods visible on the plane wing over Lieutenant Eastman's right shoulder (courtesy George M. Eastman).

loaded the wounded onto the helicopters. Once the wounded were loaded, we then began putting the KIAs onto the floor of the aircraft, where they were unceremoniously stacked one on top of another. This grotesque scene strangely reminded me of stacking fence posts into our little two-wheeled cart back on the farm. During this gruesome process, I noticed most KIA were hit in the head or upper body. Most likely, the casualties were lying flat on their stomachs in the rice paddy facing the enemy. This explained the location of their fatal wounds.

In a haze, I did not recall the names of the advisors who replaced us, and it later occurred to me that I failed to brief them on the ground situation. I can only explain this basic breach of duty by my mind struggling to come to grips with the events of the past 24 hours, culminating in the way the KIAs were loaded. At some point the crew chief motioned me and Sergeants Van Blarcum and Henderson to get on board. With the bodies taking up most of the space in the helicopter, I sat on the floor straddling the pole near the crew chief/gunner compartment with my legs dangling outside and my arms interlocked around the pole. Near shock would best describe my mental state at the time.

On the short flight to the airfield the impact of what happened over the past 24 hours really hit me. The loss of life and the callous way we treated the bodies was something I had never experienced before. Those lifeless souls now lying next to me, though from a different culture and speaking a different language, just a day earlier were full of life, had loved ones and, I'm sure, had thoughts of their future. Their future now was grieving relatives and a grave for all eternity.

Once the helicopter sat down at the Vi Thanh airfield, I moved away from it as fast as my zombie-like state would allow. As I walked to the terminal building, I saw a Vietnamese ambulance and 2½-ton truck moving toward the helicopters for the grim task that awaited them. Near the terminal I saw Captain Sands sitting in a jeep. Though I barely knew him, I knew Captain Sands was the province S-1/S-4 advisor. He stood out as the epitome of efficiency and was a soldier who was usually quiet, but when he spoke, everyone listened. Captain Sands was another of the "good" captains and had an always cheerful and helpful demeanor.

Captain Sands told me to get into his jeep, and then proceeded to pick up Van Blarcum and Henderson for the ride back to the MACV compound. On the ride from the airfield to the compound, the four of us sat in abject silence. Once we got to the compound, the two sergeants and I went to the mess hall, where the staff fixed us a late breakfast. This was literally the first good meal I'd had in days, and I felt better after eating. That feeling was crushed when Captain Sands told me Lieutenant Young had died of his wounds. This sad news just made me more depressed than ever. Following breakfast, I stowed my gear, took a long shower, and crashed into my bunk.

I was roused from my sleep of nearly 10 hours by a noise within the hooch. I was surprised to see Harvey sitting at the table in the center of our room. He welcomed me back from my slumber and we discussed the recent operation. Harvey also filled me in on some of the details I had not known. He said we most assuredly had fought against elements of the 303rd VC main force battalion.[20] In the ever important metric of body count, friendly forces suffered 16 ARVN and one American KIA with probably double that number wounded. Estimated enemy losses were 30 KIA and an equal number wounded.[21] As I was listening to this, it occurred to me I had not fired a single shot.

Harvey also told me the TOC initially reported it was I, not Lieutenant Young, who was initially identified as KIA during yesterday's operation. That news was unsettling! The good news, he told me, was that Lieutenant Carlile was at the 29th Evacuation Hospital in Can Tho, and as far as Harvey knew, Lieutenant Carlile was still alive. Harvey had learned from Sergeant Henderson that Lieutenant Carlile used his radio

Chapter 8. The First Weekend in September

for protection as it, and the small rice paddy dike, were the only cover between him and the VC. As he was taking multiple hits, the VC also shot up Lieutenant Carlile's radio, ultimately knocking it out of commission.[22] That explained the lack of communications that I had noted.

Psychological relief and Harvey's questions compelled me to talk about my actions during the operation. This discussion was therapeutic as it allowed me to excise some of the traumatic events that lingered in my mind. My actions, as I believed, were not heroic, but rather, I was just doing what I was trained to do and as the situation required. Harvey disagreed with my assessment and thought my actions merited a Silver Star recommendation. I told him that I was just glad to be sitting there talking with him!

Over the next few days it seemed like everyone wanted to discuss the weekend operation, though I hardly felt like talking about it. On Monday, Captain Howard Taylor asked me if I wanted to see the battle area from the air. I eagerly took him up on his offer, and soon we were airborne, flying over the Snake River. Captain Taylor, who replaced "Jug" later in the day on Saturday, pointed out friendly and enemy locations and described the operation as he experienced it from 1,500 feet. The enemy bunker areas were easy to spot as the area was pockmarked with artillery and bomb craters around the length and breadth of those fighting positions. Captain Taylor showed me the location of my dusk helicopter insertion LZ, and I saw the lone hooch that had served as our evening command post. I also saw ashes from the MEDEVAC signal fire we had set. What I had not seen before was a small canal running right beside the hooch and the post-battle litter. Everything appeared so small and tranquil. It was hard to believe the carnage that had occurred there less than 48 hours earlier.

Several days later, Colonel LeVasseur, Captain Childress, Harvey, and I took a helicopter flight up to the 29th Evacuation Hospital at Can Tho to see Lieutenant Carlile. Rick was lying in the hospital bed with a Purple Heart medal on his bed stand and a small vial containing the 7.62 x 39-mm[23] slugs the doctors had removed from him. Obviously sedated for pain, Carlile did not want to talk much. However, I thought I noticed a slight smile on his face when Colonel LeVasseur made a comment on Carlile's grit, determination, and the attention the hospital staff was giving him. I told him he certainly looked better than when I last saw him. Colonel LeVasseur talked to Lieutenant Carlile's attending doctor, who told him that once he was stabilized, Rick would be evacuated to a hospital in either Japan or the U.S. As we left, we bid Lieutenant Carlile farewell, knowing he would not return to Team 73.

Chapter 9

Routine, Money, and Morale

During the trip to see Lieutenant Carlile, Colonel LeVasseur and I discussed the recent operation, and he told me I had done a good job. I appreciated his kind words but told him I was disappointed with the results of the operation as well as my inability to effect a better outcome. Sometime during our trip to Can Tho, Colonel LeVasseur asked me if I would be willing to take on the responsibility of managing the AIK (Assistance In Kind) fund. He could have been speaking in a foreign language, since I had never heard of an AIK fund and therefore I had no idea what he was talking about. But I had been looking for additional duties, so once I understood what was required, I readily accepted this assignment. Managing the AIK fund gave me more to do and allowed me more interaction with district and MAT members. It also required me to make a trip to Saigon every four to six weeks to replenish the fund.

Within Chuong Thien province[1] the U.S. government established an AIK fund that was allocated up to 50,000 piasters (roughly $400) per month to administer. The intent of this fund was to help the local economies, and it was used to reimburse Vietnamese civilians who provided goods and services to us. For example, the AIK fund paid for the civilian welder and the rock used on the Kien Long airfield repair project. It also paid for occasional Vietnamese labor for the district teams and MATs and purchased the most precious commodity used by these subordinate units—ice. Before I assumed responsibility for the fund, the district teams and MATs had been allocated a certain amount of AIK funds. Now it was my responsibility to replenish team funds with Vietnamese piasters in the amount of receipts/invoices received from Vietnamese vendors.

Vi Thanh felt like home whether I was returning from an operation, Saigon, or a visit to one of the districts. Life was great on the MACV compound. There, I had friends, good food, and a different movie almost every night. But the absolute cherry on the top was being able to take a hot shower. I lived in a clean and dry hooch that had a small area that was mine: Mine to stack and read books sent by U.S. civilian agencies; mine

Chapter 9. Routine, Money, and Morale

to write letters or play solitaire; or mine to just sleep! It was there in our hooch that Harvey, Gene, and I often talked about team and world events.

Since I had not attended college, I found my discussions with Harvey to be both enlightening and educational. Our discussions challenged and expanded my mind. Some of our memorable discussions were about politics. Harvey explained the basic concept of liberalism and conservatism. As fundamental as these terms are to everyone today, in 1969 I did not know what they meant. It was easy for Harvey to talk politics because he had a great intellect, an Ivy League education, and had grown up under the long shadow cast by fellow Bay Stater and moderate Democrat John F. Kennedy.

As for me, I came from a background of conservative Midwestern farmers. All I knew about politics was that both my parents and grandparents were Republicans, so I was naturally swayed in that direction. Although in my early 20s, I considered myself politically naïve and did not know what the Republican Party stood for. With my limited political knowledge and passion, Harvey was always much more able than I to state and defend his positions. When Gene Griffiths, another native of the Northeast U.S., joined our hooch in October 1969, I was ideologically outnumbered. Therefore, I avoided political discussions altogether. However, Gene added immensely to our many other light, but occasionally deep, discussions.

August 31, 1969, was a memorable day. The day before, I celebrated my one-year anniversary of becoming a commissioned officer in the United States Army. I reminisced over the many things that had happened during the past year and just how quickly time had passed. An important event for me was to come later in the evening. After dinner, but before the movie, Captain Andrews put the word out that everyone should assemble in the club. There, at the appointed time, I stood at attention facing Colonel LeVasseur as Captain Andrews read:

> Attention to orders! Headquarters Military Assistance Command-Vietnam, Special Orders number 242 dated 30 August 1969. The following individual is promoted as indicated; Raschke, John S., Second Lieutenant Corps of Engineers, to be, First Lieutenant, effective August 30, 1969, signed J.F. Harris, Major, USA, Assistant Adjutant.

Following these words, Colonel LeVasseur pinned my new first lieutenant rank onto my collar. During this "pinning," I thought it was great to no longer be a second lieutenant.

Second lieutenants—aka "shavetails," "butterbars," and other less flattering terms—described a class of soldiers who occupied the lowest rung of respect within the army and were held in a level of esteem just slightly higher than derelicts, sexual deviants, and winos. Privates, I thought, were better respected. With Colonel LeVasseur's congratulations, I thanked him, beaming with the knowledge that I had just received a nice pay raise. So, in keeping with army tradition, I proclaimed, "A round of drinks for everyone!"

Notwithstanding what one had to do to receive it, Vietnam was a well-paying opportunity for a non-college-degreed person such as myself. In 1969, the median annual income for a family in the United States was about $9,400.[2] With my pay and entitlements I was in the $10,800 per year range, of which 75 percent was nontaxable. In looking at my monthly pay slip, as a new first lieutenant I received $641.40 as base pay, $30.00 for family separation allowance, $65.00 hostile fire pay, $47.88 basic allowance for subsistence, and $120.00 basic allowance for quarters. This totaled $904.28 per month. Because I was stationed in a war zone, only $206.40 of that amount was taxable. Each month I had allotments of $80.70 for my Camaro car payment, $525.00 placed into an interest-bearing savings account, $6.25 for a savings bond, and $2.00 for Serviceman's Group Life Insurance. With collections for allotments and taxes, my net pay was about $260.00. Of my net pay amount, I sent $200 home, making do with about $60.00 per month.

Living on $60 per month was actually pretty easy. Everything I needed fit into this meager budget. I paid for my mess hall meals.[3] Once a month, I went to the compound PX and spent about $2–$3 for a carton of Salem cigarettes. I did not smoke, but usually carried a pack of cigarettes everywhere I went. This was because just about every Vietnamese soldier smoked, and giving out Salems[4] was a great way to make friends with the young soldiers. Additionally, I gave the Vietnamese MACV compound gate guards a pack of Salems as payment for cleaning my M-16. All in all, Salems were a great icebreaker and trade medium.

I also bought a case of sodas at the PX (7-Up was the most commonly available brand), and on infrequent occasions I purchased a case of Black Label beer. As with the cigarettes, I did not really drink, but I bought the beer to share with hooch visitors or have an occasional cold beer after a trying operation. I had never heard of Black Label beer before Vietnam and wondered why it was there in the PX. Here again, being at the end of the supply chain was likely the most logical reason for the surplus of 7-Up and Black Label. Strangely, opening either the soda or beer cans required the use of an old-fashioned can opener, as "pop-top" tabs were just becoming popular in the U.S. Another trait both the soda and beer cans shared was the frequency with which on opening a can I would find it completely flat, or once in a while, empty or only partially filled.

Still spending my way through my $60 each month, I would convert

Chapter 9. Routine, Money, and Morale

about $8–$10 of MPC into Vietnamese piasters. I used these piasters when I purchased items from Vietnamese vendors. I also spent a whopping 200 piasters[5] per week on maid services. Our hooch maid was Cô Yen.[6] Cô Yen cleaned our room, made my bed, and did my laundry. She received 200 piasters from probably 6–10 advisors each week. This paltry amount to us Americans was a tidy sum in Vietnam. Cô Yen was an industrious, genial young woman who spoke no English but had a perpetual smile on her face.

While some men on the compound played poker, spent time in the club, or had other ways to spend their monthly pay, I was pretty frugal. Any remaining money I had I would spend on snack items from the PX, use to finance my trips to Saigon, or save.

By the fall of 1969, events around the compound were beginning to fall into a dull pattern. The food in the mess hall continued to be excellent and became even better on those few occasions when we had ice cream. I marveled that the army was able to provide ice cream when temperatures, even during the rainy season, were in the high 90s. Also amazing was the ice cream itself. It was packaged in wax paper and wrapped in single servings that measured about 3" × 2" × 1". Ice cream days were memorable! Then too, about once every month, on Sundays or special holidays, the mess hall staff grilled steaks. This was always a special feast as the steaks were served with the standard picnic side dishes. These thoughtful gestures by the army really helped morale.

I recall being in the compound during many of the monsoon downpours. On those many afternoons in the rainy season, the sky would go from sunny one minute to dark and foreboding the next. Once the clouds set in, the skies would literally open up. The rain would come down in torrents for perhaps 20 minutes. Then, as suddenly as it started, the rain would end and the sun would be out again. The rain pounding on the roof of the hooch sounded like hailstorms I had experienced back in Illinois. This cacophony would make talking difficult, but in the afternoon few people were around. Strangely, I do not recall thunder or lightning during the monsoon rains. I do know that being caught in these downpours in the field was an unpleasant experience.

The only thing that would boost morale more than good food was mail call. Just about every day a detailed mail clerk held mail call at the improvised mail shack. Between established times, team members could stop by and see if they had received mail. Nothing was more uplifting than receiving mail, and nothing was more disheartening than not receiving mail. On average, I received a letter two or three times a week and a CARE package from home about once a month.[7] My CARE packages would include such things as Tang, Jiffy Pop popcorn, a small jar of

Lieutenant Gene Griffiths opening a "CARE" package in our hooch. "Clean" Gene and I were a great fit, the two of us (courtesy Harvey Weiner).

olives, packaged cookies, etc. Some teammates regularly received audio tapes from home. In addition to not having a camera, I did not have a tape recorder. Though I could have purchased one in-country, I thought listening to tapes from home would only make me more homesick.

I probably wrote two or three letters home each week, occasionally more when I would send my mother or grandmothers a letter.[8] I wrote Sue about the events of September 6–7. Several weeks later in one of her letters she asked that I not write about dangerous operations or use graphic descriptions as it upset her. I honored her request for the rest of my tour but felt denied an outlet for my feelings in reaction to the abnormal situations I was facing.

I really enjoyed receiving my weekly hometown paper, *The Geneseo Republic*. It was great to keep up with events in the Geneseo area. However,

Chapter 9. Routine, Money, and Morale

it was a striking dichotomy for me to read about normal life back home while Americans were fighting and dying in Vietnam. I was most interested in reading about classmates and friends serving in Vietnam. The quaintness of *Republic* articles often made it hard for me to rationalize the world I was living in.

Team personnel were almost always back on the compound by dark unless one was involved in an infrequent night operation. Evening time was when everyone was together. The primary after-dinner activity was the nightly movie. Each night around 7:00 p.m. a recently released movie was shown and most of the compound personnel showed up to watch it. These movies helped keep morale up. They provided a temporary release from the world we were living in and reminded us of our earlier lives. Just as important, the movies featured "round-eyed" women[9] and added color to our otherwise drab surroundings. Of the many movies I saw that year, I specifically remember seeing *Romeo and Juliet,* starring Olivia Hussey and Leonard Whiting. A loud cheer went up from the crowd when Juliet partially exposed herself during the wedding night scene. How those little things leave such a lasting impression is just remarkable.

Lieutenant Raschke studying a field manual (in reality, probably a *Playboy* magazine) in the hooch of "Jug" Eastman and Captain Taylor (courtesy George M. Eastman).

Although I was grateful for it, for the life of me, I never understood why the VC did not mortar us during movie time. From a military perspective, movie time was a well-established routine. Most of the team was assembled in the same area (presenting a lucrative target) and were fixated on the movie. Instead, the VC chose the early-morning hours for the use of mortars, when in the stillness of the night sounds were more pronounced. Fortunately for us, this was the VC's opportunity lost.

On those occasions when I had either already seen the movie or just did not like the one playing, I would entertain myself in a variety of ways. I would play solitaire, write letters, listen to the

Armed Forces Vietnam Network (AFVN), read, visit others on the compound, or just try to break the world record for accumulated sleep hours over the period of one year. In Vietnam, I read more books or periodicals than during any other previous time in my life. Each week we received magazines like *Time* and *Newsweek*,[10] and newspapers such as *Stars and Stripes* and *Army Times*. Then, too, there was always someone's personal copy of *Playboy* floating around the compound. This we professionals strictly reviewed for the insightful and thought-provoking articles.

Like most soldiers in Vietnam, I enjoyed *Stars and Stripes*, since it had a strong, pro-military slant and had many articles about operations and activities within Vietnam. Throughout the year, *Stars and Stripes* had several detailed articles on successful operations in Chuong Thien province. The weekly *Army Times* was much more big picture and covered the army's activities worldwide. I read *Army Times* from cover to cover and always paid close attention to the weekly casualty list to see if anyone I knew was on it. I was shocked to see Lieutenant Colonel Eugene Smallwood's name on a mid–September casualty list. Colonel Smallwood had been a classmate of mine at Fort Bragg (MATA) and Fort Bliss (Vietnamese Language School), and was the senior advisor to the 50th Regiment, 25th ARVN Division. He had served in the army during World War II, the Korean Conflict, and now Vietnam. Colonel Smallwood was a good officer, had a large family, and had a great sense of humor. Post-Vietnam, I learned a deranged Vietnamese security guard killed him and a U.S. Army major as they were entering a Vietnamese headquarters compound.[11]

On most occasions, AFVN reception was not very good on my small transistor radio. However, it was the only American station available and brought a small slice of life back home to Vietnam. Like me, I believe everyone had their favorite songs in Vietnam. Most of those favorites had something to do with going home. Songs special to me, and probably to many Americans serving in Vietnam, were "San Francisco," by Scott McKenzie[12]; "Leaving on a Jet Plane," by Peter, Paul and Mary; "Homeward Bound," by Simon and Garfunkel; and "We Gotta Get Out of this Place," by the Animals. These last three songs spoke metaphorically to me about leaving Vietnam and going back to the real world. It is hard to explain why I listened to these songs because at their conclusion I ended up thinking more about home and was always sadder than before I heard them.

Movie or not, one nightly ritual was spraying the hooch down with the army-issue bug spray to kill any insects brave enough to invade our sacred space. Harvey, Gene, or I often did this just before we went for our nightly shower. A 15-minute shower gave time for this potent aerosol to do its work and mostly dissipate. It did a great job of killing anything flying, and some of us feared it could eventually have a similar effect on those of

Chapter 9. Routine, Money, and Morale 75

us who were bipedal. The last thing I did before going to bed was to ready my M-16, ammo bandolier, flak jacket, helmet, and boots for a possible night run to the bunker. Fortunately, this run occurred only about a half dozen times during my tour.

The infrequent USO show or celebrities visiting Vi Thanh provided live entertainment and were real treats. Although I missed them, Raymond Burr (Perry Mason to me) and George E. Jessel had come to Chuong Thien in May or June. The few shows I saw featured lesser-known celebrities but were upbeat and great for morale. While these USO shows were good, they could not compare with the concerts I had attended in the U.S. The highlight of the USO shows was always seeing "round-eyed" women because this was a rare visual delicacy to those of us in Vietnam at such remote locations.

Military payment Certificate (MPC) with a 10-cent face value. This Monopoly-like money was one of several series used in Vietnam.

Around the second week in August 1969, everyone on the compound was required to exchange their "old" MPC for new scrip. This was not a big deal for me, but I wondered about the purpose of this action. Our hooch sage, Harvey, told me the purpose of this MPC replacement was to discourage black market activities and the exploitation of our currency by unsavory people. I did not believe we had this problem in Vi Thanh, and found it hard to comprehend that people would do something like this in a war zone. Harvey reminded me of my naïveté and that this change of MPC was going on throughout the country. It was an easy exchange for me as I received my new monopoly money.

Unlike Harvey and Gene, who played tennis nearly every day during post-lunch siesta times,[13] my form of noontime relaxation was either reading or sunbathing on top of the bunker outside our hooch. Later in my tour it occurred to me that I had established a rigid, time-sensitive tanning session routine. Fortunately, the VC never molested me: Another bit of good fortune for me—another VC opportunity lost. An opportunity lost, since only a chain-link fence separated me from the Vietnamese civilian area just a few feet away from the bunker—easily within grenade tossing range. Equally amazing to me was that the VC never targeted our teammates who played tennis outside but adjacent to the compound. I figured this was perhaps due to the VC having their own siesta time. As a plus for me, during the dry season, I had a tan that would rival that of George Hamilton.[14]

Throughout my tour, I had the philosophy of doing the most and best I could, but when this was not required, I conserved my energy—mostly by sleeping. Harvey, in particular, could not believe my ability to sleep more than eight hours at a time. Whether one was in a U.S. combat unit or on an advisory team, there was no such thing as a prescribed work week in Vietnam. However, on the MACV compound, when not otherwise required to be performing some sort of duty, Sundays were a day of rest for team members, a day for catching up on letter writing, reading, visiting others, or sleeping. I mostly chose the latter.

We had several community dogs on the compound. Two were of such a mixture of breeds that even guessing their pedigree was impossible. We called one Ratdog. He looked more like a hyena than a dog. For some strange reason, the "Shotgun" pilots assumed the role as Ratdog's masters. He got his name from his ability to kill rats trying to invade the compound, such as those I heard while on guard duty one night. As proof of his handiwork, Ratdog would often carry around a dead rat in his mouth and drop it at your feet to demonstrate his hunting prowess.

Another dog on the compound was Susi. Susi appeared to be mostly German shepherd but mixed with other breeds. Like Ratdog, she was a friendly dog—especially with male dogs. She was constantly having pups

Chapter 9. Routine, Money, and Morale 77

and had at least two sets of puppies while I was in-country. Susi was a constant companion of the soldiers from the 52nd Signal Detachment and they took good care of her and her many pups.

The other compound dog was Pierre. Pierre was a mixed breed but mostly resembled a French poodle. He was the ward of the airfield NCO, who never let him out of his sight. As everyone on the compound would attest (except, of course the airfield NCO) Pierre was a much too spoiled, snippy, arrogant little cur. Not surprisingly, Pierre was universally despised. In dispensing GI justice within hours after the airfield NCO DEROSed, several soldiers took Pierre to the airfield one last time. Though I was not present, I understood these soldiers ceremonially used Pierre to sight-in their M-16s.

During evening hours, officers performed the extra duty called staff duty officer (SDO) at the TOC. NCOs ran the TOC during the day and captains and lieutenants ran it at night. A duty roster, posted on a bulletin board in the mess hall, assigned officers to perform this role during the hours of 7:00 p.m. to 7:00 a.m. (1900 to 0700, using the military clock). TOC duty was always interesting. As SDO, we were required to record a narrative of each significant event into a staff duty officer's journal, DA Form 1594. These entries included the event, its start and end date and times, and the final disposition/resolution of the event. The staff duty officer's journal served as a team history where our daily team activities were recorded. Each morning the S-3 Advisor and/or the PSA reviewed the log. Ultimately, the army collected and retained these journals as a permanent historical record of organizations' activities in Vietnam, and worldwide, for that matter. Accordingly, we SDOs were cautioned to be thoughtful and professional in making our entries.

In Vietnam, "Charlie[15] owned the night." During hours of darkness, the VC conducted most of their troop and supply movements and attacked GVN personnel and facilities. However, on most nights SDO duty was reasonably quiet. During these quiet hours, one could write letters, read a book, visit with the Vietnamese soldiers performing duties in or around the TOC, or take interrupted catnaps.

The most frequent evening SDO activity was clearing the many different types of aircraft traversing the province. Aircraft needing to fly through the province would radio the TOC to ensure they would not fly into artillery fires coming out of Vi Thanh, or occasionally other locations. Each evening, the Vietnamese artillery unit located in Vi Thanh would provide the TOC with the Harassment & Interdiction target grid locations; the general time frame they would be firing on those targets, and the maximum ordinate of the projectile.[16] As SDO, we would translate the target grid locations into an imaginary clock with the pivot point of the clock hands being the location of the artillery firing unit. Using this clock, due north was 12:00, due east 3:00, due south 6:00, and due west 9:00.

As aircraft approached the province, we would tell them the firing location and the portion of the clock they should avoid. For example, we would tell them a unit was firing from Vi Thanh, that they should not fly between 8:00 and 11:00 (west-northwest of Vi Thanh), or that the max ord was so-and-so. Of course, if we had a call for a MEDEVAC pickup in one of the areas affected by the H&I fire, we would coordinate a cease-fire through a Vietnamese officer co-located at the TOC. This ARVN officer would contact the artillery unit and order them to cease fire until further instructed. These simple procedures were amazingly effective.

As they always required, pilots wanted the name of the person providing them the clearance authority. I always believed this was because in the event their aircraft was shot down, the pilot's command would have someone to court-martial. In this process, I became fluent in quickly spelling my last name using the phonetic alphabet, as in Romeo, Alpha, Sierra, Charlie, Hotel, Kilo, Echo.

TOC duty, though occasionally interrupted by some serious incidents, was a social event for me. I would spend the early-evening hours talking with the Vietnamese communications soldiers on duty at the TOC, learning their card games and listening to their Vietnamese civilian music channels with them. Then, too, after telling the American RTO (who was on duty to monitor the U.S. radio traffic) of my whereabouts, I would go outside the TOC and talk with the Vietnamese TOC security personnel.

Most nights, the Vietnamese had an M-706 armored car stationed just outside the TOC. For reasons I never understood, this armored car was manned exclusively by soldiers of Cambodian descent. These young soldiers were very proud of their vehicle and kept it in immaculate condition. They would invite me to look it over and even crawl inside. In my mind, I thought their almost boyish pride, *esprit de corps,* and friendliness meant Vietnamization had a good chance of working.

A routine event for all SDOs during TOC duty was calling for and monitoring MEDEVACs. These were invariably MEDEVACs of Vietnamese civilians. The reasons for needing medical evacuation were medical emergencies that included stepping on a land mine, experiencing a difficult childbirth, having wounds from an accidental firearm discharge or enemy contact, burns caused by a cooking fire, etc. "Dustoff" pilots, wisely, would not go to unknown/unsecured locations at night, so this meant the patient had to be transported to a district headquarters or MAT location. Typically, soldiers or other government paramilitary units would be the ones transporting the Vietnamese casualty to an advisory team's or MAT location.

Chapter 9. Routine, Money, and Morale

Once the patient arrived at the district or MAT location the team medic would assess and treat the patient. If the team medic believed the casualty was beyond his level of care, a MEDEVAC would be requested. The protocol for requesting a MEDEVAC was for the SDO to contact the 82nd Medical Detachment (helicopter ambulance) in Binh Thuy (near Can Tho) via telephone. As staff duty officers, we would identify the number of patients, the status of each patient (military or civilian), nature of the medical emergency, condition of the patient, patient grid location, the ground situation (enemy activity or none), and the frequency and call sign of the Vi Thanh TOC and/or the ground element at the pickup location.

The TOC would suspend H&I fires or divert the "dustoff" around them once the aircraft entered the province. The TOC would then monitor the progress of the MEDEVAC. Most often, the "dustoff" transported the patient to the Vi Thanh hospital, although the more critical cases were taken directly to Can Tho. As SDOs, we entered required elements of the MEDEVAC mission into the staff officer's journal.

During TOC duty, the most serious type of event was a VC attack on a Vietnamese outpost as relayed to us by our Vietnamese counterparts. These outposts were a part of winning the "hearts and minds" of the local populace by expanding government control. However, the remoteness of these outposts made them vulnerable to VC attack. All outposts I saw were built in a triangular configuration and had interior bunkers and firing positions. The area surrounding the outpost had a moat,[17] often filled with *pun ji* stakes, sharpened pieces of bamboo about 12"–18" long designed to impale anyone who stepped or fell on them, extensive barbed wire barriers and entanglements, and a mine field of anti-personnel mines extending out 50–100 meters. These outposts were manned by a PF or occasionally an RF platoon-sized unit of about 30 soldiers. The soldiers often brought their families to live with them in the outpost, which compounded the tragic effects of VC attacks.

During my tour in the province, outpost attacks occurred exclusively at night. These attacks followed a predictable pattern. The VC would initiate a mortar attack that would cause the outpost defenders to seek cover in the bunkers. Concurrent with mortar rounds landing on the outpost, VC sappers crawled forward and created lanes for the attacking force. These lanes were cleared by the sappers who cut through the barbed-wire obstacles, disabled mines, and marked the avenues of approach for the attacking force. Once lanes were cleared, the mortar fire would shift or cease and the assault force would attempt quick entry into the outpost.

I estimate that about one-third of these VC attacks were successful in overrunning the outposts and their defenders. Included in this VC success statistic was that during some attacks defenders simply abandoned the outpost or gave it up without a fight. The inevitable outcome from losing an outpost was the cost in human lives, the loss of M-16 rifles and other U.S.-made weapons, and the loss of radios. It always bothered me to think that these weapons and equipment could be used against me on future operations. Notwithstanding these military losses, when the VC overran an outpost it sent a loud message to civilians that the VC controlled the area.

The Vietnamese artillery protected friendly outposts during attacks if the outpost was within range.[18] Occasionally, the TOC would request a U.S. Air Force gunship that answered to the call sign "Spooky."[19] If "Spooky" was in the area (and this was a big "if") and could help, the pilots would employ their multiple mini-guns capable of firing 6,000 rounds per minute. Coordinating "Spooky" support from the outpost under attack through Vietnamese channels to the TOC or district team was difficult on the best of evenings. However, when used and properly coordinated, "Spooky" was awesome to watch and quite effective.

On those days when I could get a jeep, I would go over to see the Vietnamese public works chief, Ông (Mr.) Son. Ông Son was an amiable, near middle-aged gentleman who was semi-fluent in English, though fully fluent in French. Between his English and my steadily improving Vietnamese, we were able to communicate without an interpreter. Ông Son always had a big smile that displayed his gold-capped front tooth. Ông Son was well educated and by every standard was dedicated to his job. He managed the electric generating station and water purification plant for the city of Vi Thanh from a secure compound on the near outskirts of the city near the 2nd Battalion 31st Infantry of the ARVN 21st Division compound.

As best I could tell, the purpose of the public works department was exclusively to provide potable water (not sewer) and electric service to the residents of Vi Thanh. Electrical services were mostly to the local merchants and government offices. Water distribution was done through local community hydrants. The efforts we American's generally associate with public works, maintaining roads and bridges, repairing infrastructure, placing signage, etc., were not apparent to me in Chuong Thien province.

I tried to see Ông Son every couple of weeks to see if he needed anything and for the sake of making an appearance.[20] On one such visit, he invited me to share a noon meal with him. The meal was the typical Vietnamese fare and, my having acquired the taste, the food was great. After lunch, Ông Son offered me cognac. This was my first taste of cognac, and not wishing to disrespect my host (as I learned at Fort Bragg) I drank a good-sized glass of it. In my mind I could not figure out which was worse—cognac or the rice whiskey I drank during my stay in Kien Long. Having never been fond of "hard liquor," I concluded that both of them

Chapter 9. Routine, Money, and Morale

were terrible. However, that day I was happy with myself for being able to both nurse my potent alcoholic drink and save face.

In the latter part of September, I made my first trip to Saigon to replenish the AIK fund. I was fortunate to have Harvey accompanying me as I would otherwise have been completely lost in this refugee- and military-swollen bustling city. Harvey had frequent business in Saigon and knew the city well enough to navigate around. Once on the ground at Tan Son Nhut airport, we went downtown and checked into an American-leased Vietnamese hotel. This hotel had been converted to a BOQ, and once there, we unloaded our gear. Harvey had to attend to his business in another section of the city, but before leaving, he told me how best to get to my destination—Pentagon East. We established a time to meet back at the hotel, and then we went our separate ways.

In addition to turning in receipts and getting money for the AIK fund, I also had the task of turning in Lieutenant Young's M-16 and other field gear at CIF on the MACV headquarters compound. I decided to make this turn-in first, so I took one of the many military buses that had routes throughout the city to MACV headquarters. What I remember most about arriving at Pentagon East was the military policeman (MP) at the main gate. This neatly dressed MP with his starched jungle fatigues, highly shined jungle boots, MP brassard, and glistening decaled helmet liner stopped me in my tracks. He not so politely told me I was out of uniform. I was aware of this, since I was not wearing headgear. I had lost my "boonie" hat when I was directing the "dustoff" helicopter picking up Lieutenant Carlile.

I accepted this MP's admonition, but when he said he was going to write me up for this infraction I thought this was a bit too much. Deep inside I felt like butt-stroking him with Lieutenant Young's weapon that I was carrying, using a bayonet maneuver I learned in basic training. Keeping my composure, I told him I had lost my cap in the jungle and planned to get a new one at the Central Issue Facility. With as much decency as he could muster, the MP said OK, pointed to the CIF building, and gave me a snappy salute. At CIF I turned in Lieutenant Young's equipment and got another "boonie" hat. This mission complete, I took the bus back to the BOQ.

That evening Harvey and I went to one of the finest restaurants in downtown Saigon. En route to the restaurant I could not believe the sheer number and variety of vehicles: Lambretta scooters, three-wheeled scooters, pedicabs, the ubiquitous motorcycles, blue and yellow 4CV Renault taxis, buses belching black diesel fumes, jeeps and other military vehicles, and most of all people on the go. When I first arrived in Vietnam less than two months earlier I had not seen the downtown part of Saigon. The activity I saw that day made it hard for me to comprehend a war was going on just outside the city.²¹

We went to a restaurant that was situated on the upper floor of the Continental Hotel. Many war correspondents and celebrities like Bob Hope and others who had toured Vietnam with the USO sponsored shows had stayed in the hotel and dined in the restaurant. From the upper floor of the hotel one could easily see the Vietnam War Memorial statue. This statue depicted two slightly crouched ARVN soldiers symbolically advancing on the enemy. Both soldiers were wearing GI helmets and one was carrying what appeared to be a .30 caliber machine gun. This statute was a source of Vietnamese military pride.

The atmosphere in the restaurant was electric! War correspondents with military and civilian personnel were discussing the conduct of the war, the accomplishments of their sports heroes back in the States, their favorite martini recipe, and many other deep topics. Beautiful, mostly younger, and provocatively dressed Vietnamese women were sitting at the bar looking for friends. Waiters and waitresses were busily scurrying around taking and delivering food and drink orders and earning nice tips from the mostly American clientele. None of this mattered to me. Harvey said the food there was exceptional, and I was just looking forward to my first non–mess hall meal in about two months.

Harvey was certainly right about the food, as we both had an excellent meal. I had a filet mignon for the first time in my life. The steak was cooked to perfection and came with a side salad and a baked potato. We washed this delicious meal down with a bottle of Mateus rosé and a bottle of Lancers rosé. When I thought the evening couldn't get any better, the *crème de la crème* arrived, a dish of exceptional-tasting scooped ice cream! Sated, and slightly wobbly, I felt like I was on top of the world as we took a taxi back to our BOQ. During this ride I marveled at the neon lights, the slightly abated traffic, and street vendors still hawking their wares at that late hour. I was also surprised to see the masses of American and ARVN soldiers and military and Vietnamese civilian police roving around. We called the Vietnamese military police officers "white mice" due to their small stature and predominant white trimmings. They wore white helmets, belts, holsters, and gaiters. My overall assessment of all of this nightlife was that these people were oblivious to the fact that a war was going on.

Following a restful night's sleep, Harvey took me downtown to the administrative office of the AIK fund. The office was staffed with Vietnamese women, most appearing to be in their 20s, wearing their silk *áo dài*, the traditional Vietnamese dress. Most of them spoke near perfect English and were highly adept at using their adding machines. I was amazed at the

Chapter 9. Routine, Money, and Morale

ease of turning in receipts and receiving replenishment funds. I signed for the funds and in less than a half hour my business was complete. I departed the AIK office with thousands of piasters in my possession. Harvey and I then went quickly back to the BOQ to pick up our gear, and from there we grabbed a taxi to Tan Son Nhut. We boarded a plane, and almost immediately we were airborne. Unlike my first transportation experience in Vietnam, this time, my flights came off like clockwork. It seemed that we were vibrating to a stop at the Vi Thanh airfield and back home in no time at all. I was to make at least a half dozen more such AIK trips to Saigon during my time in-country.

Chapter 10

Mostly Blowing Stuff Up

Back from my first trip to Saigon, I resumed going on operations. However, remembering the casualties from September 6, I forever after wore a steel helmet instead of a "boonie" hat. In the next several weeks, I went on several operations with Sergeant Haley and one with Lieutenant Olderson. On those operations with Sergeant Haley we had no enemy contact, although I continued to learn field craft, tactics, and advisor duties from him. With Lieutenant Bob Olderson, our operation was in the general area of the Snake River. As could be expected, we got into a firefight. It was just a brief skirmish, as the VC quickly fled the area. Soldiers of our unit, the 120th RF company, did detain a suspicious "farmer."

This particular detainee was interesting. He was probably in his early 20s and appeared to be of Chinese rather than Vietnamese ancestry, since he had a round face and a stocky, almost pudgy build. It was unusual to find any military-age males in the countryside, since either the government or VC "recruiters" often conscripted them on the spot. The fact this young man just happened to have a picture of him holding a German Mauser rifle[1] put his freedom in real jeopardy. Finding these kind of pictures on their person or in their homes never worked out too well for an individual as they were immediately suspected of being VC. This young man tried to convince us he was simply an innocent farmer. This was a standard ploy used on those rare occasions when we found any military-age men in the field with such militaristic pictures. They claimed to be farmers, fishermen, merchants, etc., and they swore that it was not really them in the picture.

On that day after a brief interrogation, the RF soldiers demanded that the detained "farmer" show them where his weapon was located. We spent a little time on a wild-goose chase but never located his weapon. As this young "farmer" was supposedly leading us to the Mauser, we had contact with a VC squad of probably 8–10 soldiers. Often, a small-sized VC unit was assigned to delay or harass the ARVN as the larger VC element escaped. There was a short but intense firefight, typical of so many others

Chapter 10. Mostly Blowing Stuff Up

Staged picture of VC posing with their assortment of weapons and aiming in the direction indicated by the man standing. Note that second man from the right is aiming a U.S. M-1 Carbine; others appear to have the SKS rifle (courtesy Harvey Weiner).

I experienced. One minute the bullets are flying, the next the VC have simply vanished! During the firefight we suffered no outright casualties, although we had to evacuate a soldier when he stepped on a land mine. We took the Chinese "farmer" (who we were convinced was a VC) into custody and back to Vi Thanh for further interrogation. On the McNamara tally, during our brief contact with the VC we counted five enemy KIA with the good guys suffering one WIA.

As with the Chinese "farmer" we found that day, when a suspected VC was detained in the field he was searched for weapons and documents. We also conducted an initial on-the-spot interrogation to gather any timely intelligence that might affect the operation. If the Vietnamese commander felt detainees were VC (we sometimes detained females suspected of being so), we would take them back to the district headquarters or Vi Thanh for further interrogation. All documents found on the suspect were seized and turned over to the Intel section for evaluation and possible exploitation. Interestingly, on one operation inside a hooch we found several photos of Buddhist monks under the backdrop of a VC flag sharpening *pun ji* stakes.

In a similar fashion, VC killed in the field were thoroughly searched to gather any documents they carried. The biggest reason for examining documents was to determine if the casualty was a member of a local militia VC unit or a larger main force battalion. Documents, if found, were given to the Vietnamese commander to be taken to the district or province Intel centers for analysis. Weapons and ammunition, whenever found, were always removed by the ARVN. Weapons, flags, and field gear were supposed to be taken to the district headquarters. However, most of the time these items were kept as personal souvenirs or for use as barter materials.

My next assignment came from Major Martinson. He told me word had reached the TOC that the VC had established a dam on the major canal located near the juncture of Chuong Thien, Bac Lieu, and Ba Xuyen provinces. In reality, the dam was a tollbooth where the VC controlled access and "taxed" those using the canal. The tax was mostly rice and other food items (chickens, ducks, pigs, etc.) being taken to market, but the tax could also be money.[2] Since the province did not have engineer assets in their force structure, a squad of Vietnamese engineers assigned to the 21st ARVN Division located in Vi Thanh were given the task of destroying the canal barrier. As the province engineer officer, I was to accompany them to ensure everything went well. On this adventure I was the only American, although I did have a Vietnamese interpreter with me.

It was midmorning on Sunday, September 21 (the first day of fall), when a U.S. CH-47 Chinook helicopter came into the landing site to pick up my small task force. This LZ was just off the airfield road on the east side of the bridge heading north out of Vi Thanh. The engineers were there with their demolitions equipment as well as a platoon of soldiers sent to provide security for the operation. When I guided the cargo helicopter to a landing I was angered when its rotor wash blew off my RPAC[3] prescription sunglasses. Once on the ground, all equipment, supplies, explosives, and about 30 ARVN soldiers were quickly loaded into the cargo hold of the Chinook. Carrying my weapon and a radio, I entered the helicopter and went directly to the cockpit to confirm with the pilots the grid location of the dam and to establish a proposed landing site. Satisfied we were in agreement, we were soon airborne. During the ride, I learned just how fast the CH-47 was, as it covered the approximate 35 "klicks" in a matter of minutes.[4]

The aircraft landed in a rice paddy several hundred meters north of the VC dam/barrier, and immediately there was distant, but ineffective, scattered automatic weapons fire. The RF platoon leader quickly led his men off the helicopter, deployed them, and advanced toward the canal—reconning by fire the whole way. Since the enemy fire quickly ceased, it was most likely that the initial shots fired were those of a tax collector or two as they fled the area.

The Vietnamese engineers sprung to work once both sides of the canal were secure and the RF platoon had established a perimeter. Carrying their explosives, they jumped into the canal and began emplacing their C-4 (a military high explosive) and threading the C-4 and det cord[5] through the bamboo pickets of the barrier. I made a cursory survey of their work. and it was clear to me the engineers knew what they were doing. In less than a half hour the explosives were in place. The RF lieutenant recalled his men from the far side of the canal and the engineers strung commo wire[6] from the explosives to a firing device located near the initial LZ. We all then withdrew to a safe distance from the dam/toll booth.

Explosives set, I radioed the Long My district team and requested they notify the Chuong Thien province TOC so it could warn aircraft and the adjacent province of Bac Lieu that we would be setting off the explosives at a given time. At the announced time, the engineers triggered a tremendous explosion, sending splintered wood and a water geyser at least a hundred feet into the air. Several minutes later, the engineers and I inspected the canal and found the VC tax collection station was no more. With this mission complete, the engineers, security platoon, interpreter, and I slogged across the rice paddy to the designated PZ. There, we set up a perimeter and waited for our transportation back to Vi Thanh.

Being in known enemy territory with a relatively small force and the VC probably not very happy with what we had just done, our wait for the Chinook seemed long and definitely uncomfortable. Finally, the Chinook was in sight. After I confirmed to the pilot that the PZ was clear, I popped smoke and the CH-47 swooped in to pick us up. We arrived back in Vi Thanh in no time. At the drop-off point I reported our arrival to the TOC, gave them a recap of the mission, and proceeded to walk back to the compound. Just another exciting day in Vietnam.

As a kid, I loved playing with firecrackers, bottle rockets, and M-80s. After a Fourth of July celebration at our farm, I made a mortar using a steel water pipe with leftover M-80s as propellant. For my ingenuity and (most would say) stupidity, I ended up with a small divot in my ankle when my mortar tube exploded. But I still loved making a big bang. As I found out in OCS, army explosives produced a much larger explosion than my M-80s. In Vietnam, I felt I had at least an adequate level of training in the use of military explosives.

My experience with the VC "dam" was a precursor to an activity I performed several times thereafter in Vietnam: blowing things up. Years earlier, the VC had blown up a bridge over the *Sông Cai Tu* river.[7] Thereafter, a ferry was the only way vehicles could cross the river on their way to Kien Hung. One evening the VC blew up an old bridge pier to which the ferry was moored. This concrete pier fell onto the ferry, sinking it. The next morning Major Martinson gave me the task of removing the fallen pier and refloating the ferry. He gave me the location of the ferry, said a PF platoon was already at the site to provide security, and that I was to get there ASAP. Without the benefit of surveying the sunken ferry, my initial thought was to blow apart the fallen concrete pier to remove its weight from the ferry. With the pier removed, my thinking was the ferry would easily resurface on its own.

Mission understood, I went to the compound's ammo bunker to get the necessary supplies. I gathered up some C-4, det cord, a Claymore M-18 antipersonnel mine "clacker,"[8] commo wire, and blasting caps. I put these items and a radio into the jeep. With a young American sergeant assigned to drive the jeep and provide security for me and my interpreter, we hopped into the jeep and headed west through Vi Thanh along the canal to the ferry site.[9] I felt uneasy on this short drive as we passed by a Vietnamese cemetery with several freshly dug graves, then over a bridge the VC had blown up in the past. I breathed a sigh of relief as the three of us safely arrived in hostile territory.

When I got to the river there were already several dozen PF soldiers going through the motions of providing security and keeping an equal number of curious civilians away from the area. The thought certainly occurred to me that the actual VC perpetrators could be among those in the crowd. A PF *Trung sĩ*[10] pointed out the sunken ferry to me, since nothing was visible above the waterline. The good news was that it was close to the bank of the swiftly moving river, thereby making it easier for me to get into the river and do my thing. I peeled off my gear, shirt, and boots. Easing my way into the water, I took a big gulp of air and proceeded to grope underwater for the ferry and the pier. The pier lay across the rear portion of the ferry, about five or six feet underwater, and roughly 10 feet from the riverbank.

After this quick inspection, I did my best to determine where to place the explosives and how much to use. In Engineer OCS, we learned the army had developed elaborate tables for calculating the optimal amount of each type of military explosive necessary to destroy a given material—be it trees, concrete, or steel. Referring to demolitions section in my *Engineer Field Data* manual (FM 5–34), no table came close to the situation I faced. I had no choice but to apply the "P" formula that we officer candidates collectively invented. The "P" formula, as we joked, stood for "plenty." Following another *Sea Hunt*[11] survey of the pier, I gathered up all the explosives that I brought with me and took them and the det cord back into the river. After several diving attempts, I was able to bundle the C-4 together and to place it underneath the pier by wrapping the det cord around it. Once I had secured the C-4, I got out of the water and gave the "clacker" and the end of the wire to the NCO accompanying me. I told my driver that under no circumstances should he connect the wire to the "clacker"! This understood, I took the blasting cap that I had attached to the end of the wire and,

Chapter 10. Mostly Blowing Stuff Up

These piers were the remnants of the bridge that spanned the *Sông Cai Tu river*. It was a pier like this that the VC had "dropped" onto the ferry I was to recover (courtesy Harvey Weiner).

diving into the river again, inserted the blasting cap into the submerged C-4.

Back on dry land, I unspooled the Claymore mine wire and to its maximum length. Once there, I asked the interpreter to tell the PF *Trung sĩ* to have his soldiers clear everyone at least 200 meters from the site. I then told the sergeant with me to notify the TOC we were about to initiate the blast. After about 10 minutes, I yelled, "Fire in the hole!"[12] three times and squeezed the "clacker." Instantly, a waterspout erupted along with a muted explosion. I waited for several minutes after the explosion as I expected to see the ferry slowly rise to the surface of the water. Nothing happened. I waited longer and still nothing happened. It was then I learned that either the "P" formula does not always work or I did not have enough C-4 to qualify as "P." After several minutes I reentered the river and felt around under the water. I discovered the explosion had fractured the concrete of the pier. However, it was still on top of the ferry since the steel rebar was holding enough of the pier together to keep the ferry from surfacing.

Out of C-4 and with the ferry still underwater, I was in jeopardy of failing at this task. Mulling over what to do, I remembered that a U.S. engineer detachment had just arrived in Vi Thanh to work on the airfield. Most importantly, they had a 20-ton crane with them. I called the TOC and requested the TOC get in touch with the engineers to see if they would be willing to bring their crane to the ferry site. Several hours later, and much to my relief, I saw a beautiful OD green army 20-ton crane nearing my location.

When the engineers dismounted, in an irony of all ironies, I saw the NCO in charge. It was Sergeant Bish, the same Staff Sergeant Bish who had been my platoon sergeant at Fort Hood. We reminisced briefly, after which time I explained the problem to him. Then, as I had earlier learned as a dutiful lieutenant, I just stood back and watched as the American engineers proceeded to save the day. The crane backed up to the riverbank and a young specialist jumped into the water and hooked the crane's cable onto the fractured pier. As the crane operator reeled in the cable, slowly but surely, the pier was lifted off the ferry.

With the pier hoisted high out of the water and placed on the riverbank, for reasons I did not understand, the ferry remained submerged. Sergeant Bish and I had a brief powwow and came up with Plan B. Bish sent the same specialist back into the water, this time telling him to hook the crane's cable directly onto the near end of the ferry—which he did. Once the specialist was out of the water, the crane revved its engine, gingerly lifted the ferry to water level, and then pulled it onto the riverbank. The engineers left the ferry on the riverbank so the Vietnamese operators could make what appeared to be minor repairs.

I profusely thanked Sergeant Bish and each of the engineers for coming to my aid. I next contacted the TOC, telling them the ferry was out of the water and I was heading back to Vi Thanh with my mission accomplished. I saw Sergeant Bish several times after the ferry incident, since his engineer unit traveled around the Delta providing engineer support. Whenever Sergeant Bish's platoon was in Vi Thanh, I would coordinate any engineer projects with him. I also made sure his engineers had plenty of Black Label beer during their time in Vi Thanh.

Early one morning following a mortar attack aimed at the province chief's headquarters, I got a call from the TOC telling me there was an unexploded 82-mm mortar round sticking out of the pavement on the road going from Vi Thanh to Duc Long. Several Vietnamese soldiers had been stationed near it to prevent traffic from driving over and detonating the mortar round. The TOC instructed me to take care of the problem as soon as possible. Again, I went to the ammunition bunker. This time I only took a Claymore mine bag with me.[13] I next grabbed a filled sandbag, hopped in a jeep, and went to the location given me by the TOC. Once there, a Vietnamese soldier showed me to the exposed fins of a live mortar round embedded in the middle of the road.[14]

At the site, I took the cover off the back of the Claymore mine and pried the 24 ounces of C-4 from its interior. I took about one-half of the

Chapter 10. Mostly Blowing Stuff Up 91

C-4 to use for the explosive charge, inserted the blasting cap into it, placed the explosives on the mortar round, and with utmost care placed the filled sandbag over the explosives. Uncoiling the 100 feet of wire in the Claymore bag to its full distance, I moved my jeep to the end point of the wire to use as a protective barrier. Next, I called the TOC and told them I would be setting off the explosives at a given time. The TOC said they would warn the Vietnamese TOC, MACV compound, and airfield of the impending explosion. Hiding behind the jeep's tire, I waited until the designated time and initiated the detonation. Fearing I would be caught in a crossfire between the MACV compound and province headquarters guards, I deliberately did not fire warning shots before the impending explosion. Everything went well and the round exploded, leaving only a gaping hole in the road with no one hurt. I thought this assignment had been really easy and fun!

Another time, I had to destroy a 19-round, 2.75" rocket pod that had been jettisoned into a rice paddy after the helicopter gunship carrying it experienced some sort of mechanical malfunction. My assignment was to destroy the rocket pod rather than recover it, thus denying the VC use of any component. Before doing anything, I was to contact Lieutenant Rob Bryson*, the officer in charge of MAT 54 OIC, for particulars. I got Rob on the radio, and he gave me the grid coordinates of the rocket pod. He also said his MAT and a squad of PF soldiers would provide security and assist me in my efforts.

Knowing what I had to do, I went to the ammo bunker and picked up some C-4, det cord, and blasting caps. I then went to the Commo Section where they gave me a quarter-mile reel of WD-1 commo wire, some electrical tape, and an extra battery for the PRC-25 radio. Gene Griffiths wanted to go with me on this mission, so together we placed the supplies in a jeep and left the compound.

Gene and I took the road adjacent to the canal heading northeast from Vi Thanh toward Can Tho. During my tour this road was never safe enough to make the drive all the way from Vi Thanh to Can Tho. Once on the road, I reported my departure to the TOC and then radioed Lieutenant Bryson. Bryson had given me the grid coordinates where he was located and said the area was presently secure. After driving about 12 kilometers we reached the vicinity of Lieutenant Bryson and the rocket pod. As we pulled up to Lieutenant Bryson it occurred to me I was very near the general location of my first radio relay site back in August.

Ready to get to work, we Americans were ferried across the canal with our supplies by a local villager. Once across, Rob told me the rocket pod was several hundred meters into the rice paddy. Lugging the demolition equipment to the site was pretty easy, since it was the dry season and the rice paddy was now solid ground. On this occasion I wore a flak jacket. Being unaccustomed to the jackets, I learned how heavy and hot they really were.

When we reached the rocket pod I saw that most, if not all, of the rockets were present; however, both the pod and some of the rockets appeared badly deformed. Not knowing how the impact may have affected them, I was extremely concerned over the stability of the rockets. Each rocket was fused and had 8½ pounds of high explosives in its warhead in addition to the solid rocket fuel. I formulated a plan to place C-4 on both ends of the rocket pod and on the middle top of it. My thinking was to simultaneously blow the rockets' ends toward themselves and the pod downward at the same time. With the explosives in the rockets and my C-4, I wanted to mitigate the explosion and potentially any collateral damage.

With Gene looking on, I carefully placed the explosives interlaced with det cord as I had envisioned. Once this was done, without inserting the blasting cap, I asked Gene to hold the end of the wire as I fed out the reel. In unspooling the reel, I was shocked to discover that my quarter-mile reel of commo wire was only about 200 meters long, not the 400 meters I expected. I was *very* concerned about the short separation

Lieutenants Griffiths and Raschke rigging a helicopter rocket pod for demolition. Note the C-4 packed on the ends of the pod and Lieutenant Raschke affixing additional explosives with det cord. Also, note the flatness of the land in Chuong Thien province (courtesy Gene Griffiths).

Chapter 10. Mostly Blowing Stuff Up

distance between the rocket pod and where I stood. But I realized that at this point there were simply no other options.

I asked Rob to have the PF soldiers dig a foxhole at the place where the commo wire ran out. I would use the foxhole for shelter when I detonated the explosives. Fortunately, since this was the dry season, my shelter would not end up being a mini swimming pool. Leaving the soldiers to dig my hole, I returned to the rocket pod, reinspected my handiwork, and inserted the blasting caps. Gene and I then walked back to Rob and told him how events would unfold. I saw that the soldiers had dug an approximate 4' × 3' × 2' deep foxhole. As per SOP (standing operating procedure), I called the TOC, gave them a status update, and told them the time I would be setting off the explosion. Efficiently, the TOC sent out a warning message to the necessary parties.

I told Lieutenant Bryson to move the soldiers and gawking civilians to the line of hooches on the canal bank about 400 meters west of the rocket pod. Satisfied everything was set, I scrunched down into the foxhole with the PRC-25 battery in one hand and the end of the commo wire in the other. At the designated time, Rob fired three M-16 shots into the air to warn those in the area. I then stuck the bare ends of the commo wire into the radio battery terminals. Instantly, I heard the most powerful explosion I had heard to date in Vietnam. This was definitely one of those "Holy crap, what in the world just happened?" moments.

The blast definitely told me I should have been further away from the rocket pod as the explosion rained down clods of dirt, fire, and shards of metal onto the rice paddy and surrounding areas. None of this debris hit me, and I was lucky the explosion did not injure any of those watching this event. However, several nearby hooches lining the canal did not fare as well, since the soldiers and civilians had to move quickly to extinguish small patches of fire from their roofs.

Once everything settled down, Rob, Gene, and I had a nervous laugh over the matter as we went to the place where the pod had been located. There was absolutely no evidence a rocket pod full of rockets had ever been in the middle of the rice paddy. While there was a gaping four-foot-deep by five-foot-diameter hole present, there was not so much as a sliver of metal in the hole. I found it incredible that the explosion had essentially vaporized the rocket pod and rockets.

I told Rob I was thankful I had caused no injuries and I really appreciated his help. Gene and I then walked back toward the jeep and recrossed the canal. At the jeep, I radioed the TOC, telling them the rocket pod was completely destroyed and we were on our way back to Vi Thanh. On the drive back Gene tried to lighten my mood as I thought about the day. In reflection, I privately criticized myself for my general lack of preparation.

Before leaving the compound I had failed to ask if rockets were present in the pod, and if so, how many. I should have ensured I had at least a quarter mile (400 meters) of commo wire to provide a safer standoff distance. Moreover, I should have better understood the potential effects of the blast, which, with rockets included, turned out to be more than 90 pounds of high explosives. In the end, however, everyone was safe and the rocket pod was destroyed—mission complete.

Once or twice during my tour I was called on to destroy defective rockets and other munitions accumulating at the far eastern end of the Vi Thanh airfield. These items were discarded from helicopter gunships and even the O-1 aircraft stationed at Vi Thanh. This collection of munitions was unserviceable due to misfires, mishandling, or belonging to bad lot numbers. I learned from my experience with the rocket pod to exercise caution. Being wiser and more careful, I completed these airfield tasks without incident or humiliation.

A somewhat humorous incident occurred when I went to Kien Thien to accompany one of their RF companies on an operation. Arriving there by helicopter, I saw a single 2.75" smoke rocket inside a rocket tube. It looked like one of the rocket tubes I had seen on the O-1 "Bird Dog" aircraft. The team at Kien Thien wanted me to take it back to Vi Thanh. I had no intention of taking this rocket back with me and gave the excuse that no helicopter crew in their right mind would allow me to do it. Therefore, I asked the team to give me some commo wire. I hooked up the commo wire onto the contact of the rocket and asked for the direction of a free fire zone that I knew to be nearby. In fact, most of Kien Thien district was VC territory and therefore a free fire zone. Aiming the rocket in the direction I was given and placing it at a 45-degree angle, I fired the rocket using my radio battery. While the team was amazed this worked, I was thinking back to my days of shooting off bottle rockets. I found shooting off the rocket was the most exciting part of the day, since the ground operation I later participated in was just another "walk in the sun."

Chapter 11

Soldiers, Units, and Friends

After several months of accompanying Vietnamese units, I formed an assessment of the Vietnamese soldiers. Like the U.S. Army soldier, the average Vietnamese combat soldier was in his late teens or early twenties. Most of the enlisted RF and PF soldiers I served with grew up in Chuong Thien province. They had been recruited or drafted from there, as was normal for these types of units. This meant many of them had lived in the small villages or hamlets of the province and therefore had a rather austere upbringing with limited educational opportunities. The majority of officers I worked with were from larger cities from around Vietnam and were typically much better educated.

ARVN officers and NCOs were much more authoritarian than those in the U.S. Army. Some actions I witnessed from these ARVN leaders would never have been tolerated in the U.S. Army and would likely have ended in court-martial at best—"fragging"[1] at worst. On more than one occasion, I saw an officer or NCO slap or kick a soldier who failed to obey a command, had not moved fast enough, or misbehaved in some fashion. At least once I saw a Vietnamese leader shoot in the direction of (not at) his soldiers to get them moving. I seldom thought these soldiers' offenses were because of cowardice but, more often than not, were due to their failure to understand what they were supposed to do.

Individual training for the RF soldier was rudimentary when compared to that of an American soldier. Collective training at the squad, platoon, and company level was essentially nonexistent and consisted primarily of on-the-job-training while on combat operations. PF soldier training did not even rise to this inadequate level.

What impressed me most about the Vietnamese soldier was his incredible stamina.[2] I was convinced they could walk through the rice paddies forever without ever getting tired. With the average Vietnamese standing about five foot tall and weighing around 90 pounds, they literally skimmed across the surface of the paddies. Not only could they go all day long, they could do so carrying heavy loads such as a 57-mm recoilless rifle³ or a 42-pound 60-mm mortar. They were small but strong and wiry men. Regarding their stature, it was always funny to see the Vietnamese before they converted to the M-16. Prior to this conversion, they had the M-1 Garands and Browning automatic rifles (BARs) and these vintage weapons were almost as tall as they were.⁴

Like most young soldiers, RF and PF enlisted men had a great sense of humor and liked to tease or foist practical jokes on one another. Unless being shot at, most had a perpetual smile or grin on their face. I never found a Vietnamese soldier who was unfriendly toward me, and I always felt that I was a curiosity to them. They liked to stroke the hair on my arms, as they were devoid of arm hair and viewed it as something strange. They also often called me *đẹp* (handsome), which made me a little uneasy as I never considered myself anything but average in the looks department. Nonetheless, I was flattered by their candor. These soldiers were also inquisitive and wanted to know about me: my age, where I lived, if I was married, did I have children, did I like Vietnam, etc. Since these were basic conversational items, I could usually respond to them without an interpreter. The young soldiers enjoyed having an American who could speak their language accompany them. Sometimes I would offer them a Salem cigarette, and this always brought about an even bigger smile. Thereafter, they would approach me saying, "OK, Sa-lem," or *thuốc lá,* as they crossed their fingers, mimicking the way one would hold a cigarette as an inducement for me to give them one. These gestures helped foster a stronger bond between us.

The Vietnamese soldiers liked to show me pictures of themselves, their girlfriends, and their families, often beaming with pride as they explained the photos. At the company level they were apolitical and just wanted the war to be over and to go on with their lives. Emotionally, I found the soldiers to be accepting of hardships, and they endured them without complaint. In the face of adversity, they were determined, and the many wounded I saw were stoic, almost accepting of their fate. I learned a lot about life from these young men.

As with their American counterparts, the Vietnamese soldiers could go from the proverbial 90 miles an hour to full stop in a heartbeat. When they were not otherwise required to be alert, they would sit around in small groups talking or clowning around with one another. It was interesting to watch the interaction between them. I always marveled at the way the soldiers, and all Vietnamese, could squat down on their haunches and sit comfortably for long periods of time. As much as I tried to do it, I could never master sitting like that.

The commanders of the 113th and 987th RF companies, with whom I spent most of my time, were unflappable. Each possessed a look of strong

Chapter 11. Soldiers, Units, and Friends

determination and was a fearless and skilled warrior. Without any doubt, these commanders had the absolute respect of their soldiers. Junior and senior enlisted soldiers of the 113th and 987th companies were like their commanders; they were cool under pressure, quick to assess a situation, and decisive in executing a plan of action. The NCOs in these companies were older, battle-hardened, and virulently anti-communist. With the officers and NCOs possessing these combined traits and skills, these were two very capable units.

Vietnamese soldiers deploying after an airmobile insertion. The American advisor in the center of the photograph is unknown. This picture was taken in the wet season, as the rice is growing and the fields are filled with water (courtesy Frank Perra).

During my time in the field I typically had an interpreter, although many of the officers spoke some English. After several months in-country, their English and my Vietnamese enabled me to effectively communicate with most commanders. Despite this, I often took one of two exceptional interpreters with me on operations. One was an older *Trung sĩ nhất* (equivalent of U.S. Army sergeant first class) by the name of Song. *Trung sĩ* Song did not like going on operations, although, somewhat reluctantly, he did go with me two or three times. I believe a reason for his wanting to avoid time in the field was his age. I guessed him to be in his late 30s, or early 40s. However, he had a family and several children. This was probably the main reason for him wanting to avoid potential enemy contact. Song was an intellectual sort and was as eager to learn English slang and idioms as I was to expand my conversational and tactical Vietnamese. We used this mutual interest in one another's language as the basis for a solid friendship. Then, too, Song was invaluable in helping me translate Vietnamese requests for areas to spray with Agent Orange.[5]

The other interpreter, *Trung sĩ* Minh, was probably about my age (22) and was newly married. Minh grew up in Da Lat in central Vietnam, was Catholic, and learned English in secondary school. He was full of energy and possessed a good mastery of English. He accompanied me on many operations and often pointed out features of the Vietnamese countryside to me. Though young, Minh had great patience with me and was an excellent language teacher. Surprisingly, Minh was never issued a weapon and always went into the field unarmed. Midway through my tour, I gave him an M-3 "Grease" gun with several magazines and several hundred rounds of .45 caliber ammo. My loan of this weapon to Minh came with the stipulations he use it for his family's protection and that he not tell anyone where he got it. I had found this relic of a weapon in our protective bunker and, after test firing it, I wanted someone to be able to get some use from it.

With both of my interpreters, I would write English words or phrases into a little green army notebook I always carried with me. Into this notebook I would have interpreters write down the Vietnamese translation of these English words and tell me how to properly pronounce them. During operational lulls, we would go over these words for everyday objects, military items, or tactical phrases to ensure I understood the meaning of each Vietnamese word or phrase and how to say it. These interpreters were always by my side in the field. They were calm when under pressure, and as time went by, we became good friends.

Going on operations with the Vietnamese was an eye-opening experience. There was absolutely no uniformity among the soldiers. Some wore "boonie" hats, but most wore steel pots. Some wore the Vietnamese-manufactured black tennis shoe–like boots; others wore sandals, while others wore no footgear at all. From their heads to their toes, their uniforms never matched, but in reality it did not matter in the least. Over their many operations, they learned what to wear and what gear to carry. There was, however, a uniform item extremely important to RF or PF soldiers. That item was the distinctive unit scarf each soldier wore. This simple piece of cloth was their source of pride and their identity, similar to a unit patch worn by U.S. soldiers.

The 113th and 987th RF companies were located in or near Vi Thanh. Both companies were nearly equal in ability and tactical competence, with, perhaps, a slight edge going to the 113th company. The 113th RF company was officially designated as the province recon company (*Trinh Sát*) which is not to be confused with the Provincial Reconnaissance Units (PRUs). Although each RF company was authorized 119 soldiers per the Vietnamese force structure document, while on operations either company could field only about 60–70 soldiers. I really enjoyed accompanying these two units, as these soldiers took their duties seriously while collectively having a great sense of humor at the appropriate times.

Trung úy An was the company commander of the 987th RF company. His soldiers wore red scarves. An was about 25 years old, had been wounded in action twice, and had commanded the unit for several years. He was tactically proficient, brave, and determined. *Trung úy* An was well respected by his men and led by example. He and I could easily converse, as his English and my Vietnamese were sufficient to get us by. I liked An and spent many hours with him—both in the field and when not on operations. Together, we spent some off-duty hours drinking *Ba Mười Ba* ("33") beer chilled with ice[6] while enjoying pickled prawns.

Although I spent a lot of time with the 113th RF company, I do not recall the name of its commander. This commander was a young *Thiếu úy* (equivalent of a U.S. Army second lieutenant), taller than most Vietnamese, and he led a very solid unit. Under his leadership, the 113th RF company possessed a high level of *esprit de corps*, and being mostly *Hòa Hảo*, they were fiercely anti–communist. Being members of the province's recon company certainly promoted their sense of elitism.[7] The 113th RF company was strong at all levels of leadership, as their junior officers and NCOs were very competent. All had the respect of their soldiers. I always felt safe with the 113th company, mostly due to their *élan* but also because I had developed a strong rapport with many of its soldiers. (A side note: as a result of information received from a *Chiêu hoi*, Lieutenant Bob Noonan and the 113rd RF company had a successful operation on November 18. On that day they decimated a platoon-sized VC unit—the VC unit responsible for killing Lieutenant Donaway and Sergeant Ard. Bob told me the VC unit was predominantly made up of teenaged boys.)

I will never forget my 987th RF company bodyguard named Pham*. Pham was very alert and attentive to keeping me out of trouble. He was a *Binh nhất*, equivalent to a private first class in the U.S. Army, and of Cambodian descent. I guessed Pham to be about 18 years old, and he stood about 5'8", which was tall by Vietnamese standards. Cambodians have darker skin than the Vietnamese, and this was true with Pham.

Lieutenant Robert W. Noonan crossing a stream while carrying the radio (courtesy Robert W. Noonan).

He also had freckles, a gold-capped front tooth, and a near constant broad smile. When I was in the field with the 987th RF company, after ensuring the LZ was secure, I would hand my radio over to Pham. For the rest of the operation, Pham would remain about one step behind me. While Pham carried the radio, I had the radio handset clipped to the metal ring of my web gear suspenders. I carried the handset so I could hear what was going on, provide my periodic SITREPs, and quickly respond when the situation required.

During one operation with the 987th company and totally without thinking, I reached to pick up a belt of 7.62 × 39-mm machine gun ammo lying on the ground. This ammo belt was for a Soviet-bloc machine gun, so it had definite VC origins. Though several dozen RF soldiers had already walked by it, I attempted to pick it up. Pham nearly took my arm off when he pushed me away. Stunned, I listened as my interpreter reminded me the totally out-of-place ammo belt could have been booby-trapped. Thoroughly embarrassed, I realized my lapse of judgment and profusely thanked my young savior.

On another operation with the 987th company we were walking through a small wooded area when we suddenly came under fire from a distant tree line. For whatever reason, Pham started to run in front of me to seek cover. Being under fire and needing the radio, I yanked hard on the handset. My action pulled Pham off his feet as he was mid-stride. (PRC-25 radios were carried like backpacks or book bags.) Caught off balance, Pham landed hard, squarely on his back, dazed but uninjured. Things settled down once I was able to direct accompanying gunships onto the enemy positions. After the enemy threat was removed, I apologized to Pham and gave him a Salem. That day, and on future days, we had a good laugh over this incident.

Despite the high quality of both the 113th and 987th RF Companies, neither unit was as aggressive as a similar U.S. Army unit. Though the two units were immensely better than all other RF units I accompanied, I was quietly disappointed at this diminished level of aggressiveness. I leavened my frustration with the knowledge that I would only be in their country one year. Yet those same soldiers would have to keep looking for, and fighting, an elusive enemy for perhaps many years to come. Then, too, despite their youth, these commanders had more time fighting the VC than I had in the U.S. Army.

I always did my best to walk the fine line between polite prodding and not giving the overt appearance of pushing any commander. Sometimes I used the approach Captain McCullough taught me, asking the commander what was happening under the pretext of better understanding the situation. If their response was unsound I could tweak it by making

Chapter 11. Soldiers, Units, and Friends

a suggestion. Foremost, I wanted the commanders to know I was there to support them and that together we would accomplish the mission.

On several occasions, I accompanied RF companies (other than the 113th or 987th) as I did on those two terrible days in early September. Most of these other RF companies and the PF units were marginal on their best of days. To describe their field operations as poor may be overstating their effectiveness. Notably, on the first operation with one of them (as we were moving to our assigned checkpoints and objective) I was shocked to hear three shots fired from the lead element of the unit. Thinking it may have been enemy contact, I asked the commander what was going on. The interpreter told me this was a signal to let the commander know where his lead platoon was. I could never buy that rationale nor get those units to stop this practice. To me, these shots were to warn the VC to get out of the area. Fortunately, operations with these marginal units were mostly "walks in the sun," but I was always afraid to speculate what may have happened if we came under intense enemy fire. My primary accomplishments during operations with these subpar units were increasing my stamina, getting frustrated, accumulating leeches, and getting one day closer to going home.

After the September Carlile operation I seldom carried anything more than the meat dish from a C-ration meal with me. In the field, I ate whatever the Vietnamese soldiers could rustle up, and they were very good at rustling up food. Most soldiers carried rice in what appeared to be a sock, and they would get fish, chickens, or ducks from the villagers. Once the meat and rice were cooked, a fermented fish sauce, *nước mắm*, was used to spice up otherwise bland food. Though these meals were austere, I got used to eating them in the field and became quite proficient in using chopsticks.

By my birthday in early November, I had participated in 10 ground operations. The majority of these operations were without actual contact, though we suffered WIAs most often due to land mines. When we had friendly casualties (never once did I have occasion to MEDEVAC a VC), I would call in a "dustoff," and by November this had become a routine matter for me. The normal procedure was the same as I had performed when evacuating Lieutenant Carlile, except it was in the daytime. A Vietnamese medic would evaluate a wounded soldier to determine if a MEDEVAC was necessary. If so, I would notify the TOC with the standard elements of a MEDEVAC request. In turn, the TOC would call for a "dustoff."

Between the initial call and arrival of the "dustoff" we would move the patient to the middle of a rice paddy if the tactical situation allowed. As the "dustoff" helicopter (which was clearly marked with a red cross on its nose and doors) was closing on my location, the pilot would contact me on my radio frequency to ask for the status of the patient, the ground situation,[8] and direct me to "pop smoke." Once my smoke grenade color was properly identified, the helicopter swooped in for a pickup. While the Vietnamese were loading the patient, I would approach the "dustoff" pilot, thank the crew, and get a "business card" from them.[9] By the end of my tour, I had accumulated a sizeable collection of these "business cards." The speed and efficiency of the pilots and their on-board medic always impressed me. Often the crew was on the ground for less than a minute. Once the MEDEVAC was complete, I would report to the TOC and then continue to accomplish the day's objectives.

As my weeks in-country turned into months, I was feeling more and more confident in my ability as an advisor, and I think the Vietnamese commanders were beginning to feel more comfortable with me. On every airmobile operation I still had an incredible rush come over me when landing in the LZ, since this was when we were most vulnerable and the adrenaline was really flowing. The sound of helicopters coming in for a landing, the preparatory fires from circling gunships, the assault fire from troops debarking the helicopters, and the officers and NCOs barking orders still gave me a "high"—what a feeling! The only thing that heightened these senses more, as I came to recognize, was the very distinctive sound of AK-47 rifle fire. Thankfully for me, these sounds were infrequent.

CHAPTER 12

Command and Control (C&C) and Radios

On airmobile operations, a specially equipped C&C helicopter[1] carried a senior Vietnamese officer and an American advisor—always an officer. The officers in the C&C kept track of and coordinated events on the ground, advised the ground elements of enemy activity, facilitated any necessary support (artillery, air, MEDEVAC, resupply, etc.), resolved issues arising between the Vietnamese ground commander and his advisor, and ensured that mission checkpoints and objectives were achieved. There would be frequent radio communications between the advisor on the ground and the advisor in the C&C and/or the TOC. Mostly, this radio traffic would be concerning the situation and location of the ground elements.[2]

To follow the movement of the ground force the C&C typically flew at 1,500 feet and would periodically request the command element's location. With the limited tree cover in the Delta, most of the time the ground unit could easily be spotted. However, when queried on our location we ground advisors would look at the direction the C&C was heading and give our location relative to the dial of a clock. The helicopter's heading was always 12 o'clock. For example, in response to a C&C location request, after checking my map and overlay, I would say something like "I am currently 300 meters southwest of checkpoint Alpha at your nine o'clock." This reply would indicate I was to the left side of the helicopter and about 300 meters southwest of a checkpoint established on the operations overlay. We always gave our location relative to a checkpoint or objective and did not pass our location's grid coordinates over the radio in the event the enemy was listening.

Most American advisors in the C&C were adept at locating ground units by this simple method we used. However, Major Martinson frequently had trouble finding the ground element despite the standardization of this clock procedure. Frequently, after I gave Major Martinson my location, he would direct me to "pop smoke." Reluctantly I would throw a smoke grenade to disclose my location, but I always felt this was similar to certain RF companies firing three shots into the air. Either action allowed the VC, if they were watching (and they often were), to see our ground location and to figure out where we were headed. More troublesome to me was that by throwing a smoke grenade, the VC could determine the location of the unit's command element. In reality, though, the VC could identify the unit's command element by the concentration of radio antennas. However, if they were not sure, wafting smoke from a nearby colorful smoke grenade was a clear giveaway.

Radio communications were the life link between advisors on the ground and the C&C helicopter or the TOC. It was very frustrating when these radio links were not working properly or when there was too much radio traffic on the net (the radio frequency used that day). Weather occasionally had a detrimental effect on our radio communications ability, though during the dry season, weather conditions in the Delta were mostly good. However, during the monsoon season, with heavy rains and sporadic thick cloud cover, weather and radio communications could be terrible. Then, too, we could have other problems.

There were times when the PRC-25 radio just did not work. Water, weather, battery life, and the distance between the sender and receiver impacted our ability to communicate. In an attempt to mitigate communications problems, radio relay stations (such as I had provided in August) were established. The more reliable PRC-77 radio with its solid-state transistors began arriving in Vietnam in 1968 to replace the vacuum-tubed PRC-25. However, in 1969 and 1970, Team 73 had not yet received these new radios. But with a bit of Yankee ingenuity and by carrying several different antenna types, we managed to get by.

To test our communications ability, the C&C or TOC would periodically call on the radio. These radio checks went something like this: "Call sign[3] so-and-so, this is call sign (the C&C or TOC), commo check, over." Most times we were able to respond and said something like, "I hear you Lima Charlie," which meant we hear you loud and clear.[4] At times when we could receive a message but not transmit due to radio issues, we would respond to yes or no questions by "breaking squelch." You broke squelch by keying the mic. One would key the mic once for yes, twice for no. This was a simple, crude, and marginally effective way to communicate when all else failed.

Until I got used to it, it bothered me that on most radio conversations we Americans used the phrase "be advised," as in "Be advised I am at Checkpoint Alpha," or "Be advised we have two 'whiskeys' needing MEDEVAC." Pilots used this phrase as well. For example, "Be advised, I

Chapter 12. Command and Control (C&C) and Radios

am five-minutes out from your location." This phrase was never taught to us when we received communications training, but it was a widely used Vietnam phenomenon. This simple but grossly overused (and somewhat annoying) phrase served to prolong radio conversations but became habit-forming. Like many others, I soon succumbed to it.

My second frustration was never resolved. Most of the time there was not a problem with radio traffic, especially during our "walks in the sun." However, when we landed in an LZ or were taking fire, it seemed like everyone and his brother thought they had something of value to say at that time. The C&C would want seemingly second-by-second reports while the TOC would want a SITREP, and all while the ground element would be trying to get FAC, "Shotgun" or gunship support, etc. Confusion reigned and this was magnified by a power of ten if there were any casualties.

I was almost always calm in otherwise stressful or chaotic situations and only got on the radio when absolutely necessary. My explanations for this were that I was pretty unemotional by nature, and I also noted how cool pilots were under stress, and I wanted to emulate them. Despite the chaos on the ground, pilots often spoke in a monotone and very businesslike manner. This was most reassuring to us on the ground. I could never fully describe how these pilots, often in their late teens to early twenties, helped and caused me, and probably others, to better focus on matters at hand. I have the highest regard for those courageous young pilots. I am convinced that pilots, especially army helicopter pilots, were the true heroes of the Vietnam War. Whether they were "slick," gunship, or "dust-off" pilots, these had to be the most composed and mission-focused people I had ever known. Adopting their stoic, measured approach allowed me to put events into slow motion and enabled me to concentrate on events around me.

As for everyone else getting excited and wanting to get on the radio during crisis times, I can only guess this was either because they wanted to help in their own way, take charge, or simply they had their own adrenaline rushes. It bothered me to consider that some in the C&C were looking to become heroes at 1,500 feet. I know of at least one instance when a C&C advisor submitted himself for the Distinguished Flying Cross medal while doing little more than being a passenger in a helicopter while a ground unit was being shot up.

A last, and extremely reassuring, means of communications came from our intrepid O-1 pilots. A simple "wing waggle"[5] was the pilots' way of saying, "I see you and I've got you covered." I cannot begin to say how much this simple act meant to me.

CHAPTER 13

Holidays 1969

The Thanksgiving Day meal in Vietnam was a feast similar to what I had experienced as a kid growing up on the farm. Though we were missing family members, the army went all out to have the traditional Thanksgiving dinner with all the fixings. To me, this was a special day, and the mess hall went all out in preparing another of their delicious meals.

By late November 1969 I had completed four months of my tour and everything was going well. I was still in one piece and mentally and physically in much better shape than when I first stepped off the plane at Tan Son Nhut. Mentally, I much better understood my role in Vietnam, I had two great roommates, and the days were clicking by. Physically I was in much better shape, since the many operations had hardened my body, increased my stamina, and caused me to shed about 15 pounds.

I had TOC duty on the evening of December 16, 1969. It was passing as a typical night with the routine of giving out H&I fire information to traversing aircraft and interacting with the Vietnamese soldiers on duty. However, early in the morning of the 17th, I received information from Vietnamese sources that a helicopter had crashed near a PF outpost in Kien Thien district about 15 "klicks" southeast of "Mickey's Ears" and near the *Rach Kgan Du* river. Although details were sketchy, I entered what I knew into the staff officer's journal and made the necessary report via phone to IV Corps Headquarters at Can Tho. Then at 7:00 a.m, I turned the information and responsibility over to the TOC NCOs and headed to my hooch.

As was the practice after TOC duty, I was able to sleep in that morning. When I awoke, I learned it was an army AH-1 "Cobra"[1] helicopter that had crashed during the night. In the early daylight hours of the 17th, Lieutenant Bob Noonan and an RF company went to the crash site to search for survivors. Instead, Bob ended up recovering the bodies of the two young (in their early 20s) warrant officers, one the pilot and the other the copilot/gunner. (These warrant officers' names are inscribed on the Vietnam Memorial Wall in Washington, D.C., at Panel 15W, Line 64.) Additionally,

Chapter 13. Holidays 1969

Bob recovered sensitive communications items at the site, like the SOI and encryption device, weapons, flight equipment, and some personal effects. The pilots' remains were carefully recovered and flown to Can Tho.

As a team accompanying the recovery effort provided security, a specially trained crew rigged the wreckage of the "Cobra" for sling loading. The rigged "Cobra" was then hooked to a CH-47 helicopter and transported to Can Tho. When I later talked to Bob Noonan, his best assessment was that the crash was caused by either a mechanical failure or the pilot becoming disoriented and simply flying the helicopter into the ground, as it was a dark, moonless night. Bob based his conclusion on conversations with several PF soldiers from the nearby outpost. These soldiers reported no hostile fire in the area at the time of the crash.

Halfway through December after an evening pre-operation briefing, Colonel LeVasseur asked me to remain in his hooch. While I was quickly trying to think what I might have done to merit this meeting, Colonel LeVasseur told me he had recommended me for the award of the Combat Infantryman's Badge (CIB). I was beyond surprised when he said this, as I did not think I would qualify for a CIB, since I was an engineer officer. CIBs were awarded to combat arms soldiers/advisors who served in an infantry position for 30 or more days, *and*, while assigned in this infantry position, had been under enemy fire.

The awards branch in Saigon denied the CIB request Colonel LeVasseur had submitted, and he felt bad about this denial. However, he said he had a plan. He told me that newly promoted CPT Bob Olderson had just extended his tour in Vietnam by six months, and accordingly he would be going home for a 30-day leave in a couple of weeks. While CPT Olderson was on leave, Colonel LeVasseur said he would temporarily reassign me into the position of Assistant RF/PF Advisor. Once reassigned, the regulation requirements would apply and I might qualify for the prestigious award. I thanked Colonel LeVasseur for his thoughtful consideration but told him a CIB would not change anything I had been doing or would do in the future. At this point, I told him I simply enjoyed accompanying the Vietnamese on operations.

As Christmas was drawing near, teammates and I started receiving gift packages and Christmas cards. As great as these gestures were, the closer I got to Christmas the sadder I felt. At this time of year, my mind drifted back to Christmases past. I came from a large and poor family, and we were not especially close, yet Christmas was still a very special time of the year. Memories of Christmas Eve services at St. John's Lutheran Church; going to Grandma's for Christmas dinner with the customary oyster soup, homemade cookies, and candies (especially those from my great-aunt); Christmas carols; and snow all replayed in my brain. I really missed those things. Moreover, it occurred to me that, at age 22, this would be the very first Christmas I would spend away from my family.

Christmas Eve in Vi Thanh was memorable, too, but for different reasons. Vi Thanh had a sizeable Catholic population. In the stillness of the night I could hear the faint music and singing coming from the Catholic church downtown as the congregation celebrated midnight mass. I recognized the Christmas songs, sung in Vietnamese, by their melodies. These sounds, thoughts of Christmases past, and loneliness drove me into deeper melancholy, tears, and eventual sleep.

The combatants (U.S., GVN, NVA and VC) declared a Christmas cease-fire in 1969, so, for the most part, the province was on stand-down.[2] On Christmas Day we had another wonderful feast, courtesy of our Vietnamese cooks and the mess sergeant. Though the meal was not quite as good as Grandma made, it easily got me out of the funk I was in the night before. I cannot overstate the tremendous morale boost a traditional Christmas meal made—even though the temperature was in the 90s!

A week after Christmas Eve came New Year's Eve. Nothing really special here, though some team members made late use of the club. As for me, I wrote a couple of letters and listened to AFVN. As I lay in my bed that night, I thought this New Year's Eve was really significant in that it was not only the end of a year; it was also the end of a decade. I began 1960 as a scrawny 12-year-old kid. The decade called the Soaring Sixties was one of great transformation in the United States and for me. I learned to work hard on the farm, graduated near the exact center of my high school class of 180 students, worked a year for International Harvester Company, became a man, went into the army, became an officer, got married, and was now sitting in Vietnam. Looking back, the '60s were a fun and exciting time for me. On this New Year's Eve, I wondered how I would fare in the 1970s.

The next morning, January 1, 1970, I finally found it respectable to start counting the number of days I had remaining in Vietnam. Almost halfway—that day, I had 206 days and a wake-up!

Chapter 14

An, Saigon, and Shopping

Some days when *Trung úy* An and I were not on operations, training, or otherwise scheming to defeat communism, we would go to downtown Vi Thanh for breakfast. Breakfast consisted of a French-type bread, noodle soup, and a strong hot Vietnamese coffee spiked with a lot of condensed milk and sugar, called *cà phê sua nong*. I also went to breakfast with my interpreter, *Trung sĩ* Minh, on several occasions and enjoyed the same fare. It was nice to have a leisurely breakfast in this urban environment and observe the Vietnamese people going about their everyday business seemingly undisturbed by the war.

Sitting in an open café, I became a novelty to children on their way to school. These schoolchildren would sheepishly approach me and spend several minutes just standing there staring at me. If I said something to them in Vietnamese, either because of my accent, mispronunciation, or out of sheer amazement, they would giggle among themselves and then break into an ear-to-ear smile. Before long, I found myself surrounded by smiling boys and mostly shy onlooking girls. Interacting with these children was probably the most gratifying part of my time in-country. On one occasion some teenage boys invited me to play foosball with them. I proved to them I had never seen or played this game before as they absolutely destroyed my partner and me. It occurred to me that I was in Vietnam for them and their future much more so than I was there for motherhood, apple pie, and Old Glory.

One day, I visited *Trung úy* An's company area, which was located just south of Vi Thanh. I was surprised his soldiers lived in buildings made out of corrugated tin with dirt floors. These accommodations were very Spartan, and to me, resembled a cattle shed. As I could have expected during this visit, An had his soldiers maintaining their individual weapons and crew-served M-60 machine guns and performing other soldierly tasks. I saw that married men of the unit were able to have their families on the compound, and I was fortunate that day to meet *Trung úy* An's wife and two young sons. An beamed with pride when he introduced his family to me, and now I can only wonder what happened to this family as the war progressed and eventually reached its sad and tragic conclusion.

On one particular occasion with *Trung úy* An, we demonstrated our collective youthful foolishness. It was during the dry season and I had just finished giving a demonstration to the officers and NCOs of the 987th RF company on how to set up a mechanical ambush.[1] After this session, An invited me to go with him to lunch. Having nothing better to do and really enjoying his company, I readily accepted his invitation.

The place we went to that day was a considerably scaled-down Vietnamese version of a mom-and-pop restaurant—a thatched hut with a dirt floor. It served food and sold cigarettes, beer, and sodas. The restaurant was located just on the outskirts of Vi Thanh near the canal that ran past Duc Long. Lunch with An was relaxing, carefree, and resulted in hours of drinking. We spent the afternoon drinking 33 beer, munching on dried squid and tiny pickled shrimp with onions, and totally enjoying each other's company. In the process, we both got totally blitzed and did not realize night was fast approaching as we continued our binge.

Wisely, An had taken his bodyguard with him. This older, totally expressionless *Trung sĩ* must have realized he was the only responsible adult present and that he needed to do something with these two drunks. Somehow, that night I ended up back at the MACV compound unaware how I got there but otherwise safe. Several days later, I saw An. Neither of us remembered leaving the restaurant but admitted we thought we had a great time. As I later thought about this incident, this would have been an opportune time for the VC to easily snatch or kill two reasonably high-value targets. Fortunately, they did not.

In 1970 during a year's tour in Vietnam, those serving in-country were entitled to receive two-, five-, or seven-day[2] Rest and Relaxation (R&R) reprieves from the war. Military personnel could go on R&R to any of the approved sites at no transportation cost to them and non-chargeable as leave. I think most married soldiers went to Hawaii to meet their wives during their R&Rs, while the majority of single men went to the other more exotic locations.[3] Each of these locations had U.S. military and civilian personnel on site whose mission was to ensure those on R&R had an enjoyable time.

In January, Harvey went on R&R to meet his wife in Hawaii. When he got back he told me about the great time he had, and that he and his wife went to the island of Kauai and stayed at the Coco Palms Hotel on Poipu Beach. Harvey's discussion prompted me to think about my own R&R, which I soon requested. After a week or two, I received word that my R&R was approved. I made travel arrangements through military channels and a reservation to stay at the same hotel as Harvey. I scheduled my R&R for

Chapter 14. An, Saigon, and Shopping

February 28 through March 6, seven months after my arrival in Vietnam.[4] As was the prevalent pastime in Vietnam, I counted the number of days until my DEROS and, certainly, my Hawaii R&R. It was good to have the days until my R&R be in double, rather than my DEROS's triple, digits. Little bites at a time, I thought.

By January, I settled into a routine of going to Saigon to replenish the AIK funds. With several trips under my belt I could maneuver the process of arranging travel and passing through airports to easily get to Saigon and back. Once in Saigon, I could navigate my way around with relative ease. I never again ate at such a posh restaurant as I visited on my first trip to Saigon, settling, instead, for the mess hall at MACV Headquarters or a place close to the BOQ where I stayed. At night, I just stayed at the BOQ.

On a couple of occasions while in Saigon I went to the bar on the top floor of the BOQ. In the bar, the B-girls[5] were working the crowd, charming men who were 10,000 miles from home and lonely. The typical approach of the provocatively dressed B-girls was to sit with the men and have the men buy them a "Wikkey" Coke. These drinks cost the equivalent of $2, as I recall, and they were allegedly all Coke with no whiskey. To not expose the deceit, the male patron's drink was properly prepared. In addition to substantially increasing the bar's profits, it was widely believed the B-girls received a kickback from each drink purchased. Like other arrivals in Vietnam, I received a warning of such "Wikkey Coke" scams during my initial in-country orientation. I heeded this warning, but by the looks of it, many others didn't. After watching them awhile, I could only guess that other services were available from the B-girls. It was interesting to watch the men who fell prey to their own loneliness. The dynamics going on within the bar reminded me of the poem "The Spider and the Fly."

In addition to the B-girls, another staple in Saigon were the many places offering steam baths and massages. A respite from the war or desk duty, these establishments were little more than fronts for prostitution. GIs commonly referred to these places as going for a "steam job and blow bath." Just as I shunned the B-girls, I never went to those establishments. Truthfully, I wasn't interested, as my religious upbringing and my fear of getting some hard-to-pronounce sexually transmitted disease convinced me to abstain. For me, a big night in Saigon was getting 12 hours of sleep and taking a long hot shower in a shower that was mere feet from my bed.

My other Saigon activity was watching outside events from the top floor of the BOQ. The level of activity was amazing. There were civilian and military vehicles going up and down the streets below, occasional flashing lights and sirens from MP or White Mice jeeps and ambulances, and "dustoff" helicopters landing at a hospital that appeared to be close to Tan Son Nhut airport. As I stood on the balcony one evening, I was surprised to see green tracers[6] arcing into the sky, probably about a half mile away. I thought this sight was unusual in this capital city, but then I thought back to news reports from less than two years earlier. During Tet 1968, the VC were running throughout Saigon, including Cho Lon,[7] the U.S. embassy, the racetrack, and the Vietnamese radio station. Like most everyone else, I could visualize the picture of the brigadier general of South Vietnam's National Police executing the VC prisoner on the streets of Saigon during Tet and Walter Cronkite proclaiming the war was lost. I was really glad that I missed Tet '68.

Since I frequently had to go to Saigon for purposes of the AIK fund, I was often tasked to stop at the Central Issue Facility and turn in equipment from a hastily departed team member or casualty, such as I had done for Lieutenant Young in September. On one such trip, I turned in an M-16 rifle that had its barrel bent at about a 30-degree angle. I could not, for the life of me, ever even guess how this happened. It was as if the barrel was heated and subsequently bent.

In early December I was returning from an AIK/CIF trip when I stopped at the PX complex in Can Tho. On this compound near the airfield was a throng of military, civilian, and Vietnamese people walking around who apparently did not know there was a war going on. Military personnel were readily identifiable by their uniforms and their Nikon cameras hanging around their necks. All seemed to be carrying cartons of cigarettes or bottles of alcohol. Blaring out over the speakers in the complex at the time was a Johnny Cash recording of his then popular hit song, "A Boy Named Sue." What a weird song!

For me, I had an express purpose for visiting this PX area. Harvey told me of a Hong Kong–based merchant who offered tailor-made suits and shirts. I thought it would be a good idea to purchase a business ensemble for my eventual return to the "world"[8] and civilian life. After looking at product samples and making my selections, the merchant took my measurements and gave me a receipt for my down payment. I purchased a suit, sport coat, vest, two pairs of slacks, and five monogrammed short-sleeved shirts for $141.25. With this purchase, I thought those male models I had seen in *Playboy* magazine would have nothing on me! Now all I had to do was to wait about six weeks as I wondered what this wardrobe would have cost in the U.S.[9]

Happy with myself and somewhat cocky over my wise and thrifty clothing purchase, I went to the Can Tho airfield officers club to get a bite to eat while waiting for the next plane to Vi Thanh. There, I was surprised to run into Captain Howard Taylor, our FAC. I had gotten to know Captain Taylor rather well as I spent a lot of time in the hooch he shared with Lieutenant Eastman. Captain Taylor had taken me up in his airplane

Chapter 14. An, Saigon, and Shopping

several times, including a fly-over of the Carlile battlefield. When I rode with Captain Taylor, with few exceptions, I believed his singular purpose was to make me airsick! He failed in his attempts.

As we sat at the bar and had a snack together, I made a completely insane bet with Captain Taylor regarding the camouflage pattern of air force majors' and lieutenant colonels' rank insignia. We both wagered a month's pay on our positions. Not surprisingly, Captain Taylor, being an air force officer, was correct. Rather than calling my bet and showing me how stupid I was, he settled for me buying him another soda. Food, sodas, and wagering complete, Captain Taylor offered to fly me back to Vi Thanh and I gladly accepted.

Chapter 15

The Dry Season

As the months passed, I considered myself lucky to have my other duties increase. One of these added duties was translating Vietnamese requests for defoliation using Agent Orange. Reviewing these requests with my language dictionary in hand, I would translate them to the best of my abilities and then have *Trung sĩ* Song go over my work. These translations required exactness and, with *Trung sĩ* Song's meticulous review and tutelage, this exercise greatly helped me expand my Vietnamese vocabulary. I performed this translation duty perhaps three times during my tour. In retrospect, I am thankful that, thus far in my life, I have not contracted any of the diseases presumed to be associated with Agent Orange. I unequivocally know I traversed areas sprayed with that potent chemical.

A major construction project happened on the MACV compound during the dry season. Soldiers from the 52nd Signal Detachment and a squad of engineers built a communications'/command bunker at the near center of the compound. Being the resident engineer, I periodically reviewed the progress of this project and reported my observations to Colonel LeVasseur. The huge bunker was made of structural timbers, PSP, and many layers of sandbags.[1] Near the new commo bunker, space that had previously been an open storage area became the parking lot for team vehicles. Several other lesser compound improvements were also undertaken in the dry season. These included relocating the main gate from the north to the east side of the compound and converting the former parking lot (near the mail and orderly rooms and the mess hall) into a volleyball court. The volleyball court was Colonel LeVasseur's idea and was a real boost to team morale. Volleyball games were held on most evenings, and for those who seldom got off the compound, these games promoted physical fitness. In total, these projects hardened our communications ability, provided a more robust command center on the compound, enhanced our security posture by moving the main gate, and helped us stay in better physical shape.

During my tour I had to prepare a base development plan for the compound. For me, this was an unnecessary, almost silly, task, since the U.S.

was gradually handing the conduct of the war over to the South Vietnamese, as we were reducing our number of troops in Vietnam. In my opinion, the compound was more than adequate with the improvements described above, and I did not like the idea of spending unnecessary dollars or wasting my time. Since the thought of expanding or improving upon the compound did not make sense to me, I took this matter to Colonel LeVasseur to seek his advice on how best to respond to this requirement. Per his request, I asked for a new and higher chain-link fence around the compound and a paved parking lot. I would have liked to request air conditioners for each hooch but thought this might be a bit too much.

In January 1970, I decided to extend in the army for an additional year, since my two-year officer service obligation was up in August. By extending, my new ETS (Expiration Term of Service) would be August 30, 1971. I knew that by extending I would be eligible for promotion to captain on the one-year anniversary date of my promotion to first lieutenant. At that time in my life, I was reasonably certain I did not want to make the army a career, but extending would give me time to decide what I wanted to do after the army. Extending would give me time to get reacclimated to life in the "world," explore college options, and/or allow me to find a good civilian job. With my request for extension, I submitted my post–Vietnam assignment request. These requests were rightfully called "dream sheets," since you had to be dreaming if you thought the army was going to reassign you to any of your requested installations. Nonetheless, I requested to be stationed somewhere in the Midwest. Predicated solely upon approval of my extension request, I would receive reassignment orders from the Department of the Army in the next several months.

January 21, 1970, halfway around the world and unbeknownst to me, my mother gave birth to her tenth child. My youngest brother, Bradley, entered this world!

Each month an officer from the MACV compound was assigned the special duty of Class A agent. In the U.S. Army, a Class A agent received the total payroll for his assigned unit from the Finance Office, broke down[2] the payroll and paid the soldiers. I pulled this duty in February 1970, and easily took care of paying personnel on the MACV compound and the district teams. Paying this last group was made easier, since the Class A agent received priority on the daily "swing ship" going to the districts. However, it was downright difficult and sometimes scary paying the outlying MATs. To pay the MATs, I had to determine their location and schedule a time to pay them when everyone was present.

Most of the time, the Class A agent could use the "swing ship" and get in and out of the MAT's location in short order. For some reason, as Class A agent, I had to drive to one MAT's location somewhere east of Long My to pay that team. Neither the young sergeant who was assigned to me as a driver/guard for the payroll nor I had been in this area before. Also, since I was carrying and responsible for other soldiers' pay, this made for a tense afternoon. I was given the location of the MAT and, using a map, we proceeded to drive the jeep several kilometers down a dirt path adjacent to a canal. As we traveled this route, we had vegetation slapping at both sides of the jeep until we arrived at the MAT outpost. Everyone from the MAT was present and I quickly paid the team.

Soon, the sergeant and I were retracing our harrowing route. This time I told the sergeant to drive the jeep as fast as he could. I knew this speed may have been unsafe; but my rationale was that perhaps the VC saw us earlier going down this desolate path. Knowing our jeep would have to take this same return route, the VC could have planned an ambush on us two imperialist GIs transgressing their turf. Fortunately, we arrived safely back in Vi Thanh and likely made Indy 500 qualifying speed to boot. Thankfully, this was my only time as Class A agent in Vietnam.

One day during the dry season, I decided to accompany a team convoy going from Vi Thanh to Can Tho and returning. This convoy was on a routine resupply run and consisted of several 2½-ton trucks and several jeeps. I chose to go along simply for something new and different to do, and I rode in one of the jeeps with Captain Sands. To get to Can Tho one had to take a circuitous route of about 70 kilometers over rutted gravel roads. Riding in the jeep that day I saw another aspect of Vietnam. I was surprised to see the Vietnamese hooches so close to the road and the many young children playing around these hooches. Beyond the road were massive rice fields that had already been harvested. That day there was no enemy activity and we safely made it back to Vi Thanh by dusk. It was a peaceful, idyllic, change-of-pace day, and I really enjoyed my ride in the sun.

Chapter 16

Grenades and Airplanes

On January 8, 1970, I went on an operation with Staff Sergeant Tolson*, the team's Riverboat advisor.[1] On this operation I was with the 113th RF company carrying a newly procured "special" 30-round M-16 magazine. This magazine consisted of an M-16 magazine affixed atop a modified AK-47 magazine. The impetus for my wanting a 30-round magazine was seeing a Navy SEAL carrying a 30-round magazine in his M-16 while on the MACV compound. The SEAL suggested I send a letter to the Colt Firearms Company requesting they send me several 30-round magazines. Colt, the M-16's patent-right holder (but one of several M-16 manufacturers), politely responded to my letter by saying I should get the requested magazines from my supply channels. In 1970, only special operations personnel (Green Berets, Navy SEALS, Recondo Teams, etc.) received 30-round magazines. So, after failing with Colt, I obtained a "special" 30-round Rube Goldberg[2] magazine. For the low price of two packs of Salem cigarettes, a Vietnamese soldier made this magazine for me. As with test-driving a car before buying it, prior to tendering the cigarettes I test-fired the magazine and it worked fine.

On this particular airmobile operation we landed in a cold LZ and proceeded on to our checkpoints and objective. An hour or so into the operation we made contact with an estimated squad-size VC unit. A platoon-size element of the 113th RF company was sweeping the tree line while the command group and I were walking in the dry rice paddy. The commander's radio crackled with excitement as the platoon suddenly began exchanging fire with VC in the tree line. It was soon after the shooting started that, after four and a half months in-country, I saw my first live noncaptive VC up close and personal.

I saw the lone VC running in the open rice paddy about 100 meters from me going from my left to right. This VC was carrying a weapon and doing his best Jesse Owens[3] impersonation. From my position in the middle of the rice paddy, I quickly shouldered my M-16, flipped the safety off, and squeezed the trigger. Bang! I missed my target, as just a single round left the barrel of my now jammed weapon. I pulled my weapon's charging handle back and saw my "special" magazine had failed to feed, and a round was cockeyed in the magazine. I could not believe it, just when I needed it most—nothing. Hurriedly, and with great disgust, I threw my 30-round magazine on the ground and slammed a regular 20-round magazine home.

Now reloaded, I was unable to get the VC in my sight and fire again as he ran into a small bunker about 200 meters away. Focused on his escape, the VC did not attempt to fire at us. While others provided overwatch, several RF soldiers, my bodyguard, and I ran in a crouching manner toward the bunker. I was propelled by both frustration and the excitement of the moment. Cautiously, we approached the bunker, watchful of the area in front of the entrance. At about 20 feet from the bunker I shouted, *"Lựu đạn! Lựu đạn!"* (Grenade! Grenade!) to my Vietnamese comrades. I removed the lone grenade from my web belt (one that I had carried on many earlier operations) and moved closer to the bunker entrance. I pulled the pin, let the spoon fly, and calmly tossed the grenade into the bunker opening. As I flattened myself in the rice paddy, I heard a muted swoosh as the grenade exploded. We later found the bunker was half-full of water.

After the sporadic firing ceased and the command group rejoined me, I asked an RF soldier to inspect the interior of the bunker, mostly because I wanted to recover the VC's weapon. Dutifully, he complied. When the RF soldier reappeared, he said he could find neither the VC nor his weapon. This could have been due to an underwater entrance/exit to the bunker that was on a canal bank. (The VC normally constructed bunkers with such an exit.) Or perhaps the RF soldier simply did not try hard enough. Whatever the reason, I was disappointed I did not get my war trophy. Rather than being able to admire my anticipated souvenir, I left one of the ace of spades cards I always carried with me on top of the bunker. On the card I wrote in grease pencil, *"VC chết đây Đại đội 113,"* which translated to "VC killed here Company 113." This gesture greatly amused the soldiers around me, and many of them commented and patted me on the back as we then proceeded on to our objective.

We claimed seven VC were killed during this operation, five killed by air (KBA),[4] which meant either by gunship, by FAC or "Shotgun" rockets, or by high-performance aircraft. On this operation, the FACs got the credit, since they were on duty overhead. Our two-enemy KIA statistic attests to the elusiveness of the enemy and what poor shots we ground soldiers were.

I only employed or witnessed high-performance aircraft attacks about two or three times while on operations. The procedures for using close air support (CAS)[5] went something like this. I would identify the target by passing the grid location and target type to the FACs. I would also give the FAC my location so he could ensure we would be at a safe stand-off distance from the ordnance the CAS was carrying. (On at least one occasion, the FAC moved us away from the target area to ensure our safety.) Once the "fast movers" (jets) were in the area,[6] the FACs communicated with them and marked the location of the target with a smoke rocket. From the marking round the FAC would adjust the ground attack pilot onto the target by direction and number of meters from the smoke rocket impact. Only after the CAS pilot identified the target, which the FAC then confirmed, would the pilot roll the aircraft in for a bombing run. Though the use of close air support sometimes involved a lengthy and cumbersome process, it was both truly terrifying and exhilarating to witness its actual employment.

Once, I waited for nearly two hours for two USAF F-4s to arrive "on station" (overhead) and attack a small number of VC who had a good sniper in their midst. We were unable to maneuver, since the sniper's accurate fire had us pinned down in a nearby tree line and my counterpart told me we were out of artillery range. I passed the target information to our FAC, who called for close air support. Once the F-4s were on station, the FAC identified the target, fired a smoke round, and passed the necessary information to the pilots. The F-4 pilot acknowledged the correction from the FAC's smoke rocket and lined up for a bombing run. About 30 seconds out, the FAC told me to warn everyone to get down as low as we could, since we were only about 400–500 meters from the targeted VC location. Reminding me of films I had seen of attacking World War II Stukas, the F-4s swooped low and dropped a load of 500-pound bombs followed by the second aircraft which dropped napalm. The bombs were the loudest explosion I heard in Vietnam. The scream of the jets with their roaring afterburners combined with the bomb blast and characteristic heat and smell of napalm were truly frightening. I could not comprehend being on the receiving end of this ordnance.

Once the jets expended their bombs, we cautiously approached the smoldering area. Giant holes in the ground, crumpled and splintered trees, little fires, and the smell of napalm and burning flesh greeted us at the VC bunker complex. Scattered among the debris we found some body parts, but no bodies or weapons. At that moment, I recalled General William Tecumseh Sherman's maxim, "War is hell." Thankfully, the rest of the day's operation was uneventful and I did not attempt to assess a KBA count. I left this imprecise science to the air force and their statisticians. For that day, however, the win went to the good guys, as we suffered no casualties.

Less impressive, though equally lethal, was an attack by two Vietnamese Air Force (VNAF) A-1E Skyraiders I once witnessed. These Korean War–vintage propeller-driven aircraft could loiter over an area for a long time and, in addition to their 20-mm cannons, could be armed with rockets and bombs. To me, the best thing about the Skyraiders was that they were flown by Vietnamese pilots. Completing the trifecta, the Skyraiders were directed onto targets by Vietnamese FACs, and those targets had been identified by Vietnamese ground commanders. I saw A-1Es in the later part of my tour, and it was encouraging to see that Vietnamization was making progress!

I frequently worked with army helicopter gunships, as they were more available than fixed-wing air support. As was routine, every time we made a helicopter insertion into an LZ we had gunships overhead. Most of these gunships were model UH-1C[7] "Hueys." These helicopters were armed with M-60 machine guns manned by the crew chief/door gunners and were armed with a combination of either rockets, mini-guns or a 40-mm grenade launcher. Gunships were, in my experience, always employed in pairs and would sweep around a landing zone providing suppressive fire to protect the vulnerable "friendlies" as we debarked the "slicks." With the "slicks" landing in the middle of rice paddies, it was normal for the gunships to shoot up any armed individuals and/or VC positions in the tree-lined areas surrounding the paddy LZ.[8]

During one operation, the troops had disembarked the "slicks" and were spreading out to perform the normal procedure of assaulting the wood line. That day, a gunship pilot or door gunner held his trigger a bit too long, which resulted in a round ricocheting off the standing paddy water and hitting an RF soldier in the leg. Fortunately for the soldier, it was a superficial wound, but it did require my shouting into the radio for the gunships to cease fire. As it was now a cold LZ, a "slick" pilot (perhaps feeling culpable for the mistake of one of his brethren) returned to the LZ and evacuated the injured soldier to the Vi Thanh hospital.

An embarrassing thing happened to me on the day when I yanked the radio handset and pulled my Cambodian bodyguard off his feet. We had cleared the rice paddy and were walking in the tree line when we came under intense, but inaccurate, VC fire. On this day, we had helicopter gunship support available. These C Model "Huey" gunships had a nose-mounted 40-mm grenade launcher system[9] that I had never used before. Under fire, I determined my location, which I passed to the pilots. Then, using my compass, I gave the pilots an azimuth and distance from my location to the VC firing positions. Despite this simple and widely used target location method, I was unable to get the gunship pilots to locate the target. After going back and forth on the radio, I finally loaded a special magazine I always carried. This magazine was filled with 20 rounds of tracer ammunition. Once loaded and when the gunships were in a position where they could observe, I fired the tracers at the VC locations. This worked, and with the VC locations identified, the gunships rolled in to attack the target.

As they commenced their attack, I radioed the gunships, telling them they were receiving what I thought was .51 caliber machine gun fire.[10] They

Chapter 16. Grenades and Airplanes 121

made a partial gun run, then pulled off. I told the gunships that the VC ground fire we were receiving was unabated, so they attacked the VC positions a second time. Again, I told them they were receiving heavy caliber machine gun fire. The gunship pilots challenged me on this assertion because they could see neither VC muzzle flashes nor the green tracer rounds from a machine gun. They made another pass on the VC position and I heard the same weapon's report this time as well.

Pausing a moment, it finally occurred to me the staccato bloop, bloop, bloop I heard was not the cycling of a Soviet-bloc heavy machine gun, but rather the sound of the gunship's 40-mm grenade launcher. On the third pass I was quiet as the gunships silenced all enemy fire. It was then that I reluctantly reported to the gunship pilots what I had done. Despite my amateurish error in misidentifying enemy fire, the gunship pilots, like most other pilots I encountered, were polite and professional. However, later that night in their base officer's club, I'm pretty sure the crew had a great laugh over the "rookie" advisor they worked with that day.

That same day after coming under fire we were all keenly aware we were in enemy territory. As we stopped at a small collection of hooches for lunch, we came upon an elder Vietnamese man who, though a Ho Chi Minh look alike, I guessed to be a farmer. A Vietnamese NCO interrogated this old man and determined he was probably not a VC. Following lunch, but still in the presence of this elderly man, the command group took their siesta. During siesta time[11] I intently observed this man and soon began to feel very sorry for him. Although he could have been a VC battalion commander (unlikely), I thought him to be the epitome of the population in rural Chuong Thien province. I could tell by his slow, determined movements and sad countenance that he just wanted to be left alone. However, since he was a local and perhaps familiar with where VC mines may have been located, *Trung úy* An decided to use him as a guide the rest of the afternoon.

We successfully closed on our objective. At near dusk the "slicks" announced they were en route to pick us up. As they neared, I radioed the lead aircraft pilot the necessary pickup information, popped smoke, and told him we had a Vietnamese civilian we would be leaving in the PZ. I told the flight lead that the civilian was wearing white "pajamas," and once all troops were loaded he would remain in the rice paddy when we took off. Then in very specific terms, I told him I did not want this elderly man molested.[12] As we left the PZ I kept my eyes on this man until he was just a disappearing white speck. For today, we and our charge were safe and especially for the latter, I was thankful.

When not on operations, I spent a number of hours flying in the backseat of an O-1 airplane. Most of this time I flew backseat with Warrant Officer Ralph Howard on what were primarily reconnaissance flights. Ralph would fly over known VC areas looking for armed men, suspicious-looking sampans, or anything appearing out of the ordinary. On finding something matching this criterion, he would radio the TOC and describe the sighted activity and its grid location. In turn, the TOC would coordinate with the Vietnamese officers at the TOC to determine if there were any friendlies in the area. If Ralph received word that there were no known friendlies in the area, it was assumed his spotting was enemy activity and he was cleared to engage. With this clearance he would engage the enemy by firing his onboard 2.75" rockets. These rockets were aimed by using a reticle the pilots had drawn on the Plexiglas windshield of the plane with a grease pencil. With this rudimentary sight system, the rockets were notoriously inaccurate, although they invariably hit the ground somewhere.

It was nearing dark after a lengthy reconnaissance flight and Ralph was heading back to the airfield, since he had used all of his rockets. On the way, he spotted a rather large sampan with a tarp over its midsection and traveling on a canal in a known VC area. Since this was a free fire zone, Ralph could engage without clearance from the TOC. However, since he had no rockets left, I asked if I could engage the sampan with my M-16. Ralph reluctantly agreed but expressed his concern over hot brass flying around the cockpit. I told him I would be careful. As he banked to take a pass over the sampan, while maintaining his altitude of 1,500 feet, I fired a 20-round magazine loaded with one tracer round every fifth round. Watching the tracers, I could see I did not come anywhere close to hitting the sampan. I failed to consider the effect of inertia imposed by the path and speed of the airplane. Making the mental adjustment, on the second pass my rounds landed close enough to the sampan to cause its occupants to jump into the canal. Convinced we had, at least temporarily, impeded the VC's delivery of supplies, Ralph headed for the airfield and my afternoon as a waist gunner on a B-17 was over.

Though not the enemy's, an aircraft that struck fear into the hearts and minds of senior officers on Advisory Team 73 was an OH-58 Kiowa.[13] Specifically, this was the OH-58 flown by, or having as a passenger, John Paul Vann.[14] In his capacity as Deputy CORDS for IV Corps, Vann flew all over the Delta, sometimes superimposing himself as C&C during a "hot" operation. Vann, an outspoken and no-nonsense professional, literally caused a panic when his Kiowa set down on the small helipad nested between the road and canal right in front of the "old" compound front gate. From my lowly perspective, it was interesting to see the effect Vann's presence had on career-minded officers.

Chapter 17

Tet and Rest and Relaxation

Tet, February 16, 1970, was the beginning of the Year of the Dog in the Chinese lunar calendar. Unlike the previous two anniversaries of the day in 1968 and 1969, Tet 1970 was mostly quiet in Chuong Thien and throughout the country. To the Vietnamese, Tet was a holiday equivalent to New Year's Day, the Fourth of July, and Christmas in the U.S all rolled into one. Tet was a joyous time: a time for family; a time for looking forward to spring, a time to remember ancestors, and, especially, a time for celebration. Tet, for Advisory Team 73, was a time to honor the customs of our Vietnamese friends, and therefore it was a day with no planned operations.

For Tet, Lieutenant Bob Noonan invited me to Duc Long to share the day with the district team and their Vietnamese counterparts. I had been to Duc Long a number of times and had enjoyed the company of Captain Childress, the previous district senior advisor, Lieutenant Noonan, and Lieutenant Dave Nickinovich, who arrived in December. During those earlier visits, I enjoyed playing with the team pet—a rhesus macaque monkey named Bridgette. Bridgette was a friendly and playful sort who enjoyed jumping on one's shoulders to inspect their hair for nits or lice. Bridgette must have done a great job, since no one in Duc Long ever had head lice.

On this Tet celebration the Vietnamese woman who kept the advisors team house in order and cooked some of their meals prepared a traditional Tet meal for the team. In particular, I remember her using what I called a volcano cooker. This particular item had a chimney-like protrusion in the middle under which a small fire kept the food warm. For our Tet meal, she had prepared a pork, vegetable, and bamboo dish, spring rolls, rice, and nước mắm. We also had iced tea and a variety of sodas. It was a splendid meal. It humbled me to think a Vietnamese woman who had so little was willing to share it with us who had so much. This spoke volumes about the Vietnamese people and was another of the many ironies of Vietnam.

February 20 was just an ordinary day for me. I did nothing in particular, yet that date stands out in my memory. That day, Colonel LeVasseur, the province Chief, Harvey, several other Americans, and a small Vietnamese entourage traveled into the countryside to celebrate the opening to a previously impassable stretch of road and view a sizeable weapons cache. The cache location had recently been disclosed by a VC who "rallied" to the government's side.[1] For today's "show," with the intent of capitalizing on these two positive events, five or six jeeps proceeded down the road heading to Kien Hung.

Harvey's vehicle was the lead vehicle in this small convoy, with the overcrowded province chief's jeep following closely behind. For inexplicable reasons the province chief's vehicle stopped at an intersection and turned down a lesser road. This action deviated from the planned route. The other vehicles in the convoy stopped at the intersection of the two roads, thinking the province chief might have taken a wrong turn and would soon turn around. After a brief pause, Harvey's vehicle decided to follow the province chief and proceeded to catch up. Then, perhaps 200 meters away to his immediate front, Harvey heard a loud explosion. Through the dark smoke he saw the lead jeep being catapulted into the air—the victim of a large VC mine.

When the dust settled, several Vietnamese (a combination of police, civilians, and soldiers) were dead with two others wounded. Miraculously, the province chief and his driver escaped this near-death experience with concussions and other lesser injuries. Harvey helped tend to the wounded and to loading those killed onto the MEDAVAC. (The province chief, despite his injuries, refused the MEDEVAC and decided to continue his planned activities that day.) Later in the evening as Harvey was relating this event to Gene and me, it was clear this incident really unsettled him.[2] I was just thankful he was safe. No Americans were hurt, but this incident reminded us how a quirk of fate can either save your life *or* kill you.

After Tet, it was less than two weeks before I was to go on R&R, and during this period time seemed to stand still. Finally, the day arrived and I packed my few civilian clothes and put on my khaki uniform prior to heading to the airfield. There, I was lucky enough to board an Air America (the clandestine CIA contract airline) PC-6 Porter aircraft and got a nonstop flight to Saigon. Once in Saigon, I went to MACV Headquarters and converted my MPC into real money. I also received a $200 partial pay that the army (in their wisdom) was providing soldiers going on R&R. Cash in hand, I went to Tan Son Nhut airport, where I boarded a chartered Pan Am 727 filled to capacity with smiling GIs.

The flight from Saigon to Hawaii felt like it took forever, prolonged by our interim refueling stop at Clark Air Force Base. However, neither the torturous flight time nor the refueling stop could dampen the spirits of the onboard passengers. Finally, about midmorning the plane touched

Chapter 17. Tet and Rest and Relaxation

Aftermath of mine explosion on February 20, 1970. RF soldiers are in the foreground, with American advisors and Vietnamese soldiers in the background attending to the wounded. Captain Weiner miraculously escaped the fate of the passengers in the overturned jeep (courtesy Lawrence J. Hickey).

down at Honolulu International Airport, where several military buses were waiting to take us to nearby Fort DeRussy.

Arriving at a reception building at Fort DeRussy (which was located on Waikiki Beach), I could see a mass of women milling around and, in the far distance, Diamond Head. We were given a "Welcome to Hawaii" greeting by a civilian who came onto the bus and who gave us a reminder that things might be different with our loved ones. Then, in a sentence that deflated our then soaring spirits, our greeter told us we needed to be back at Fort DeRussy at a certain time on March 5 or we would be considered AWOL (Absent Without Leave). "Enjoy your R&R" were the final words I heard before I joined the surge to get off the bus. I saw Sue in the crowd, and once reunited, we slowly walked to the line of cabs near the reception building.

A cab took us to the airport, where we boarded a small commuter airplane for the flight from the island of Oahu to the island of Kauai, a short hop away. On Kauai, we rented a small Datsun so we could drive around the lush green island. I have two memories of seemingly insignificant events that occurred while driving around Kauai on R&R. The first memory was that we encountered a large number of frogs or toads on the road as we drove from the airport to the hotel and later around the island.

The second was hearing the song "ABC," by a relatively new group, the Jackson Five, on the car radio.

On Kauai, we enjoyed the beaches, the beauty of the volcanic mountains, the acres of pineapple fields, and our time together. On our last evening on Kauai, we went to a restaurant located on a beach on the west side of the island. There, as we were eating the best seafood we had ever tasted, we watched the crimson sun slowly setting into the Pacific Ocean. We had never seen anything like this before and were amazed at the spectacle of seeing the sun actually moving, slipping away under the watery horizon. The setting sun sadly reminded me that my time on R&R was also quickly sinking away.

All too soon we were turning in the rental car and doing everything in reverse. Back on the main island, we spent our final night at the Holiday Inn near the international airport. The next morning we did some shopping, where I purchased a U.S. demolition knife before returning to Fort DeRussy. After one final kiss and embrace with my wife, I boarded a bus filled with the quietest, most dejected-looking bunch of men I had ever seen. A bus took us back to the international airport, where we boarded the plane for our return flight to Vietnam. On the flight back there was little talk, as most of us were either reliving our all-too-brief R&R memories or catching up on sleep we had forfeited the previous couple of days. Hours later, we were sweating again as we deplaned at Tan Son Nhut and began taking in those signature "Vietnam smells." In a strange kind of way, I felt I was back home as the C-7 Caribou I boarded in Can Tho landed with a clattering thud at the Vi Thanh airfield. About four and one-half months to go!

CHAPTER 18

Pride, Volunteering, and Annoyances

March 10, 1970, was my proudest day in Vietnam. Refreshed from my recent R&R, that evening in the presence of team members assembled in the club, Colonel LeVasseur presented me with the Combat Infantryman's Badge. As the adjutant read MACV Special Order Number 63, dated 4 March 1970, I could barely contain myself. While I had not thought about this award before Colonel LeVasseur mentioned it to me in December, after that discussion I had become obsessed with the thought of receiving this beautiful piece of sky-blue and silver metal.

To bring me to this moment, Colonel LeVasseur had me reassigned as the assistant RF/PF advisor during the five weeks Captain Olderson went back home on his extension leave. This was in January and early February. During this temporary reassignment, I had been on six combat operations; and notably, I had been under enemy fire during my defective magazine/grenade/ace of spades operation with the 113th RF company. Once my CIB was awarded, I was elated. It was visible evidence I had fought an elusive enemy called "Charlie."

As happy as I was at receiving my CIB, the next day I began to feel bad for some of my fellow advisors. There were several I could think of who had been on more operations than me, yet they had been denied this honor. At the top of this list was Lieutenant Bob Noonan. As the Phoenix advisor in Duc Long district, Bob was not in an infantry position. A true warrior, Bob was as gung-ho and brave as anyone in the province, in fact, braver than most. Over his many months in-country Bob had volunteered to accompany the Vietnamese on many, many operations, and he had been in far more difficult fights than I had. It was incomprehensible to me that an action could not have been taken that would have allowed Bob to be eligible for a CIB. Of course, being the true professional he was, there was no complaint from Bob.

Even though my principal duty had been going on operations, this was not steady work for me. I continued to volunteer for other activities to fill the time gaps and stay busy. One of the more interesting duties I performed was accompanying MEDEVAC missions. I would do this when there were no American advisors on the ground and the ARVN unit needed a patient medically evacuated. The way this worked was the TOC would contact me to see if I was available to accompany a MEDEVAC. They would tell me the general and medical situation and inform me a "dustoff" was inbound and needed an interpreter.

"Dustoff" pilots did not like to pick up Vietnamese casualties without an American present, preferably on the ground. Rightfully, they feared they could be flying into an ambush prepared by the VC claiming to be friendlies. If a "dustoff" was en route to pick up the casualty or patient and found no Americans on the ground, they would request an American to accompany them to coordinate the patient pickup. I volunteered for this duty often and, when I did, I would request the "dustoff" crew stop at the Vi Thanh hospital landing pad to pick me up.

Before getting on the helicopter, I would verify the information given to me by the TOC with the pilot. This included the grid coordinates of the pickup site, type of patient (military or civilian), their medical condition, and the situation on the ground. Having this information confirmed, I would board the helicopter with my radio frequency tuned to the Vietnamese unit on the ground and don a radio headset for an intercom connection with the pilot. The pilot would fly to the general location and then tell me on the intercom when we were near the pickup coordinates. On this signal, I would use my radio to contact the ground unit using their call sign, saying something like *"Tôi là cố vấn Mỹ vẽ phi-cò trực thăng. Ông có khói maū không? Hiệng trái khói."* This translated to "I am an American advisor on the helicopter. Do you have a smoke grenade? Pop smoke." On this command I would look for a colored smoke plume and identify it as, for example, *"Vàng!"* (yellow), to which the ARVN RTO would then reply with *"đã"* (yes) or a simple OK. With this confirmation, I would tell the pilot it was safe to make the landing to pick up the patient, who was in the vicinity of the smoke. On the ground I would help load the patient, and I'm happy to say I never had to perform this task when the ground unit was under fire. With the pickup successful, the "dustoff" would drop me (and most often the patient) at the Vi Thanh hospital. I felt gratified in performing this duty.

During the dry season I volunteered for an adventure that afterward made me shudder. A PF platoon was building the typical triangular-shaped outpost on the south bank of the *Sông Cai Lon* river and about eight kilometers southeast of Kien Hung. Over the course of several years the Vietnamese perfected the method of constructing outposts. They would dig a moat around the proposed perimeter of the triangular outpost and use the

Chapter 18. Pride, Volunteering, and Annoyances

Vietnamese soldiers loading a wounded comrade onto "dustoff" helicopter of the 82nd Air Ambulance Detachment, as indicated by the "82" inside the red cross painted on the door. "Dustoff" pilots were certainly "Angels of Mercy" during the Vietnam conflict (courtesy Frank Perra).

excavated mud to build the outpost walls. The moat was usually filled with *pun ji* stakes.[1] Beyond the moat were several rows of barbed or concertina wire entanglements. When available or practical, the Vietnamese would place Claymore mines at strategic places around the outpost.

Within the outpost a small headquarters area and soldier living quarters were constructed inside the hollow mud and palm log walls. These very dark and dank rooms had logs and corrugated steel or PSP for the interior roof and walls. When the outposts were completed, the families of the PF soldiers often lived in the them. The sight or thought of anyone, military or civilian, living in these outposts was unimaginable. To me, the rickety old barn on our farm seemed far more habitable.

As this particular outpost was nearing completion it required additional barrier materials: barbed wire, pickets, sandbags, tin, etc. Only riverboats or helicopters could bring in these items, and given the unavailability of a CH-47 helicopter, riverboats were chosen. A platoon of *Trung úy* An's 987th RF company was assigned to accompany and provide security for the boats on their journey and to help the PF platoon in constructing the fledgling outpost. Wanting to do something different, I decided to go along.

I boarded the Vietnamese Navy "Mike" boat in Vi Thanh. The landing craft mechanized (LCM) was referred to as a "Mike boat." With building materials and the RF platoon onboard we proceeded down the canal to the river and then south to the outpost. It was a journey of about 20 "klicks." The most exciting part of this trip was when the Mike boat's .50 caliber machine guns shot up the riverbank at a potential VC ambush site. This was the first time I was near a firing .50 caliber other than on a designated range. I was amazed at the ease at which these weapons, with their one-half-inch diameter bullets, splintered and chopped down trees along the riverbank. After the .50 calibers finished their devastating fire, any VC in the ambush site faced one of three possible outcomes: killed, wounded, or taking a time-out to go home and change their black pajama bottoms.

We safely arrived at the outpost and it took the soldiers and boat crew the rest of the day to unload the barrier materials. I went on this outpost building adventure on pretty much a lark, and as such, I did not take another American or interpreter with me. However, I did take a radio with extra batteries so I could have radio contact with the district team in Kien Hung who were my gateway to the rest of the world. I also took my weapon, field gear, poncho and poncho liner, several days' worth of C-rations that I carried in an old Claymore bag, and a reasonably strong back.

During my time at the outpost I helped the Vietnamese install the outpost obstacles. This was actual engineer work and the soldiers seemed delighted to have me working alongside them. I was glad to be doing something different and enjoyed my time with the soldiers and the few family members who were present. Despite the hard work, the isolation of the outpost, and the primitive conditions, I was amazed at the positive attitude everyone possessed.

Three days after my arrival, a helicopter landed and took me back to Vi Thanh. It was only after getting back on the compound that I thought about what I had just done. Establishing an outpost on the frontier was a clear sign to the VC and the populace that the government was claiming territory that formerly had been up for grabs. The VC certainly understood the message a newly constructed outpost conveyed. Remote outposts, which sounds redundant, were frequently attacked. Often the results were

Chapter 18. Pride, Volunteering, and Annoyances

Vietnamese soldiers and civilians building an outpost in Chuong Thien province in early 1970. The mud collected from digging a moat was used to construct the walls for the outpost (courtesy Frank Perra).

disastrous to the ARVN but favorable to the VC. I was just thankful the VC spared the outpost during my brief time there. Fortunately, the most serious thing to happen to me during my stay was that someone appropriated my C-rations while I was helping install the barrier obstacles.

My stay at the outpost, in retrospect, was foolish and unsafe, but it was not my closest brush with death. That distinction goes to an operation on which an accompanying American advisor almost killed me. This soldier shall remain nameless, but he was a young, noncombat arms staff sergeant on his first operation. We had just made a successful helicopter landing into a cold LZ, secured the tree lines surrounding the rice paddy, and were proceeding toward our first checkpoint. So far, everything was quiet, safe, and routine. On this operation I was advising a company I had never been with before; therefore, I did not have an assigned bodyguard/RTO, so I was still carrying the radio. The command group was walking single-file with the company commander and interpreter right in front of me and the American NCO directly behind me.

We were walking along and I was talking to the TOC when, all of a sudden, I heard a burst of 6–10 rounds from an M-16 on full auto being fired just feet behind me and slightly off to my left. The suddenness, the noise, and the near-impacting rounds caused me to almost jump out of my skin! The firing stopped as quickly as it began and I turned to see what had just happened. The "green" NCO walking behind me had failed to "safe" his weapon and had absentmindedly pulled the trigger—unleashing the rounds. Fortunately, he was carrying his M-16 in the low-ready position (pointed downward), which allowed the errant rounds to miss me and other friendlies, but this miss was by mere feet. As soon as I regained composure, I screamed some rather choice words at this idiot and told him to "safe" his weapon and walk in front of me. I'm pretty sure those were the last words I spoke to this sergeant, as I fumed about that incident the rest of the day. As it turned out, the operation was just another "walk in the sun." It was just as well because after this incident I had zero confidence in this individual. Needless to say, I never took this NCO with me on another operation.

Vietnamese Marines moved into the province in early to mid–January. Their mission was to move into the U-Minh forest to engage and dislodge enemy forces there. On the evening of January 22, 1970, there was a major battle on the eastern outskirts of the forest near Kien Long. It was probably the 273rd VC Regiment (accompanied by NVA regulars) that initiated the battle with a preparatory 100-round mortar and recoilless rifle fire attack. This indirect fire attack was followed by a ground assault against the Marine base camp. When the battle ended the government declared it a major victory, since they counted 89 enemy killed while the Vietnamese Marines losses were light.[2]

What I remember most about the Vietnamese Marines operating in the province (though not in the battle just mentioned) was that they had several 155-mm howitzers set up on the Vi Thanh to Duc Long road right across from the MACV compound. When these howitzers fired, and it was typically at night, they often fired over the compound. The howitzer muzzle blast and subsequent concussion rattled the roof and shook books and other items off the shelves within our hooch. Over the previous months I had gotten used to the nightly H&I fires coming out of Vi Thanh. Of course, they were 105-mm howitzers that were located 2–3 kilometers away, not 155-mm howitzers located just 200 meters from our hooch. I could easily sleep right through the "normal" H&I fires. However, it was near impossible to sleep with all of this noise and commotion caused by the 155-mm howitzers blasting away.

When Vietnamese Marines were operating in the province their American Marine advisors could occasionally be seen on the compound. These advisors lived a nomadic life, as their units were assigned missions throughout the country. They wore the American equivalent of the Vietnamese tiger-striped uniform plus a camouflaged "bush" hat that looked like a very small inverted U.S. Navy seaman's cap. I once approached a U.S. Marine captain on the compound and tried to barter with him to get his

Chapter 18. Pride, Volunteering, and Annoyances   133

neat-looking wrist compass. I offered him a VC flag for his compass, but he apparently already had a VC flag or perhaps knew how they were sometimes produced.

I spent many days throughout my tour doing mundane things. Meeting with the Public Works chief was one of those tasks lumped into this group. Although I had a good relationship with Ông Son, there was little to nothing I could contribute to his efforts. When we were together, we most often talked about his family or what life was like in the U.S.

Every couple of months I served as certifier for the destruction of classified documents. I guessed this was because I had a top secret clearance and I was in no way associated with the documents being destroyed. In accomplishing this task, an NCO would individually show me the documents for destruction and I would verify each document was listed on the form he supplied. He would then burn the listed classified document in a garbage can and stir the ashes. Once the fire fully consumed all the listed documents, I would sign the form certifying the classified documents were destroyed. Once this important job was done, I considered myself to have had a productive day.

It was sometime in January when Intelligence Analysts at some level received information that the enemy was planning an attack against the Vi Thanh MACV compound. Accordingly, Colonel LeVasseur decided officers and NCOs would walk guard duty at night on assigned interior positions of the compound. The purpose of the guard duty was to alert the compound of any suspicious ground activity or distant mortar firing. Each "guard" performed a two-hour tour of duty, and we did this for several nights. I had two memorable events during my guard duty tour. One was hearing rats scurrying around the far corner of the compound. It was amazing how (in the stillness of the night) noisy these nasty rodents were. Alerted to this noise, I investigated it but found no enemy sappers—just huge rats. Ratdog needed to step up his anti-rat campaign.

As unnerving as the rats were, the second event was quite reassuring. While walking my guard duty tour early one morning, I observed (off to the northeast of the compound and probably 20+ kilometers away) "Spooky" was engaging ground targets. "Spooky" was sometimes erroneously called "Puff the Magic Dragon"[3] due to the arc of tracers belching from the plane's three mini-guns. These luminous rounds resembled a fire-breathing dragon. "Puff" was the call sign of the larger four-engine C-130 aircraft that was much more heavily armed than "Spooky." Whether "Puff" or "Spooky," it was an awesome sight to see those streaming tracers being fired. That sight made me wonder how anyone on the receiving end of that firepower could survive the 3,000–6,000 rounds per minute from the mini-guns. Each mini-gun fired a 7.62 × 51-mm NATO round, and reportedly a single gun could place a round into each square yard of a football field in less than a minute.

The nights of guard duty tours were finally over and I was grateful the intel analysts were wrong, but by this time in my tour I realized that getting faulty intelligence was a pretty common occurrence. My realizations from guard duty were that rats were disgusting creatures, and I was thankful for the air force and their awesome weaponry in Vietnam. Regarding this last thought, I knew I had to refrain from saying anything positive about the air force in front of Captain Taylor or Lieutenant Eastman.

I had one other experience with a mini-gun. I was at the Vi Thanh airfield one day when a hunter-killer team[4] was there refueling and re-arming their aircraft. Somehow, I got to talking with the LOH ("Loach") pilot and he invited me to ride along with him on a mission. I had never been in this type of helicopter before, so this sounded exciting, and I simply could not resist the invitation. Once airborne, the pilot did his thing of flying fast and low, darting around in known VC areas—daring the VC to engage him. On this brief flight the mission was a bust with no enemy activity. However, the pilot, on the way back to the airfield, decided to give me a personal firepower demonstration. He spotted a sampan half-submerged in a canal[5] and said, "Watch this!" He positioned his aircraft into a low hover and then cut loose with tremendous BRRRRRRRRR-UP as his mini-gun totally chewed the sampan into small splinters. I was literally blown away by this demonstration as the mini-gun was located less than five feet from my seat and the sampan was about 50 feet away from me. When the mini-gun fired I could feel the torque the gun applied to the helicopter. It was all just incredible. Seeing this, I thought America, with its incredible technological advantage, could not possibly lose this war.

Chapter 19

Food and Customs

With pun intended, Vietnamese food was certainly foreign to me. Before going to Vietnam, I would not so much as put mustard on a hot dog because it made it too spicy for me. Vietnam changed all of that. The advisor's course at Fort Bragg made it abundantly clear: if your Vietnamese host offered you something to eat, it was an insult to turn it down. With this in mind, I ate foods given to me and tried just about everything the Vietnamese ate. In the field I ate chicken, duck, rat,[1] snake,[2] eel, different kinds of fish,[3] pineapple, watermelon, and many other local foods. My taste buds definitely came alive in Vietnam.

Though not exclusive to Vietnam, coconuts, and especially coconut milk, were my absolute favorites. Coconut milk, even when quite warm, always tasted great. There were several times on long operations when, after my two frozen canteens had been exhausted,[4] coconut milk made the difference between having the energy to complete the mission or repeating my disgusting performance on my very first operation. As great as the coconuts were, the process of getting them was nearly as enjoyable. Vietnamese soldiers would often shinny up a palm tree to knock down coconuts. Sometimes, we tried to impress or outdo one another by shooting coconuts from the trees in an attempt to sever the coconut stem from the tree. (Yes, I knew this was as bad as firing the three "warning" shots I talked about earlier, but at least this was not as frustrating.) Once our prize was on the ground, Vietnamese soldiers were proficient in carving open the coconut husk without spilling any of the precious milk. I carried my M-7 bayonet for the express purpose of getting at this refreshing drink.

Then, there was fish sauce—*nước mắm*. *Nước mắm* was a product one did not want to see being made. On operations in the dry season I often saw a latticework outside a hooch filled with sliced fish draped across it baking in the unrelenting sun. Below this latticework was a drip pan that collected the liquid produced when the fish literally rotted in the sun. The drip pan contents flowed into a clay vessel. I never saw the final steps in the process but must admit *nước mắm* greatly spiced up the blandness of rice and the meat dishes I had in the field. It was strong and on the salty side, and once I had *nước mắm* I could not eat Vietnamese food without it.

I recall one time on an operation when our noon meal main course was chicken that had been procured from a local farmer. When I say chicken, this included the feet, beak, and head with comb. On this particular day, I was accompanying a Vietnamese company commander that I had not been with before. At lunch this commander placed a chicken head complete with comb, beak, eyeballs, and brains into my rice bowl.[5] I later was told this gesture was to honor me by giving me the "choice" part of the chicken. I did not know how to handle that situation and was disturbed by the way the chicken head was staring at me while sitting atop my small bowl of rice. I nodded thanks to my thoughtful counterpart, picked up the chicken head with my chopsticks, and tried to eat it. The chicken's beak scraped the roof of my mouth. In slight pain, and unable to chew, I just held the chicken head in my mouth, nearly gagging, as I desperately thought about what I should do. Frantically I tried to come up with a face-saving solution. Fortunately for me, the commander's attention was diverted to respond to a radio message, so I was able to escape this dilemma. In a flash, I turned my head, spit the chicken head into my hand, and then shoved this "delicacy" into my jungle fatigue cargo pocket. I felt rather certain neither my host nor others saw my sleight of hand, which would have made the great Harry Blackstone[6] proud. Following this memorable meal, siesta time began. During this brief intermission from the war, I said I had to relieve myself and walked to the rear of a hooch. There I tossed that nasty chicken head as far as I could into the nearby rice paddy.

Betel nut was an item most middle-age or elderly Vietnamese women chewed in a manner similar to the way men chewed tobacco in the States. This "nut" came from a species of the palm tree and produced a strong caffeine-like buzz in those who used it. You could always tell those women who chewed betel nut. Its consumption caused red-stained teeth and, judging by the Vietnamese women's lack of teeth, tooth loss. The red juice ran down the chins of its users, most of whom used the back of their hands to remove this crimson saliva. This really was a gross sight! To see a middle-age or older well-wrinkled Vietnamese woman squatting outside her hooch, basking in the sunshine, and chewing betel nut was a sight best forgotten. On the other hand, it was my observation that most Vietnamese women in their late teens to early 30s were beautiful. Sadly, they tended to prematurely age, and this was especially true in the rural areas, where life was far more arduous, primitive, and medical and dental care were essentially nonexistent.

Something I could never forget about the Vietnamese was their sanitary practices. The typical communal bathroom was over the closest water source—a river or canal. With great originality, we advisors called them "shitters." The facilities were always similar in construction to one another and were built on stilts driven into the canal floor or riverbed. On these stilts sat a small hut with sides of about three feet each. Walls were constructed of thatch, being about two to three foot high, with one wall having a small door. The "shitters" had no roof but had a slit in the floor enabling one to squat and do their business. In order to access these primitive facilities, one had to balance oneself on a precarious three- to five-foot-long gangplank leading from the bank to the "shitter." At high tide, these bathrooms sat several feet above the waterline. It was in these quaint little "shitters" that the Vietnamese tended to nature's calling. Whether by road or by sampan, it was common to go past these "shitters" and see a head sticking over the wall.

If these "shitters" were not strange enough, it was common and appalling to see people swimming, bathing, or occasionally washing a water buffalo within mere feet of these facilities. The sight of someone bathing in the near vicinity of a "shitter" was enough to make me want to gag, but seeing people squatting on the shore brushing their teeth close to these "loos" was absolutely sickening.

In remote villages and hamlets the primary source for cooking and drinking water was huge clay jugs that collected rainwater off the hooch through a crude downspout system. This worked out well during the rainy season, but the fecal infested waterways were the main water source in the dry season. My overall observation was the Vietnamese lacked a general understanding of sanitation compared to us Americans, but, fortunately, they had strong constitutions.

As I was with Vietnamese soldiers and children, I was a curiosity to the Vietnamese civilians I encountered in the field. Of the civilians I met on operations, most were either young girls or women, since they were not subject to proselytization by the government or VC—though they could willingly assist either side. If I met any males at all they were either elderly or young preteen boys. I can truthfully say that in every field encounter I never met a Vietnamese civilian who was unfriendly toward me. At the absolute worst, I sensed only indifference. If I were passing through a village or hamlet I would see or feel dozens of eyeballs staring at me. I found this attention both interesting and flattering. Whenever possible, with the hope of fostering goodwill, I would try to engage in light conversation with the villagers. In addition, aware of Vietnamese and Asian culture, I was always courteous and deferential to Vietnamese elders.

At the Fort Bragg advisor school we got a healthy dose of Vietnamese culture and were instructed on cultural no-nos. Among the taboos I remembered were never touch a Vietnamese on the head, never point the soles of one's foot toward a Vietnamese's face (even as innocent as crossing one's legs while sitting in a chair), and never motion for a Vietnamese to come to you in the way we do it in the U.S. with palms up and motioning with your fingers. To the Vietnamese these were all disrespectful gestures. When summoning someone in Vietnam, you would place your palm down and made a welcoming motion with your fingers. However, one of the customs the school forgot to tell us was that it was common for adult Vietnamese men and women, when walking with a person of the same sex, to be holding hands. This sight shocked my Midwestern values and took a while for me to get over.

Other normal life actions were different in Vietnam—like getting a haircut. Like many products of the '60s, longer hair was in vogue, and I wore my hair in Vietnam slightly beyond army regulations. For my haircuts I went to a Vietnamese barber whose shop was set up near the TOC. He gave a haircut using the old-type clippers that were hand activated by a squeezing motion. The barber gave a good haircut, but I always got a little nervous when he got out the straight razor to shave the back of my neck.[7] Apparently, Vietnamese men had their ears shaved as well. That was one custom I would not allow. I could picture myself in later life having more ear hair than Bridgette the monkey, and that was something I did not want to encourage.

I had converted to Catholicism prior to my marriage in 1968. I was a Lutheran as a boy and attended the country church my grandparents, parents, and many other relatives attended. The church actually abutted our farm, and on many occasions, my brothers, sisters and I walked to church, Sunday school, or vacation Bible school. Now at 22 years old, I considered myself religious and expected to find regular services of some type available in Vietnam. Catholic masses in Vi Thanh were infrequent. Maybe quarterly, we would have a Catholic chaplain hold mass, though Protestant chaplains did show up slightly more often. Chaplains did perform fitting memorial services for Lieutenants Donaway and Young and Sergeants First Class Ard and later Walker. In all, I was disappointed at the lack of religious services on the compound. I tried my best to make up for this by reading the little New Testament Bible I received from the Gideons at the Chicago Van Buren Street Military Induction Station on February 20, 1967.

It was around the 20th of March when I received orders approving my one-year service extension assigning me to Fort Leonard Wood[8] with a report date NLT August 31, 1970. I had never been to Fort Leonard Wood, but a number of my college graduate OCS classmates had. Those classmates enlisted in the army with the express purpose of attending Engineer OCS. Accordingly, they took their basic training and engineer advanced individual training at Fort Leonard Wood in the October 1967 to February 1968 time frame before reporting to OCS in early March. My OCS classmates said wintertime at Fort Leonard Wood (derisively called Fort Lost in the Woods) was incredibly cold. Some compared Fort Leonard Wood's winter to what they heard from their father's, uncle's, or neighbor's experience during the Battle of the Bulge or Korean War. Being from Northern Illinois, I was not bothered by the cold. Most importantly, I now had a one-year extension in the army, which added a bit of clarity to my life. Reassignment orders to Fort Leonard Wood gave me something to look forward to and served as a reminder that someday I would be going home from Vietnam. As a bonus, Fort Leonard Wood put me about 6–7 hours from my family in Geneseo.

CHAPTER 20

Night Flight into Sickness

Early on the morning of March 21, 1970, the CQ (charge of quarters) roused me from my typical deep sleep.[1] The CQ told me an outpost was under attack and I was to immediately get my gear and meet Captain Bob Olderson in the orderly room.

I hurriedly got dressed, grabbed my M-16 and field gear, and went to the orderly room. It was a little before 4:00 a.m. and Captain Olderson was already there talking with Major Martinson. Major Martinson said a PF outpost in Kien Thien district on the banks of the *Rach Nuoc Trong* river was under attack. The outpost was near "Mickey's Ears," and, for reasons never explained to me, someone had decided to send in an Eagle Flight[2] to relieve the besieged outpost. This was the first and only Eagle Flight I had during my time in Chuong Thien. On this inaugural night operation, I was more than thankful I was accompanying Captain Olderson, as he was experienced, brave, and steadfast. Deep down, I felt honored I had been chosen to go on this operation, as I took it to be a recognition of my tactical competence.

Since my arrival in Chuong Thien province, the VC had attacked perhaps a half dozen outposts. Those attacks always came at night and the VC were successful in overrunning several of them. Major Martinson gave Captain Olderson and me a quick situation update and our mission. He said helicopters were currently inbound from Soc Trang to the Vi Thanh airfield. The "slicks" would pick up the 416 RF company and land this relief force about two kilometers from the outpost. Once there, we would advance toward the besieged outpost while another RF company with advisors from Kien Thien would close on the outpost coming in from a westerly direction.

As it was so early in the morning neither Captain Olderson nor I had breakfast, and because I was required to get ready so quickly, I failed to take a C-ration meal with me. Food notwithstanding, on the short bouncy drive to the airfield, I had many concerns. Foremost of these concerns was that I had never worked with the 416 RF company and I knew nothing

Chapter 20. Night Flight into Sickness

about them: Were they any good? Guessing the VC were at least at company strength of about 50–80 men (which would give them a favorable assault ratio against the PF platoon outpost), I wondered whether we would we be landing in a hot LZ and perhaps be outnumbered. How do you control troops and friendly fires in the dark, especially with converging forces? How do you control air attack assets in the dark? Was this going to be a textbook example of the VC besieging an outpost and then ambushing a relief force? Land navigation in the Delta was always difficult—in darkness it had to border on the impossible. Could I see and engage enemy soldiers in the dark? Though I had these and other thoughts, I kept them to myself as Captain Olderson and I got to the airfield at the same time the "slicks" were landing. As the "slicks" landed, my concerns intensified.

Captain Olderson went over the details of the operation with the flight lead pilot while I waited near the helicopter door with the radio. Once the briefing was over, Captain Olderson motioned to the RF company commander to gather with us so we could quickly discuss the concept of the operation. The commander could speak enough English and I could speak enough Vietnamese that we were able to converse without an interpreter. In fact, no interpreter was present or probably even made aware of the operation. Once this briefing was complete, the commander ordered his soldiers to load onto the "slicks" as he and his RTOs got into the lead helicopter with Captain Olderson and me. Soon we were airborne and en route to the LZ.

During the approximate 15-minute flight to the LZ, I was constantly looking in the direction of where I believed the outpost to be, thinking I might be able to see red and green tracer rounds being exchanged. However, I saw no tracers or explosions and made no sighting of the outpost. I felt unbelievably calm (without as much as the normal adrenaline rush) even though this was my first night assault into an area where there was known recent VC activity. I think I felt safe believing the darkness prevented the enemy from seeing me. Soon I might be testing that theory.

The darkness of the night was beginning to turn to gray as we landed in the LZ. Unlike other operations, this morning the gunships were not swooping around providing suppressive fire as the "slicks" set down. This was probably due to concern over possible friendlies in the area, either hiding or perhaps being held as POWs. Jumping off the helicopter as I was looking around, I thought I could see distant morning breakfast fires coming from hooches lining the river in the distance. Once on the ground we got our bearings and Captain Olderson verified the azimuth to the outpost with the company commander. Slowly, the company began to move across the rice paddy in the direction of the outpost with platoons abreast. During our movement we heard no shooting, encountered no enemy fire, and saw no VC. All of these were good signs. However, as we neared the outpost, we began to see some bloodstained first-aid field dressings, wrappers, and spent cartridges lying on the ground. All of this was evidence something had happened nearby.

After we had moved some distance we heard on the radio that the RF element with the Kien Thien advisors had made it into the outpost. We monitored their SITREP to the TOC, where they reported no friendlies or their equipment were present in the outpost, although they did find the bodies of several PF soldiers who had been killed during the attack. Listening to this report, I thought back to my stay at the outpost under construction near Kien Hung. I silently thanked God that the remote unfinished outpost had not been attacked during my stay there, as the results could have been similar to what we found this morning. I had other dreadful thoughts: more M-16s and radios had fallen into the hands of the enemy, and on this my very first Eagle Flight, we did not encounter the enemy, free any possible POWs, or recover any captured weapons or military equipment. With the experience of eight months in-country, I considered this a failed mission. That day I questioned Vietnamization.

Once the fate of the outpost was determined, the Vietnamese operational commander in the C&C ordered the 416th to reverse course and head east—proceeding parallel to the river. We were to see if we could find the VC or signs of the PF soldiers who might have escaped the outpost or who may have been captured. With one platoon in the tree line near the river, my morning's efforts turned into a lengthy walk in the rice paddies. We found absolutely nothing. As we progressed on this trek, I became very hungry.

Around noon we finally stopped to eat—something I had not done for about 18 hours. The meal that day was my most memorable one in Vietnam, although, as I was to later learn, for the worst of reasons. That meal, prepared by a Vietnamese villager, reminded me of a dark Creole shrimp gumbo with, of course, rice and *nước mắm*. I wolfed down the meal and it satisfied my hunger. After eating I looked forward to taking a siesta in the field—knowing that Bob Olderson would remain alert. My sleep came easily. Following siesta time, we proceeded several more klicks downriver with exactly the same results as in the morning—nothing.[3] Later that afternoon we were airlifted back to Vi Thanh.

Little did I realize the shrimp gumbo I enjoyed for lunch that day would nearly kill me. A day or so later, I began constantly throwing up in between spasms of diarrhea. I had never been sicker in my life, and SFC Ramirez could do nothing to help me. After a week of this misery, spent mostly in my bed or running to the latrine, I was ordered by Frank Gillis to go to the 3rd Surgical Hospital[4] in Can Tho. Not wanting to wait for the

Chapter 20. Night Flight into Sickness

next plane to take me, I went to the Vietnamese hospital in Vi Thanh and waited. Before long a "dustoff" helicopter landed and dropped off several patients. I talked with the Binh Thuy–based crew and they agreed to take me to the U.S. hospital located in Can Tho.

I arrived and checked into the 3rd Surgical Hospital around April 1. At admitting, I completed a questionnaire, after which the hospital staff took my vitals and gave me a cursory physical exam. I provided the requisite specimen samples, and without receiving any treatment,[5] I soon found myself assigned to a hospital ward, one devoid of patients.

At the hospital, I do not recall ever being seen by a doctor, but a nurse did occasionally stop in to take my vitals and question me on my condition. From the stool sample I had given upon admittance to the hospital, a nurse told me the hospital determined I had contracted cryptosporidiosis. This debilitating disease was caused by ingesting food or water contaminated with human feces, likely from a waterborne source. Once I heard this, right away I thought about the Vietnamese "shitters" and the gumbo I ate on the day of the Eagle Flight.

I took the pills that had been prescribed and spent my hospital time mostly in bed or in the latrine. I never received a meal while in the ward and guessed that, being ambulatory, I was expected to go to the hospital mess hall. In truth, it did not matter, since I was far too sick for food and could not keep anything down anyway. I spent most of my time sleeping between my trips to the latrine.

While in the hospital, I just stayed in the ward, one that smelled foul and like death itself. It became obvious that this was a ward for soldiers suffering from some sort of illness, like myself. To me, a trained medic, the ward was dirty and far from being clinically clean. A corpsman visited the ward during the days and brought me more pills, but I felt no better than when this whole episode began. On the second night I was really getting disgusted with the hospital, my inability to do anything, the smell, and the fact I was not getting the quick relief I expected. Bored, but not better, I watched a movie at the hospital outdoor theater that evening and enjoyed seeing a large congregation of "round eyed" nurses.

As almost seemed appropriate, the VC closed out my miserable second day by mortaring Can Tho and the area around the hospital that evening. Once the attack began, I realized I had not been given instructions as to where the bunkers were located. With mortar rounds impacting and my safety imperiled, I just rolled under my bed and pulled my mattress on top of me. Besides, since I had been under mortar attacks in Vi Thanh, I could tell the rounds were not really that close. But the mortaring was the last straw, and I could take no more of this hospital!

The next morning I located a phone in the hospital and called an OCS classmate of mine, Lieutenant Virgil Allan. Virgil was assigned to the 120th Transportation company stationed in Can Tho. I asked him if he could come over to the hospital, pick me up, and take me to the Can Tho airfield. Virgil readily agreed and he soon showed up in a jeep. As we drove to the nearby airfield we talked about OCS, the loss of Lieutenant Lee, the status of some of our classmates, and our current duties in Vietnam. During our chat, I told Virgil I had not been released from the hospital; I was just walking away from it since it was not doing me any good. I told him that he was abetting me in going AWOL and if I was court-martialed for it, I was taking him with me. We chuckled over this and on arriving at the terminal building I thanked Virgil for picking me up. Thereafter, Lieutenant Allan went his direction and I went mine, and I never saw him again in Vietnam. From the airfield, I caught an afternoon flight back to Vi Thanh.

I was really disgusted with my treatment (or rather, lack of treatment) at the 3rd Surgical Hospital. Apparently, I was a low-priority patient, since I had all my extremities and was not shot or blown up. It bothered me that my condition did not rate so much as a visit from a doctor. This hospital experience greatly affected me in a very negative way. (In my post-Vietnam life, I truly hate hospitals and feel uncomfortable when within their walls. I attribute this to my experience in the Can Tho hospital. That uneasy feeling has led me to the point where it is difficult for me to go to a hospital—for my own medical issues or even to visit those whom I love.)

Back on the MACV compound, I continued to struggle with an illness I knew the name of but could not pronounce. Soon after my return from the hospital, MAT and district teams contacted me and told me they were low on AIK funds. Therefore, sick or not, I would have to go to Saigon to replenish the AIK fund. Miraculously, out of nowhere and prior to my heading to Saigon, one of my best boyhood friends, Bill Pobanz, contacted me.[6] I had written a letter to the editor of the *Geneseo Republic* several months earlier to rebut one written by a Geneseo High School graduate who was then stationed in Vietnam. This Specialist Fourth Class criticized the American presence in Vietnam, the general character of the Vietnamese people, and the ARVN. From my article, Bill knew my team assignment and location, and somehow he figured out how to contact me by phone. It was almost surreal to talk to him on what I thought was a primitive phone system.

Bill was in the air force stationed at Cam Ranh Bay. I had lost track of him since last visiting him when he was going through basic airman training. He was at Lackland Air Force Base, near San Antonio, while I was stationed at Fort Hood in early 1969. I had no idea Bill was in Vietnam, but I was really glad to hear from him. During our phone call I told Bill I had to go to Saigon on a certain date and, with luck, we might be able to get together. Bill said he would find a way to get the time off, so I told him where I planned to stay while in Saigon. We agreed to meet.

Plans set, I left for Saigon on the scheduled date and Bill and I did manage to meet, though I was still sicker than a dog. I completed my AIK fund business and Bill and I spent about two days together. We reminisced about our life in Edford Township on the farm at a time when we were young and innocent. We got caught up on life events over the past year, and we talked about our Vietnam duties. As good as it was to see Bill, my sickness clouded most of our time together in Saigon. Soon, our time in Saigon was over. Somehow, I was able to make my way back to Vi Thanh, though I have no recollection of it.

A day or two after I got back from Saigon and seeing Bill, I bumped into Frank Gillis. Frank freely volunteered that I looked terrible and asked me about my experience at the U.S. hospital in Can Tho. All Frank could do was shake his head as I was relating my story. As I talked, Frank better understood my condition and told me I should go to the Vietnamese hospital located just up the street from the CORDS compound and across the road from the MACV compound. The Korean doctors there had treated Frank when he contracted a similar disease, and he had nothing but good things to say about them.

Without delay, I followed Frank's advice. Soon I found myself, an American, lying on a gurney in a Vietnamese hospital being treated by a Korean doctor and nurse. After the doctor inserted an IV into my vein, I lay there for about four hours as the solution slowly dripped from one glass bottle, then another, into my body. As the second of the 500-milliliter bottles was emptying, I was certain my bladder would explode. When my treatment was finally complete, all I could think about was finding the nearest latrine. Going to the bathroom after that IV treatment was probably the most pleasurable sensation I had during my time in Vietnam.

As Frank had wisely predicted, my recovery was slow but steady after my treatment by the Korean doctor. During the next several weeks, I gradually began to regain my appetite and believed I was on my way to feeling healthy again. During the four to five weeks of my illness I lost 20–25 pounds, as I was not able to eat much. The little food I did eat I threw up or quickly expelled during my bouts with acute diarrhea. In late April my uniforms were literally hanging on me, and those around me were not hesitant to point out how bad I looked.

Once cured, I was mad that the U.S. doctors did not help me during my stay at the Can Tho hospital. However, the Korean doctor, without the benefit of specimens and a questionnaire, fixed me up in a matter of about four hours. Upon reflection, I have a difficult time reconciling these two facts. My illness and experience in the U.S. hospital was without question my worst time in Vietnam—both physically and mentally!

Chapter 21

Something Funny or Frustrating Just Happened

As I remember my time in Vietnam, it is easiest for me to recall the many humorous things that happened. These were mostly fleeting but nonetheless funny events. It is just strange the way one's mind works. Here I was in a foreign land, carrying a weapon to kill someone who wanted to kill me, and yet, I could find things to laugh about. Then, too, I've learned throughout the years that soldiers tend to develop a perverse or twisted sense of humor.

Crossing what we advisors called a "monkey bridge" was akin to being a member of the Flying Wallendas. These bridges were aptly named, since only a monkey could safely cross them. They were made of palm tree trunks that were cut down and laid on supporting uprights over a small canal or stream. "Monkey bridges" were designed to facilitate a single person crossing at a time. They had to be elevated six to eight feet above the water level to allow sampans to navigate the waterway beneath them. This meant they were constructed with a short tree trunk approach ramp from the bank to one or more longer palm tree trunks spanning the canal or stream. The approaches were laid on an incline and these bridges had a flimsy handrail to help the crosser maintain stability. Still, they were a challenge to use.

During operations, most of the time it was faster to cross a waterway using a nearby "monkey bridge" than by wading through the water. The downside, however, was that the more soldiers who crossed over on the bridge, the more slippery it became. This slipperiness was due to the mud or water the soldiers had on their boots. Invariably, someone in the unit crossing on a "monkey bridge" would fall into the water. As long as this was not me, it was always funny.

It was interesting to see the Vietnamese navigate a river or canal when no "monkey bridge" or sampan was available. In those instances, these diminutive soldiers would raise their weapons over their head and walk

Chapter 21. Something Funny or Frustrating Just Happened

under the water to the other side. Many times the only things visible were the tops of soldiers' heads and their arms with rifles or radios slowly moving through the water, their bodies completely submerged. It was hard to believe that the Vietnamese soldiers could hold their breath that long. As I watched river crossings unfolding in front of me, they also reminded me of a cartoon scene I had seen as a kid in which the characters were walking on the bottom of a river.

The worst part of this kind of crossing was when it was my turn to get into the water. But I figured if those little soldiers could cross in this manner, so could I. When I crossed in this way I was often not completely submerged, so it was easy. But getting out of the water was always a chore for me, since the banks were steep, and by the time I got there it always seemed the banks were slippery. Once out of the water, we would all perform a near-ritualistic leech search. It was amazing the number of leeches one could pick up on such a short journey across a river or canal.

On another occasion, I remember our coming across a series of unoccupied VC bunkers tactically located in a tree line with their firing ports facing the rice paddy. The commander I was accompanying decided we should destroy these bunkers to deny the enemy future use. As other soldiers took on this task, I decided I would lend a helping hand. Therefore, in a manner replicating a scene from the movie *Sands of Iwo Jima*, I took the grenade off my web belt, pulled the pin, let the spoon fly, and casually threw the grenade into the bunker's opening. What I failed to consider before my "Sergeant Striker" move was that the ground was slippery due to the recent rain. Immediately after tossing the grenade into the bunker, I tried to make a quick escape to avoid grenade fragments. Just feet from the bunker door, I fell completely on my butt. Making matters more embarrassing was the way I frantically clawed at the ground trying to get away from any blast. I managed to escape the grenade effects, but I did not escape the laughter of the Vietnamese soldiers who saw my dramatic performance.

Viewed with typical GI humor, one of the more hilarious, though costly events I saw in Vietnam was an experiment Major Martinson conducted. He was looking into the feasibility of rapidly unloading supplies at the Vi Thanh airfield. The concept was to have a C-130[1] transport plane fly 5–10 feet over the landing strip and deploy a device called a drogue chute that would then pull a standard USAF 463 pallet from the aircraft and onto the landing strip.[2] The aircraft would not land but would safely and quickly deliver its load. At least that was the plan.

Gene Griffiths and I,[3] charter members of the Major Martinson fan club, went to the airfield to watch this demonstration. We were standing near the terminal building while Colonel LeVasseur, Major Martinson, the Vietnamese province chief with members of his staff, and many "straphangers" were standing closer to the PSP landing strip where the demonstration was to be conducted. As the aircraft approached from the eastern horizon, Major Martinson radioed the C-130 pilot and told him everything was in place. He directed the pilot to commence the delivery demonstration.

The C-130 is a large lumbering four-engine aircraft. As it lined up on the landing strip and continued on a downward flight path, I was certain it was going to crash. Then, about one-third of the way down the airstrip the crew deployed the drogue chute, which was soon fully filled with air. At the one-half runway mark, the C-130 began a climb as the pallet, filled with four 55-gallon drums of gasoline, exited the rear of the aircraft and began skidding across the top of the PSP. At first, we saw sparks flying as the aluminum pallet, propelled by the inertia from the plane, skimmed across the steel plate landing strip. The sparks triggered a huge fireball and explosion as the drums containing the gasoline burst into flames. Despite the taxpayer dollars lost in this experiment, Gene and I laughed until we had tears in our eyes. Fortunately, Colonel LeVasseur, Major Martinson, and others were too concerned with the fire to notice our outburst. Our laughter had everything to do with the fact that Major Martinson was in charge of the demonstration.

During my time in-country, the VC mortared Vi Thanh about a half dozen times (all at night), hitting the interior of the MACV compound two or three times. Once an attack was detected the CQ activated the high-pitched siren that sent sleep-interrupted teammates scrambling to their assigned bunkers. Heard over the wailing of the siren was the clanking of dropped steel pots and weapons hitting the PSP or concrete, and the curses of men as they ran from their hooches to their bunkers while bumping into one another, stubbing toes, or hitting unseen obstacles. These human-inspired collateral noises were always amusing.

Then, too, there was the sight of the team First sergeant.[4] He was a middle-aged rather rotund man with skinny legs who had seen service during the Korean War. During these alarms, it was common to see the first sergeant dash from his hooch to his bunker wearing his steel pot, with his weapon in hand, but wearing nothing else but BVD briefs. This scene always reminded me of those dancing hot dog commercials we used to see during a drive-in movie intermission. After several sightings of the first sergeant making his bunker run, the junior officers' cabal christened him "Big Balls."

Once, on an AIK trip to Saigon, I took an Air America flight that went by way of Rach Gia, the capital of Kien Giang province just northwest of Chuong Thien. Rach Gia was situated on the eastern coastline of the Gulf

Chapter 21. Something Funny or Frustrating Just Happened

of Thailand and was the home to MACV Advisory Teams 54 and 55 as well as elements of the U.S. Navy Mobile Riverine Forces. I had never flown into Rach Gia before, and while sitting on the aircraft parked on the airfield, I was surprised when two navy junior officers (ensigns or lieutenants junior grade) boarded. Both men were wearing their spotless white (Good Humor man) summer uniforms, had deep tans, Hollywood smiles, aviator sunglasses, and carried tennis rackets. I found it amusing that in the midst of a war (with me wearing muddy boots and jungle fatigues and having experienced the September 6–7 operation) here were two officers who appeared to be untouched by the war. Seeing them also infuriated me. To think they were receiving the same amount of hostile fire pay as I was. That very moment, I remembered my father suggesting I should go into the navy because the navy always had three hot meals a day and a dry place to sleep. (Not that my father served in the navy—he didn't. He had a farming deferment during World War II and served in the Illinois State Militia.) And now, after seeing these boarding passengers, I thought, yeah and nice clean uniforms and recreational activities, too!

Late one afternoon, Gene and I were in our hooch doing nothing in particular except waiting for the evening meal. As we chatted, we suddenly heard a gunshot come from the hooch next door. Our next-door occupants were two captains, one a "Shotgun" pilot, the other our S-2 (Intelligence) advisor (on his second tour of duty in Vietnam) and warrant officer, Ralph Howard. All of these men were quiet and mild mannered, so I dismissed the idea that one of them shot the other in a fit of anger. Following the shot, I heard voices of surprise and a commotion coming from next door, so I ruled out suicide. Cautiously approaching their hooch, I knocked on the door, which slowly opened. Inside I saw one very embarrassed captain sitting on his bunk. He had unwittingly shot a hole in the hooch floor with his .45 caliber pistol as he was preparing to clean it. Just as easily, he could have accidentally shot his hooch mate or fired through the thin hooch wall separating them from Gene and me. Upon finding out what just happened, I returned to my hooch and told Gene. We both had a guarded laugh over this incident and commented how glad we were that neither of us had been the one to fire the shot.

One story going around the compound was that a Vietnamese hooch maid was seen wearing men's white briefs. A soldier noticed this when the woman squatted down, in typical Vietnamese fashion, as she was performing a cleaning chore. He saw the elastic band of men's briefs showing from the top of her pajama-like pants. Likely, she "borrowed" these underwear from someone's laundry. By her diminutive stature, it had to be from one of the smaller 52nd Signal Detachment soldiers. (There were probably a dozen Vietnamese women who worked on the compound as hooch maids.) For several days we speculated on who had their laundry borrowed. I was certain they were not mine, but overall, found this an amusing story.

In a way, Vietnam reminded me of what I had learned about medieval Europe and the early days in our country. In Vietnam, there was constant bartering for things. I traded cigarettes to have my M-16 cleaned, for a crappy 30-round magazine, and for good will. I also traded a pair of U.S. jungle boots to the Vietnamese major (*Thiếu tá*) who was the province S-3 (operations officer). These boots were the same ones the departing lieutenant gave me on my first day in-country at the Pentagon East BOQ. Anyway, I traded these boots for a brown-speckled camouflage uniform worn by the RVN National Police Field Force. I found that after my bout with food poisoning, I was actually able to fit into a size large Vietnamese uniform.

It was normal to trade with outsiders who came to our compound. American engineers, transportation soldiers, and especially aircrews were constantly looking to acquire war trophies. At the top of these souvenir seekers' want lists were VC pistols, SKS semi-automatic rifles,[5] and VC flags. For these items the Americans would pay in the form of cases of beer, bottles of booze, cartons of cigarettes, steaks, building supplies, MPC, or any combination thereof. Some enlisted men on the compound and advisors in the districts ran a rewarding enterprise. They had friendly villagers make VC flags that they would then splatter with chicken blood and/or fire bullet into so as to suggest the flags' authenticity. I think in most instances the proceeds from exchange of these "captured" items benefited the team rather than an individual. In a way, these actions reminded me of Joseph Heller's classic novel, *Catch-22*. I read this book for the first time in Vietnam and saw that the deceit of Heller's character Milo Minderbinder of M&M Enterprises was alive and well in Chuong Thien province. I am sure this industry was not localized to our province and just wonder how many of these flags ended up as a centerpiece in some veteran's den or trophy room.

A frustrating but nevertheless funny experience was using the MARS (Military Auxiliary Radio System) to make an overseas telephone call. MARS enabled a military member to connect with someone in the States via a military long distance communications network and licensed civilian HAM radio operators. Vi Thanh did not have a MARS station, so it turned out I only used this once—during an AIK trip to Saigon.

When a soldier wanted to place a call, he would have to go to a military MARS station and schedule a radio/telephone call, giving them the name and phone number of the call recipient. Then at the scheduled time a HAM radio operator in the area of the intended recipient would call the

Chapter 21. Something Funny or Frustrating Just Happened

phone number given them by the MARS station. Once connected, the HAM radio operator would inform the MARS operator[6] that the connection had been made. With this accomplished, the MARS operator would inform the military member to go to a designated phone booth to talk. Yes, it really was this complicated.

Once the call was established, the HAM operator held his radio mic next to the telephone handset so both parties could hear one another. Annoyingly, just as with military radios, after you communicated a thought, you had to say "Over" so the HAM operator would know to key his mic and let the other person talk. This whole complex and impersonal procedure was very frustrating, and I'm sure it was designed to keep conversations short. Just saying, "I love you … Over" in the presence of several other people was just too much for me to do more than once.

Though not quite as bad as MARS, the MACV compound telephone system could also prove frustrating. I do not pretend to understand how I could talk to someone in Saigon, Can Tho, Bac Lieu, or anywhere outside of Vi Thanh, though this was not only possible, it was incredibly reliable. On the MACV compound, the 52nd Signal Detachment soldiers were responsible for connecting us with the rest of Vietnam and the local places. This included the TOC, airfield, orderly room, hooch to hooch, etc. To initiate a call, one would crank the handle on the TA-312 telephone and an operator[7] would answer. You told the operator who or where you wanted to call, and *voilà*, he would perform his magic to make the connection. So far, so good, and no frustration. However, as you were talking, the operator would ask (it seemed like every 10 seconds), "Are you working?" On a somewhat lengthy or complex conversation, this simple question and interruption drove me nuts. The operator did this to determine if he could "unplug" the connection, since there were a limited number of available circuits, and leaving a circuit open limited someone else's ability to make a call. While this was annoying, I also realized it was just soldiers from the 52nd Signal Detachment following their army training.

Chapter 22

Getting Close

As the early months of 1970 were passing by, I was getting closer to going home. My homeward progress was measured when my friends, to whom I owed so much, reached the end of their one-year tour of duty. Sergeant Haley left country in October 1969 though thankfully after he taught me enough to survive. Captain Childress departed Chuong Thien in November 1969. Lieutenant "Jug" Eastman received his traditional water salute (though his was champagne) commemorating his last flight in February. Captain "Buddy" Shieldes, the district senior advisor in Kien Hung, headed home in March, and both Lieutenant Bob Noonan and Captain McCullough said goodbye in April. It was really sad to see these comrades

Lieutenant Chauvin Wilkinson on TOC duty. To his immediate left is the "cubby hole" room in which the MACV RTO was situated. To his rear is a map of the province (courtesy Chauvin Wilkinson).

Chapter 22. Getting Close

in arms and others leave Vi Thanh. While I was happy for them, it was disheartening for me to think that, most likely, I would never see these men again.

What hit me the hardest was when Harvey had his going away party in the club on the evening of May 10. As had become the custom with others, Colonel LeVasseur presented Captain Weiner with the traditional farewell gift and told everyone assembled about Harvey's contributions to the team and his outstanding character. This was followed by several individuals offering impromptu toasts followed by more drinking. Later that evening, Harvey, Gene, and I, along with a stream of other well-wishers, spent time commiserating in our hooch. It was a late night.

For those friends, now forever my brothers, I knew their departure dates were coming, since we constantly counted and compared the number of days we had left in-country. Still, attending their farewell parties in the club made concrete the finality of their tours. Saying a final goodbye and seeing them depart the compound with a duffel bag in hand was a very sad experience.

With Harvey's departure, I was happy to have Gene Griffiths with me in the hooch. I was even able to talk Gene into going on an operation with me. Within a week of Harvey leaving, Lieutenant Roger Dykes* moved into the recently vacated corner of our hooch. Roger was a Quartermaster Corps officer commissioned through ROTC, but other than that, I really do not recall much about him other than that he had a very distinctive laugh. I still enjoyed Frank Perra's occasional visits to Vi Thanh and befriended a recent arrival, Lieutenant Chauvin Wilkinson. Chauvin was a Louisiana State University graduate and an armor officer commissioned through ROTC. Chauvin had a dry sense of humor and was unflappable, witty, and smart. He was initially assigned as the assistant RF/PF advisor, but later became the province agriculture advisor.

During a mid–April airmobile operation, Lieutenants Noonan and Nickinovich were accompanying the 987th RF company on an operation where it destroyed a VC company. This multi-RF company operation was the most successful of its kind during my time in Chuong Thien. The enemy, located in what was later determined to be a VC headquarters area, was caught completely by surprise. Escape for the VC was impossible. They had a river to their backs, open rice paddies to their front and flanks, other RF companies in blocking positions, and helicopter gunships patrolling the skies like vultures. *Trung úy* An's 987th RF company skillfully pressed the attack. Through the effective use of close air support, gunships, artillery, and maneuver, the 987th RF company and their American advisors killed 57 enemy and captured a number of items—including documents and individual and crew-served weapons. This operation

Lieutenant Dave Nickinovich boarding a helicopter before an operation (courtesy David G. Nickinovich).

occurred just days before Bob's departure from Chuong Thien and, in retrospect, seemed a fitting exclamation point to his Vietnam service. For their valorous actions that day, there was little doubt in my mind that both of those American lieutenants should have received the Silver Star.

After nearing full recovery from food poisoning, I began going on operations again. On one particular operation, for reasons that made absolutely no sense to me later, I chose to emulate *Trung úy* An by wearing a flak jacket and carrying only a .45 caliber pistol. On that operation this worked out fine, since we had no contact. Another time I carried only an M-79 grenade launcher.[1] I did this toward the end of my tour. My reasoning was that on previous operations I really had not fired my M-16 that often anyway, so I could just lighten my load. I liked the M-79, since it was easy to carry and I was fairly proficient with it.

Colonel LeVasseur surprised me when he said he wanted to accompany me on one of my last operations. Since he had never accompanied a ground unit during my time in-country, I was flattered he wanted to go with me. I took his request to mean he had confidence in my abilities. The PSA and I had an uneventful airmobile operation. I have to admit, I was disappointed when we had no enemy contact because it would have given me the ability to demonstrate my combat prowess to the colonel.

On my very next operation Major Martinson decided to accompany me. Again, this was a first. I surmised he wanted to demonstrate to

Chapter 22. Getting Close

Colonel LeVasseur and others that he was equally the "warrior." My operation with Major Martinson that day was just another "walk in the sun," but this time, I was thankful it was. Throughout the operation, I had uneasy thoughts as to what might happen should Major Martinson and I come under enemy fire. Even though he was an infantry officer, I did not have a lot of confidence in his abilities—especially his map reading. At least with Major Martinson on the ground beside me, I was able to conserve smoke grenades.

On April 30, 1970, we heard over AFVN that U.S. and ARVN forces had taken the fight to the NVA in Cambodia. No Team 73 advisors accompanied the ARVN, as this operation involved, primarily, U.S. and ARVN division- and brigade-sized units and their support elements. Units from the ARVN's 21st Division (some stationed in Vi Thanh) did get into Cambodia. *Trung úy* An had an officer friend in the 2nd Battalion of the 31st Regiment of the 21st Division who made the cross-border trip. This friend told An that the Vietnamese units fighting in Cambodia went in with apprehension, but they returned with soaring morale. All Vietnamese soldiers considered it a huge success.

It was this same friend who gave *Trung úy* An a silk-embroidered picture of Ho Chi Minh, a fistful of NVA scrip, and a new SKS rifle—all of which he gave to me. These items, all captured from an NVA base camp in Cambodia, were in pristine condition. Of these gifts, I especially cherish the Ho Chi Minh picture, since *Trung úy* An wrote the inscription, "*Mên i Ặng LT Raschke,*" which roughly translates as ("Sincerely presented to my dear friend LT Raschke") 14–6-70 *Phan Ngọc An Viet Nam*. I have framed this embroidery and fondly remember *Trung úy* An every time I look at it.

Following the successful Cambodian incursion (the Nixon administration did not want to use the term "invasion") we read of the massive protests in the United States that culminated in the shooting death of four students at Kent State University in Ohio. By all accounts, Operation *Cửu Long* (Mekong), as it was called for the IV Corps effort, was a huge tactical, and perhaps strategic, victory for the U.S. and our ARVN allies. It was hard to for me to comprehend that this positive development in Southeast Asia could result in something so tragic in the U.S.—10,000 miles away.

It was my observation that most, but not all, Team 73 members had a similarly positive view of the Cambodian operation. For me and others, the operation demonstrated the Nixon administration's willingness to do what it took to successfully conclude the war. We applauded this effort, since it would likely slow the introduction of NVA soldiers (derisively called *Bắc Việt* by the ARVN), equipment, and supplies into Chuong Thien province.

Though the NVA had been in Chuong Thien for a while, their build-up in the province became much more apparent at the beginning of

1970. It was then that we saw signs of larger numbers of NVA soldiers in the province. Intelligence had picked up radio traffic by the NVA,[2] clandestine sources reported seeing them in their distinctive uniforms, and ARVN forces had captured a small but growing number of them. To us on Advisory Team 73, the increasing number of NVA in the province was a worrisome development, since the NVA were better trained, equipped, and led than their local Viet Cong cousins.[3]

The increase in anti-war demonstrations, including the formation and activities of the Vietnam Veterans Against the War, was quite demoralizing. Because of the protesting students, their radical organizations, and the anti-war veterans, I personally felt betrayed. While some team members may have lost their ardent support for the war, most were still dedicated to the effort of helping our Vietnamese counterparts. Seeing the reporting in *Time* magazine and the anti-war bias in *Playboy* was disheartening. It made me wonder how helping the ARVN forces and Vietnamese people, something that seemed so noble, could be so vilified at home. Hadn't the people in the U.S. heard of how we were pacifying previously disputed areas, helping build new schools, visiting orphanages and giving them donated items from back home, building more roads, and, most importantly, giving the people of South Vietnam the right of self-determination? With what I saw, pacification and Vietnamization were working and the population was becoming more pro–government. Why weren't the positive aspects of our efforts being reported?

With the departure of Bob Noonan, I came to better know Lieutenant Dave Nickinovich. Dave was another incredibly smart, brave, aggressive, and competent tactician from Duc Long. Like Bob, Dave was also fun to be around. Nearing the end of my tour, I went on an airmobile operation with Dave. On that day, we were accompanying a PF company, which, during my time in-country, was unusual because the PF normally operated as platoons—not companies. The PF company performed well that day and suffered no casualties. We counted five VC KBA (Killed By Air), in this case, by Viet Nam Air Force (VNAF) A-1Es. Once we made it to our final objective, we were told "slicks" were not available for our extraction. We would, therefore, have to walk approximately six kilometers back to Vi Thanh. This trek would take us about two hours, and darkness was falling. Being with an unfamiliar company and knowing that "'Charlie' owned the night" made our walk back to Vi Thanh a bit on the tense side. My thought during this hike was that I was with Dave Nickinovich and I just dared Charlie to do anything. We safely made the journey home.

On May 26, we received word through the TOC that Sergeant First Class George Walker, the medic on MAT 56, had been killed by a land mine explosion while on an operation. I did not know Sergeant Walker, but his death was alarming and again brought the cost of war closer to home. Although there had been eight U.S. military personnel killed in Chuong Thien province since Lieutenant Young's death on September 6, most had been aircrew members. As cold as it sounds, these other deaths, though tragic, had little impact on me or, I believe, the mood of the team. Sergeant Walker, however, was one of us and the first Team 73 member killed in 8½ months. We knew combat operations were dangerous, and weekly, often daily, we heard of our ARVN comrades suffering multiple KIAs. With Sergeant Walker's death it, again, was personal. I think we collectively asked the same question we asked at the death of other advisors: "Why Sergeant Walker? Why him?"

By early June I was into the serious phase of counting my days remaining in-country. On June 1, I had 55 days remaining in Vietnam, and to use a Nixon/Kissinger phrase of the day, I could see "light at the end of the tunnel." I did not participate in many operations in June. It was not my desire to shrink back and avoid operations or other efforts, since it was important to me that I not adopt a "short timer's attitude." My lack of field time had more to do with the district teams controlling more operations. As for me, I continued to translate Agent Orange requests and monitor the AIK funds. June 1970 also found me spending more time with Mr. Son, the Public Works chief.

A significant boost to ARVN and team morale came on June 13. Though I was not on the operation, I got the details from someone who was—Lieutenant Dave Nickinovich. Dave related how he and *Trung úy* An's 987th RF company were part of a multi-unit ARVN force searching for a suspected Viet Cong Main Force battalion. The VC had overrun a Popular Forces outpost located about 10 kilometers southeast of Vi Thanh the previous evening.

Dave and the 987th had conducted an airmobile combat assault into the suspected area of the VC battalion. On the ground, pressure from the 987th company forced the VC battalion elements to retreat and smash into, and nearly surround, one of the PF platoons that had established a blocking position. The VC maneuver resulted in a fierce firefight with the PF. To rescue the greatly outnumbered PF platoon, Dave and *Trung úy* An moved the company toward the beleaguered platoon and began calling in massive gunship and artillery fires onto the now firmly fixed VC battalion location. When the gunship and artillery firing slackened, the 987th RF company assaulted the Viet Cong positions, severely mauling the VC battalion. The remnants of the VC battalion escaped under the cover of darkness. For his actions, Dave was awarded the Silver Star and *Trung úy* An received the Vietnam Cross of Gallantry. For his heroic actions, Dave became the most decorated Advisory Team 73 soldier[4] during my tour in Chuong Thien province.

CHAPTER 23

The End and a Beginning

Sunday, June 21, 1970, was a significant day for me. It was the first day of summer and, unbeknownst to me when I awoke, this would be my last day with Advisory Team 73. The evening before, I had attended the operations briefing in Colonel LeVasseur's hooch and learned the company I was to advise was doing an airmobile operation in the area near the Snake River. Anytime we went into that area after September 1969 I was always concerned. However, I had volunteered for this operation, since I was now one of the more experienced advisors on the Vi Thanh compound. After a good night's sleep and early-morning breakfast, I grabbed my weapon, gear, and radio and departed with my NCO for the airfield. Once at the airfield I met my interpreter and company commander. We quickly went over the plans for the operation to ensure we were both on the same page. I had never been with the company I was to accompany that day. In fact, I had never even heard of them. I believed they were *Hòa Hảo,* since they wore purple scarves. Going with a "new" company was never a good thing, especially in an area known to harbor *beaucoup* VC.

As I stood on the airfield PSP waiting for the "slicks" to arrive, with my apprehension level building, a jeep with a junior enlisted man from the compound drove up to me. He told me I had a call from the Red Cross and I needed to immediately return to the orderly room with him. Handing off the radio and map overlay to the NCO, I hopped into the jeep. As the jeep sped its way back to the compound, numerous bad scenarios were going through my head. Why had the Red Cross called me?

Arriving at the orderly room, I was soon on the phone talking to a Red Cross agent in Saigon. He told me there had been an accidental shooting involving a family member in East Moline and I needed to get home right away.[1] The agent was unable to provide any specifics concerning the shooting, and the call left me both worried and confused. Momentarily, I did not know what to do, but the sergeant on CQ duty told me to get packed, as he would start the process of getting me home. A movement specialist, whose job it was to arrange air transport for team members,

Chapter 23. The End and a Beginning

supplies, etc., was assigned to Advisory Team 73. The CQ told him of my situation and he quickly swung into action, making arrangements for me to get from Can Tho to Saigon.

Thankfully, it being Sunday, Gene was not working and was in our hooch when I told him of my emergency. Gene and I talked as I packed my uniforms, meager civilian wardrobe, and a few other items. Before leaving my hooch, I called a soldier from the 52nd Signal Detachment as he had expressed an interest in my Colt .25 caliber automatic pistol. I was afraid to take my pistol home with me as the U.S. was experiencing civilian aircraft being hijacked to Cuba. I was afraid I might be detained if authorities found my pistol. The young soldier came to my hooch, we agreed on a price, and I relinquished my constant companion and source of security. I suddenly felt naked! Packing complete, and pistol sold, I hugged Gene and told him how glad I was to have known and spent time with him. Holding back tears, I told him that I hoped one day we would meet again.

I looked over my hooch one last time and thought about the day I had arrived in Vi Thanh. With sadness, I sought out Colonel LeVasseur to say goodbye and thank him for his support. When I inquired at the orderly room, the CQ told me Colonel LeVasseur was flying in the C&C ship for today's operation and was, therefore, off the compound. I knew this, but with the excitement of the morning, it had slipped my mind. My next concern was how to get to Can Tho? The movement specialist said he had me manifested to get from Can Tho to Saigon and was working out the details to get me from Vi Thanh to Can Tho. He had just talked to the TOC, who informed him that an inbound "dustoff" would soon be landing at the Vietnamese hospital located several hundred meters from our compound. He said it should be able to take me to Can Tho.

The same young soldier who came to the airfield telling me about my Red Cross phone call loaded my duffel bag into his jeep and took me to the hospital landing pad. I did not have to worry about turning in my weapon or field gear, since someone else would take my equipment to CIF, a task I had done for others on several occasions. Several minutes elapsed before I saw the silhouette of a helicopter approaching from the northwest. As it got close, I could see it was marked with bright red crosses. It was the "dustoff" helicopter the TOC mentioned and it soon landed at the hospital helipad. I remained out of the way as the Vietnamese doctors and medics removed several wounded soldiers from the helicopter.

The TOC told the "dustoff" pilot I needed a ride to Can Tho. Once the less severe casualties were offloaded, the medic, who also served as crew chief, motioned for me to climb aboard. I stowed my duffel bag near the compartment where the gunner on a "slick" would normally sit and then got onboard. As I was buckling in, I looked around the interior of the helicopter. The medic was feverishly working on four seriously wounded, litter-bound RF soldiers who were being taken to the American 3rd Surgical Hospital in Can Tho. I was unnerved to see the wounded on the aircraft. They were members of the same unit that I had stood beside at the airfield several hours earlier—the unit I was to accompany! I could tell this as they wore the identical purple scarves I had seen earlier in the morning.

As the helicopter lifted off, I had one last glimpse of the MACV compound. It was a sad sight to see. This place had been my home for the last almost 11 months, and I had made friends there. I had both good and bad experiences on that compound, and I knew that I would never see this place again. Despite the casualties beside me and my uncertainty over family events back in the U.S., I silently wondered to myself if I had done a credible job. Did I make a difference?

Focusing back to reality, I will never forget the sight of a wounded RF soldier seated next to me on that "dustoff." This man had been shot through the cheek, with the bullet exiting on the opposite side of his face. Blood had soaked through the field dressing on his face and was slowly dripping onto his uniform. I guessed this soldier to be about 18 or 19 years old. This *Binh nhí* (soldier) painfully mumbled to me, "*Tôi bị thương*" (I've been wounded). I said, "*Tôi biết.*" (I know) and showed my sympathy to him by putting my hand on his shoulder and holding him during the approximate 20-minute flight to Can Tho. Seeing this injured young soldier was very hard on me. I knew I was leaving Vietnam and heading to the safety of the United States. This teenage soldier symbolized, in my mind, all of the dead or wounded ARVN soldiers I had seen during my time in Chuong Thien province. I could only speculate on his future and the number of casualties yet to come.

The "dustoff" crews were stationed at Binh Thuy, which was on the far side of the Can Tho airfield. Over the intercom the pilot told me it would be fastest and easiest if I got off at the hospital and hitched a ride from there to the terminal. At the hospital landing pad, marked with a giant bright red cross, I carefully helped my young wounded RF soldier off the helicopter and into the waiting arms of a medic who walked him into the hospital. Then, with my bags in hand and acting on the pilot's advice, I asked a nearby medic how I could get transportation to the Can Tho passenger terminal. The terminal was only a few minutes away, he explained, and once the wounded were triaged, he would take me there in an ambulance.

True to his word, the medic soon returned with an ambulance. I threw my gear into the back and we were soon heading to the airport. Arriving and checking into the terminal, I found that the movement specialist in Vi Thanh had done his job well. I was listed as a priority passenger on the next flight to Saigon.

Chapter 23. The End and a Beginning

While I sat waiting to board my flight from Can Tho to Saigon, I could not help but believe divine intervention was at work that morning. I certainly did not know what had happened to the unit I was supposed to advise that day except that they had taken casualties: at least eight wounded by my count. The "dustoff" aircraft was full when it picked me up, and casualty evacuation prioritized removing wounded rather than KIAs from the battlefield. Therefore, I could only surmise it had been a bad fight that morning, one with many friendly casualties.

The only logical explanation I could come up with for my missing the operation was that it was totally God's will! I would have accompanied the RF company that had been badly shot up had it not been for the Red Cross call, or if the orderly room jeep had arrived 10 minutes later. Being safe and on my way home, I was haunted by the thought of what happened to Lieutenants Carlile and Young the previous September near the same area as that day's fight. My missing that bad fight on the first day of summer 1970 is a miracle that has remained in my mind all of my life.

Wheels up, I soon departed the Can Tho and the Mekong Delta forever. My flight landed at Tan Son Nhut in mid-afternoon. On the ground in Saigon, I took the bus to Pentagon East, where I expected someone would tell me what I needed to do next.

At MACV headquarters the personnel specialist told me he could start, but not complete, my out-processing as they were short-staffed on Sundays. The specialist completed as much of my out-processing as he could, then told me to be back at his desk early the next morning. He suggested I go to the BOQ, the same one I stayed in on my first night in Vietnam. At the BOQ, I thought back to the lieutenant who gave me his clay-encrusted jungle boots and the latrine "VC" I encountered. I left my gear near a corner bunk and went to the mess hall. Despite not eating since earlier in the day, I found I really was not very hungry. I had just too many emotions going on inside of me. But I knew that I had to take advantage of the opportunity to eat. After dinner, I felt myself starting to get antsy and eager to get out of Vietnam.

I got up early the next morning after a fitful sleep, ate a good breakfast in the mess hall, and went straight to the personnel office. There, the clerks finished my out-processing and booked me on the next flight out of Vietnam that was scheduled to leave Bien Hoa airport around noon. Because I was going home on emergency leave, and therefore a priority, I was given a Vietnamese civilian driver to take me to Bien Hoa airport, about 40 kilometers (or about an hour and a half) away. The driver, at the wheel of an army sedan, arrived promptly. Along the way, he exposed me to sights I had not seen before. There were large numbers of American and Vietnamese military vehicles weaving through traffic to avoid other vehicles, people, and, dogs and I saw throngs of Vietnamese buying and selling produce at the many makeshift stands along the road. The whole sight was incredibly chaotic. I thought myself lucky to have been in a much more tranquil place like Vi Thanh.

Arriving at Bien Hoa, and after being checked through security at the main gate, the driver dropped me off at the main passenger terminal. There, I went to the outbound flight desk and reported to an air force sergeant, who verified I was on the next flight. He told me the flight departure time, pointed toward the boarding gate, and then sent me to a screening area manned by U.S. MPs. Though I had no reason to be, I was concerned about going through this checkpoint. The MPs did a thorough search of my belongings. Although it appeared they were looking more to confiscate and keep unregistered war souvenirs,[2] their stated purpose was to prevent the removal of any military gear and/or illicit drugs from Vietnam and to detain those carrying such items. I had no problem at the security checkpoint, and in no time I was boarding a plane filled with over 150 very happy Americans.

The airplane door closed once all passengers were checked off the manifest and on board, blocking the already stiflingly hot Vietnam air and smells from entering the cabin. Anchored in my seat, the next thing I knew we were taxing down the runway. Airborne, a cheer arose from several voices on the plane at the sound of the landing gear locking into the hold. A few minutes later, when the pilot announced the aircraft had cleared Vietnamese airspace, a tumultuous roar arose, and on some faces, tears appeared. By the grace of God, we had survived.

I sat in stoic reflection as we flew over the South China Sea, mulling over the last 10+ months. The civilian chartered plane was headed for landings in Japan and then Anchorage, Alaska. We deplaned at both stops. It was good to get off the plane, stretch my legs, look around, take in different smells, and just feel somewhat normal. Although I was deeply concerned about what had happened in East Moline, I was less apprehensive on this flight than I had been on the flight to Vietnam. I think this had much to do with my not having a one-year tour of duty in front of me and my heading back to a more familiar environment. Accordingly, I was actually able to catch some sleep on the plane, which seemed to make the flight to the U.S. go much quicker.

Our final stop was Travis Air Force Base, California, the starting point for my departure flight to Vietnam. Most of us on the plane cheered when the plane taxied to a stop near the gate. After deplaning and reaching the bottom of the stairs some of the men bent down and kissed the ground. I thought that gesture was unnecessary, as I didn't want to slow down my getting into the terminal building. At that point, I was just anxious to get

Chapter 23. The End and a Beginning

home. I thought it ironic that the plane that just brought me home was probably now changing crews and refueling so it could take another load of unhappy men to Vietnam.

I proceeded inside the terminal building at Travis, where an airman checked each passenger's name against the manifest. With my name checked off, I went into a nearby restroom and changed from my jungle fatigues into my summer khaki uniform, slathered on a layer of deodorant, and got into the queue for the bus going to the San Francisco airport. With absolute military efficiency, and remarkably no stragglers, the bus departed Travis on time. The bus ride from Travis AFB to San Francisco International Airport was a total blur about which I have absolutely no memory. Like most on the bus, my thoughts were now several hours into the future.

The transportation specialist I had seen in Saigon had me booked on commercial flights from San Francisco to Chicago and from Chicago to Moline. After I checked in for my flight to Chicago, I made a collect call to Sue to find out what the emergency was and to tell her my flight number and the time I would be arriving in Moline. Though not fast enough, both my flights went off without a hitch. However, on this flight I did not get first class seating or complimentary champagne—two amenities my absence from the country should have earned.

The sound of the Ozark Airlines plane's tires hitting the tarmac at the Moline airport snapped me out of the trance I was in and brought me back to reality. Staring out the aircraft's window, I just could not believe I was home, even though I had left part of my otherwise good hearing and about 35 pounds of weight in Vietnam. As I deplaned and walked toward the terminal building, I scanned the crowd. There I saw Sue and, surprisingly, my father. I'm sure we talked, but I was still taking in everything around me. I felt like I was in a different world, or perhaps, a different planet. The colors, the fragrant smells, well-dressed people, clean streets, and birds singing were things I had never appreciated as much as I did that day. As we walked to the parking lot I saw a white 1968 Camaro. With all of this around me, I knew I was home.

Epilogue

As with all of Vietnam, Chuong Thien province fell to communist forces in April 1975.

Safely home, I searched to find meaning from my time in Vietnam. I knew from what I had experienced there that my life from that point forward would be changed. On the positive side, I returned home uninjured, without the physical scars of the war, and, I think, my mental scars were minimal. I enjoyed my time with the Vietnamese soldiers and people and truly believed I had done something to help others less fortunate than myself. I made some good, though fleeting friends—both Vietnamese and American. My most significant and positive realization from Vietnam was that God is totally in control of everything in this world and every life plays out according to His plan. This had been taught to me as a child attending Sunday school and church; it became manifest to me in Vietnam and forevermore. I take great comfort in this fact and look at difficult life events in this context.

I believe it is beyond human ability to fully comprehend or rationalize tragic events, be they a death in combat or a traffic accident or a dire health diagnosis. I knew that I needed to be careful in Vietnam, but came to believe the old cliché, If my number was up it was up! I never understood how I could go on a "walk in the sun" operation one day, while the next day an advisor or ARVN soldier was killed or wounded in the same area. The tragic events I witnessed or that happened in the province were many: being hit by a VC sniper or small-arms fire, stepping on a mine or detonating a booby-trap, being killed or wounded in a helicopter that is down, being killed by a VC mortar round on the MACV compound, or walking or motoring into a VC ambush. These were things that happened to others, but not to me. Surviving Vietnam, I realized God had other things in store for me.

I have positive reflections on the members of the Chuong Thien province advisory effort—military and civilian. To me, it was just amazing that men from different backgrounds (social, economic, religious, and educational; civilians, career soldiers, young enlistees, draftees, and junior officers with a defined service obligation) all came together and performed their tasks, enabling the team to accomplish its collective mission. Not only did our team do its jobs well, but we shared a belief in our efforts and in one another. In this process, it appeared that most team members genuinely liked one another, and certainly in the reflection after over 50 years, some strong bonds have remained. In all, I truly believe everyone on the team was committed to the advisory effort and to helping the Vietnamese people.

I do carry some negatives from Vietnam. Memories of death, severe injuries, brutality, suffering, and the fear I saw in the eyes of Vietnamese women and children are images I can't forget. I cannot forget these tragic sights, as they were not present in my life before Vietnam. However, like many others who have experienced war since the beginning of time, I was able to push these terrible events into the far recesses of my mind. Over the many years since my service in Vietnam, the tragic memories have seldom surfaced.

I think it is beyond debate that the war profoundly affected anyone who served, especially those who experienced the brutality of war in life and death situations. Some who served in Vietnam (as well as those from past and current wars) suffer from post-traumatic stress disorder (PTSD). I was never diagnosed with PTSD, and I am thankful I am able to cope with the memory of my experience in Vietnam. I believe my coping may be attributable to my years growing up on a farm. There, my life was harsh, austere, and filled with witnessing sometimes gruesome farm and hunting activities.

My experience in Vietnam negatively affected me in two ways. The first of these is an annoyance, the second a persistent curse. When I hear an unexpected sound or experience someone's sudden appearance or movement,[1] I duck, flinch, or jump. I attribute this subconscious response to a heightened "fight or flight" reaction. Since I did not have this problem before Vietnam, I can only guess it is a result of having been under enemy fire. Though this problem is uncontrollable, at worst it is only embarrassing.

The second, and I believe more severe, problem I have lingering from Vietnam affects my relationships with others. Post-Vietnam, I am much more emotionally detached from people and events. While I can still empathize with others, few things faze me. In fact, I seldom get excited or mad. I tend to measure unpleasant events against a scale that has death at the far extreme. Since few occurrences in life rise to that level, I find I can accept tragic events (accidents, deaths, etc.) more easily than those around me. I attribute this detachment to what I saw in Vietnam, seeing others killed, wounded, or suffering greatly. In Vietnam, while in the midst of the horrors of war, I learned to set aside emotions and just deal with the situation at hand. Combat requires clarity of thought, and for me, that meant turning off my emotions. During a hectic or crisis situation, I learned you just cannot call a time-out or have an emotional meltdown. In Vietnam, those normal human responses simply were not an option. For me, after Vietnam it has often been difficult to find the emotional "on" switch.

Psychologists would tell you that talking about things that bother you is the best medicine. Shunning this good advice, I do not dwell on my experience in Vietnam and seldom talk to anyone about it. I have always believed I did not do anything particularly noteworthy in Vietnam and never wanted to sound like a braggart or portray myself in heroic terms. Lastly, not wishing to sound condescending, I reasoned that those who had not experienced anything similar to what I did in my time in Vietnam simply would not understand what I went through. For me, not talking about my Vietnam experiences did not result in my keeping demons bottled up inside me. Nor did my silence about Vietnam make me feel like I was ready to explode at any moment or cause me to walk around constantly thinking of my time in-country. I simply moved on.

Like other war veterans, I believe I am pretty normal. Normal notwithstanding my wife, Jane, telling me on occasions as late as in the 1980s that she would be awakened in the middle of the night to find me speaking in a foreign language she believed to be Vietnamese. During these infrequent episodes, I didn't recall having nightmares. I was most probably having a simple conversation with *Trung úy* An or other Vietnamese soldiers.

While I can say I returned from every operation soaking wet, including those days in the dry season, I really didn't experience fear in Vietnam.[2] Any fear I may have brought to Vietnam dissipated after my first operation with Captain McCullough. Now, I will certainly admit that I was always concerned about going into certain areas of the province and was always pumped up on adrenaline heading into a landing zone as my senses were heightened and my attention put on full alert. However, this was not fear! Most of my operations were just "walks in the sun," and after a while, I think I became lulled into the expectation of safety. Though I knew it was ever present, I became impervious to danger. On those few occasions when I experienced being shot at, events seemed to go in slow motion, and I didn't think—I just did as I was trained to do. It is an absolute fact that I often did not realize the seriousness of some of the situations I was in and was perhaps too foolish to comprehend the consequences. After all, I was in my early 20s and invincible, but not afraid.

I honor *all* who served in Vietnam, as they did their duty for this great nation. I believe many Vietnam veterans, like myself, held the belief that we were fighting communism and, by doing so, we were allowing the Vietnamese people the right of self-determination. That said, I have a hard time with the minority of Vietnam veterans who have allowed themselves to become victims upon returning home. The Vietnam veterans I call victims are those who define their military service by the mistreatment they received in the U.S. *after* Vietnam—rather than their service *in* Vietnam. Some of these victims tell of being spit on or having items thrown at them while in uniform, often happening at an airport as they were returning home. Others talk about being berated or shunned by family or former friends because of their Vietnam service. Still others just had a hard time adapting to civilian life as a result of Vietnam.

Did these things and more happen to some Vietnam veterans? Absolutely yes! My problem is that the view that some Vietnam veterans are victims has been wrongly characterized as pertaining to *all* Vietnam veterans. This treatment, related by the victims, tends to denigrate the service of all. Without the benefit of a psychology degree, but after 70+ years of life, I believe those Vietnam veterans who talk about these isolated negative events do so for the express purpose of evoking sympathy. My philosophy has always been pretty simple: war is horrible and life has its fair share of good and bad—just deal with it.

Another group that bothers me are those who just cannot get over their (real or invented) service in Vietnam. These are the ones who are often seen wearing camouflaged shirts or jackets plastered with military medals, their "boonie" hats replete with little pins and patches, and, of course, combat boots. This group in their standard "uniform" was most often seen in the 1970s and 1980s. To me, this garb begged for attention and recognition that was intended to elicit conversation. I label this group "cornfield commandos." Some of these festooned veterans are often more than happy to tell how they "killed some gooks," were "often high on drugs in Vietnam," were on "secret ops" and therefore cannot discuss their incredibly dangerous missions, or perhaps that they should have received medals for their numerous valorous actions but were denied this by their vengeful and often inept officers. This group bothers me because, in my opinion, they reflect poorly on my special brotherhood—Vietnam veterans. I was first exposed to these types while sitting with a lifelong friend and Vietnam veteran during an initial veteran-related membership meeting in 1972. Hearing these "war stories," I chose not to become involved with any veterans organizations after I returned from Vietnam.

Then there are the outright phonies who seek recognition for deeds they never performed. Whether they are those who served in Vietnam or those who never served, I fundamentally dislike those braggarts, embellishers, and outright imposters. My view seems to be the consensus of opinion in this country, as the Stolen Valor Act of 2013 was signed into law to create criminal penalties for individuals fraudulently claiming/wearing certain combat medals. Apparently, these imposters have the need to tell their "war stories" as a way to gain admiration, sympathy, or something. Who knows? For me, Vietnam was a memorable and noble time—a time when I learned a lot about myself and life. I dislike those individuals whose words and actions tend to take away from the honorable service of millions of silent Vietnam veterans.

Another group for whom I have little respect are those who protested our involvement in Vietnam—with my special scorn reserved for campus protesters and draft dodgers. In retrospect, I see many errors the U.S. government made in the prosecution of the war. However, during my time in Vietnam, which was also the time of those protests and of draft-age men fleeing to Canada, I always felt that we were doing something to help the Vietnamese people. I took the protests personally as I felt they were all directed against those of us who served rather than against the government. These protesters lived in the freest country on earth—one that had given and promised to give them incredible opportunities. Yet led by campus radicals and some prominent Americans, the protesters and draft dodgers fell prey to anti–American/anti-war propaganda. As it was later determined, some of these anti-American activities were formulated in Hanoi and the Soviet Union.

Then there were those who used the anti-war movement for personal recognition and fame. At the top of this list of people is Jane Fonda, a well-known actress of the time. I think it is accurate to say Jane Fonda is universally despised by most Vietnam veterans. Fonda's actions as an apologist and propagandist for the North Vietnamese have been well publicized. Most notorious of her activities was a picture taken of her while sitting on a North Vietnamese anti-aircraft artillery piece, a weapon whose sole purpose was to shoot down American aircraft. Her actions in support of an enemy we were fighting were a great propaganda boost for the North Vietnamese and, to me, were beyond contemptible. My disdain for Ms. Fonda is just slightly more than my low regard for ex–naval officer and Vietnam veteran John Kerry.

Mr. Kerry parlayed his (as the navy Swift boat veterans say, phony) medals and service in Vietnam into becoming the poster boy for disgruntled Vietnam Veterans.[3] As spokesman for the Vietnam Veterans Against the War, Kerry testified before the Senate Foreign Relations Committee.[4] In his opening remarks he stated his testimony was for a "very much larger group of veterans in this country," and he proceeded to talk in general terms about the many war crimes being perpetuated in Vietnam. He certainly was not speaking for me! Kerry read his well-scripted condemnation of atrocities and U.S. policy in Vietnam as he testified while wearing his navy fatigue shirt replete with rows of medals. Little effort was made to challenge Kerry's remarks by the assembled senators. Regardless, the expected damage was done, and Kerry's political career was launched. No doubt, his congressional appearance on April 22, 1971, was just Act 1 of his well-conceived plan, a plan that took him to the U.S. Senate, to a presidential run, and eventually to Secretary of State.

Then there are the lesser-known anti-war leaders and organizations: Abby Hoffman and his Yippies; Bill Ayers and Bernadine Dohrn and their FBI-designated "domestic terrorist" organization, the Weather Underground; the Students for a Democratic Society; and others who also turned the tide of support against U.S. involvement in Vietnam. For some of us who served in Vietnam, their collective actions were despicable and personal.

I have said (at least a thousand times since my service in Vietnam) that I adore the South Vietnamese people and am most thankful to have served in Vietnam as an advisor. Living and interacting with the Vietnamese people was incredibly rewarding. Though the war did not turn out the way I hoped it would, I was proud and honored to have helped people who were less fortunate than myself. Seeing and living with those of a different culture made me appreciate that I was an American living in the freest and most prosperous country on this earth.

Some Americans who served in Vietnam criticized the Vietnamese for their cautiousness, lack of American-style aggressiveness, and political corruption. Let me address these points. The Asian culture looks at life in terms of the long game. Being thoughtful and deliberate are respected attributes of the Vietnamese and most Asian cultures. I was also constantly reminded that the Vietnamese had to deal with the war and its consequences long before I got there and long after my one-year tour was over. The American in Vietnam had a calendar that lasted 365 days—the calendar of the Vietnamese lasted well into the future.

Aggressiveness is a function of training, leadership, and unit cohesion. As the war progressed, the South Vietnamese military expanded at an exponential level. When the U.S. involvement began to expand in the late 1950s and early 1960s, the ARVN training base (facilities, instructors, equipment, and doctrine) was nearly nonexistent. As the war progressed, especially after 1964, the Vietnamese training base matured, but it appeared that it was sacrificing quality for quantity. In a country at war, the level of individual training the ARVN officer and soldier received was never to the level of those in the U.S. Army. Collective training at every level consisted primarily of active operations against a formidable enemy. Combat teaches harsh lessons to those inadequately trained.

Leadership was taught at Vietnamese military institutions. I believe, however, that leadership (the ability to get others to do difficult tasks) is mostly innate. You either had it or you didn't. I saw the range of bad to excellent leaders while an advisor. From the company commander who insisted on the three warning shots to *Trung úy* An, the men under their command responded accordingly. In fairness, there were bad to excellent leaders in the U.S. Army as well.

Except for elite organizations (ARVN rangers, Marines, Special Forces, and airborne forces), unit cohesion was seldom apparent. I was fortunate to advise units like the 113th and 987th Regional Force companies, both of which possessed the necessary qualities for a successful combat unit. To see how the factors of training, leadership, and unit cohesion came together for the ARVN, one should look to the performance of the ARVN's 18th Division in the defense of Xuan Loc, April 9–21, 1975. That division, led by Brigadier General Le Minh Dao (a former province chief in Chuong Thien province) fought off the NVA's 4th Corps, which consisted of three NVA divisions. This determined and heroic action achieved with limited support resources was unmatched in the long annals of Vietnam War history.

On the issue of corruption of Vietnamese politicians or military leaders, I did not see evidence of it at my lowly level but heard enough stories to believe it existed. Corruption at the top levels of the South Vietnamese government methodically worked its way down through successive layers of bureaucracy and into the military. While I do not intend to make excuses for corruption, Vietnam had a history of being conquered and ruled by other nations—most recently, the French from 1887 to 1954. As a fledgling democracy, one could easily make the argument that South Vietnam's leaders were not prepared to lead. At the national level, this theory is borne out by the many South Vietnamese heads of state the between 1954 and 1975. Could this inexperience, the succession of national leaders (each with their bureaucratic appointees), and the millions of dollars the U.S. was putting into the war effort lead to corruption? I would say the conditions were ripe for corruption. So, if the individual ARVN soldier saw corruption, did this affect his willingness to fight with total dedication and vigor?

Like some others on Advisory Team 73, I soured on the war toward the end of my tour. I never wavered in my mission or determination to help the Vietnamese people, but I became disgusted with the way the war was being waged. I lived through and saw a time when politics trumped military strategy, and this was quite demoralizing. The most graphic example of this was in May 1970. The Cambodian operation was an extremely positive development that temporarily offset the nearly constant barrage of anti-war reporting that we read about in magazines. The brief "high" we got during the initial phase of the operation was soon followed by a depressing low when the U.S. abruptly abandoned the operation and withdrew.

The politics of ending the campaign to neutralize North Vietnam's presence in Cambodia disappointed me and caused me to question just what our government was doing. To use the old cliché, our government's actions seemed to "snatch defeat from the jaws of victory." My bitterness sprang from wanting to be on the winning team of South Vietnam *and* America. To me, the end of the Cambodian operation vividly proved our government would not let us win.

My reflections on the effectiveness of the training I received prior to going to Vietnam are mixed. In OCS we learned the secondary mission of an engineer was to fight as infantry, however, we received little infantry training at Fort Belvoir. Had it not been for the tactical training I received at the Fourth Army NCO Academy at Fort Hood and individuals like SFC Bill Haley and Captains Howard McCullough and Bob Olderson, I think I would have been little more than an oversized target in Vietnam.

I have a similar sentiment pertaining to the map-reading instruction I received in OCS versus that I received at Fort Hood. Here again, the NCO Academy excelled. Map reading was probably the most important skill an advisor could possess on operations. You had to always know where you were on the ground to report reaching checkpoints and objectives, to pinpoint the enemy, and sometimes, just to stay out of the line of fire. Accurate target location was a critical component of the information I passed to FACs, "Shotguns," helicopter gunships, or MEDEVACS for engaging or avoiding enemy positions. It is no understatement to say that accurate map reading could mean the difference between life and death. I was OK at map reading at the beginning of my tour in Vietnam and quite good at it by the end. My expertise was a function of good training prior to going to Vietnam and the nearly one-year on-the-job training I received in-country.

The advisor and language training I received at Fort Bragg and subsequently at Fort Bliss was exceptional and well prepared me for Vietnam. The training I received on Vietnamese culture was invaluable for it allowed me to better understand the Vietnamese people. This said, I think many Americans went to Vietnam with a strong cultural bias. Not being able to understand the Vietnamese, it seemed American soldiers sought ways to assert themselves over them. On occasions I heard Americans calling the Vietnamese pejorative names such as "Gook," "Slope," "Dink," and others. I also saw American crew members literally kicking Vietnamese soldiers off helicopters. (As a qualifier, I neither heard nor saw any of these actions by an American advisor.) By having a rudimentary understanding of Vietnamese history, culture, and especially by having a basic working knowledge of the language, I enjoyed an advantage most other American soldiers did not possess. I consider this knowledge (gained through my pre-deployment advisor training) to have been my strongest asset in Vietnam. This training helped me help them.

In comparison with others who served in combat or in engineer units in Vietnam, I consider my service as an advisor to have been great duty. While the work was at times demanding, I did not spend days or weeks in the field as did many of my American counterparts. I was not under frequent attack, ambushed by the enemy, nor did I have to work 12- to 16-hour days for days on end. I had great amenities on the MACV compound, and most of all, I really enjoyed the Americans and Vietnamese I worked with. When I consider the privations soldiers and Marines in maneuver units went through in Vietnam and in previous wars, I realize I had a pretty easy tour of duty in Vietnam.

With the advantage of 50 years of life after Vietnam, I look back at the many things I did there. The words that quickly come to mind are that I was young and foolish. In this book I have recounted some of the many reckless things I did. In reflection, I think my actions were typical of soldiers throughout time. As I look back many years later at my service in Vietnam, I cannot believe how foolish, and on many occasions, how downright stupid I was. I shudder to think of some of the dangerous things I did and attribute my survival to a force far greater than me.

In Vietnam I believed I was invincible. While I saw death around me, I could never imagine it happening to me. My greatest concern was never about dying. I was more afraid of losing a limb or of being grievously disfigured. However, after the first several weeks in-country I fully resigned myself to my destiny. I recognized my fate was totally in God's hands and I was OK with that.

For my service in Vietnam, in addition to a Combat Infantryman's Badge, I received a Bronze Star for meritorious service, an Air Medal, and a Vietnamese Cross of Gallantry with Palm. While not denigrating its award to anyone else, I consider my receiving the Bronze Star to be the equivalent of being awarded a Good Conduct Medal[5] for my service in Vietnam. I say this because I do not believe I did anything extraordinary to merit the receipt of this prestigious award. The Air Medal resulted from my time participating in combat assaults, "dustoff" missions, or flying backseat recon missions with either the FACs or "Shotguns." My Vietnamese Cross of Gallantry was an award given by the Vietnamese to departing American advisors, especially those who served in combat or combat support roles. This Vietnamese award was available in many different classes, and mine was essentially a "thank you for your service" type of award.

Of these awards, the CIB is my most cherished symbol of my service in Vietnam.

I received two OERs in Vietnam—the first upon the completion of six months in Vietnam and the second upon my departure. An OER rates an officer on a number of traits, provides a narrative of the officer's accomplishments during the rated period, and assesses his/her potential for future service in the army. My second OER, written by Norm Olsen upon completion of my tour of duty, was more impressive than the narrative portion of my Bronze Star citation. I was humbled to read the words he had written about me: "*LT Raschke performed two functions in Chuong Thien province.*[6] *He was an infantry advisor with RF/PF units and the province engineering advisor. As an RF/PF advisor, he did an outstanding job. His courageous, competent performance under enemy fire earned LT Raschke the respect and admiration of all he worked with, both Vietnamese and Americans. Of all the advisors in Chuong Thien, LT Raschke was the one the RF/PF desired to accompany them into combat. This was because he could be depended on to rise to the occasion no matter how heavy the enemy fire.*" I learned during my 31 years of commissioned service that OERs tend to slightly embellish one's accomplishments, and perhaps Mr. Olsen had done that in my OER narrative. However, his kind words were the most complimentary and meaningful to me of any I ever received.

Fast forward to 2008 when I happened to be in Washington, D.C., for a work-related meeting. That evening I met with John, my eldest son, for dinner, and as was our practice, we later went to a bookstore. It was at this bookstore that I found the book *A Dragon Lives Forever*, by a former Advisory Team 73 teammate, Tom Hargrove.[7] I read Tom's book[8] and saw where he had been in contact with other teammates during its writing. I became intrigued with the prospect of reconnecting with former teammates and was able to find and contact Tom. In our phone conversation, we decided to find and contact other team members for the purpose of having an Advisory Team 73 reunion.

Military reunions. I would like to describe my experiences with Advisory Team 58/73 reunions and military reunions in general. Military reunions are so important to giving past, present, and future veterans a sense of closure in their lives. This is how we Chuong Thien province teammates got together.

Shortly after talking to Tom, I began a concerted effort to locate those who served in Chuong Thien province—military, civilian, and Vietnamese. I started by asking "found" teammates for the names of those they remembered from Vietnam and repeated this query for every newly found member. Then, knowing a name, I used Google, WhitePages.com, the army officers register (for selected years), Fold3.com, Facebook, and other websites or search engines to get a phone number or address for the veteran. Using these methods, over the intervening years, I have found the names of about 550 individuals who served in the province. Of that number, some have passed away, some have proven impossible to find, and a small number do not wish to be reminded of their service in Vietnam. In total, I have had actual contact with about 180 of these men who served their tours in Chuong Thien province from 1964 to 1973.

With a handful of teammates located, we had our very first advisory team reunion in St. Louis, Missouri, in June 2009. To date, we have had seven reunions (St. Louis, Denver, Tucson, Las Vegas, Washington, D.C., San Antonio, and Springfield, Illinois) at two-year intervals. Despite our getting older, at each reunion we have a growing number of attendees.

Reunions typically span four days as we tour local sites within the reunion area, though companionship is the real focus of our time together. All reunions have featured a meal at a Vietnamese restaurant, and when available, Vietnamese beer. On the final night of the reunion we hold a very solemn memorial service for our teammates who were killed or died in Chuong Thien province. A highlight of the reunion is getting a group picture of all those in attendance.

These reunions are cathartic, and have included everything from hearty laughs to an outburst of tears! Seeing men reunite after being separated for 50+ years and rekindling those long-ago friendships is truly amazing. Our reunions have allowed us to relate our memories and experiences in Chuong Thien province and to remember our fallen teammates. They have proven to be helpful for the teammates' spouses as well, since in the end, they have a better understanding of what their loved ones went through.

Probably the most important thing to come out of our reuniting is that attendees are able to more freely talk of their time in Vietnam and, in my opinion, to "exorcise demons" they may have been carrying with them for so many years. A very often heard phrase is an attendee saying, "I have never talked with anyone about this, since they would not understand." In the end, we all had the common experience of being advisors in a contested province in Vietnam, and we truly consider ourselves a band of brothers. Our incredibly strong bond is to each other and to the country whose uniform we once wore.

At reunions our universal regret is that in the end our government left our Vietnamese allies. This is not a judgment on the war itself, but rather the uncertainty of knowing what happened to our Vietnamese counterparts and their families once the country fell to the communists. We know our Vietnamese counterparts had families and aspirations for themselves, their loved ones, and their country's future. In the end, we left them. I, and many of my advisor brothers, feel terrible at the fate our surviving Vietnamese comrades suffered beginning in April 1975. Our only solace is to see those who escaped Vietnam and have become doctors, lawyers, engineers, small business owners, and successful citizens of the United States. That is our legacy!

Those in This Book

Within this book, I have mentioned many people. Some I knew as just acquaintances, while others were comrades in arms and some were friends. Since 2009, I have been able to reconnect with some of these veterans, while others have passed on. There are a number of others I have been unable to locate. Below is what I know about my brothers in this book.

Trung úy An, *Trung sĩ* Minh and Song, and *Ông* Son. After leaving Vietnam, I lost all contact with my Vietnamese friends. I often wonder what happened to them after I left and especially after the communist takeover. They, like so many ARVN soldiers and GVN civilians who worked directly with the Americans, were most likely sent to "re-education" camps, that is, if they survived to April 30, 1975.

Chief Warrant Officer Two Robert W. Aberle got out of the army shortly after his return from Vietnam. He continued to fly helicopters by joining the National Guard and flying for the State of Illinois. Bob passed away in Illinois in 2021 at the age of 73.

Sergeant First Class Howard Carlton Ard lives in the memory of his family, friends, and his Advisory Team 73 teammates. His name is inscribed at Panel W19, Line 58 of the Vietnam Memorial Wall in Washington, D.C. Howard was 38 years old.

Captain Jim Bugansky, after serving in Chuong Thien province, went to Rotary Wing flight school, qualified as a helicopter pilot, and returned to Vietnam for a second tour. In 1972, Jim decided to leave the army. Now living overseas, Jim works in the natural rubber (plantation) industry and travels worldwide.

Captain Al Bundons made the army a career and retired as a colonel. Al passed away in Kansas in 2014 at the age of 73.

Lieutenant Richard Carlile survived his many wounds suffered on September 6, 1969. In addition to the Purple Heart, Rick received the Bronze Star for his valorous actions on that terrible day. Rick stayed in the army for several more years after Vietnam, serving in the U.S. and Germany. Leaving the army, Rick became a very successful restaurateur in his hometown in the Southeast U.S.

Major General Patrick F. Cassidy served as the chief of Army Personnel Operations from 1968 to 1969. He would later become the commanding general (lieutenant general) of the Fifth U.S. Army. He retired in 1975 with 34 years of service and died in 1990 at the age of 75.

Captain Richard "Dick" Childress stayed in the army and ended up working in the Reagan White House on the National Security Council's (NSC) Southeast Asia desk. At the NSC, Dick was the director of Asian affairs and dealt with 10 assigned countries in the far Pacific on matters such as Vietnam POW/MIA issues, refugees, narcotics, maritime issues, and other U.S. interests. Since his retirement in the late 1980s as a colonel, Dick remains active in POW/MIA matters. He has made numerous trips to Vietnam and neighboring countries working on MIA issues. Dick resides in the southeastern U.S.

Brigadier General Le Minh Dao was captured by communist forces following the fall of South Vietnam and spent 17 years in "re-education" camps. Through the efforts of Colonel Dick Childress and the State Department, General Dao was given asylum in the United States in May 1992. A towering figure in the U.S.-Vietnamese community, General Dao died in Connecticut in March 2020 at the age of 87.

Lieutenant Ralph Diaz, like most other lieutenants in 1969, was sent to Vietnam. There, he served in a combat engineer company and was wounded in action. After Vietnam, Ralph served with the U.S. Army Corps of Engineers in his beloved New Orleans. Facing orders to Germany, Ralph got out of the army and eventually became a tugboat captain while serving in the Army Reserve. Ralph retired as an Army Reserve colonel and lives in the Deep South.

Lieutenant Knute Dietze left the army after completing his two-year service obligation, most of which was as a tactical officer at Fort Belvoir. He subsequently went to law school and practiced law in the state of Texas. Knute passed away in 1998 at the age of 56 in Victoria, Texas.

Lieutenant Robert Hughes Donaway lives in the memory of his family, friends, and his Advisory Team 73 teammates. His name is inscribed at Panel W19, Line 59 of the Vietnam Memorial Wall in Washington, D.C. Bob was 25 years old.

Lieutenant George "Jug" Eastman stayed in the air force and served in a number of U.S. and overseas flying assignments, finally retiring as a major in 1991. Following retirement from the air force, "Jug" worked for the Pima County Sheriff's Department, followed by a stint as an aircraft avionics and maintenance instructor, and finally as a technical writer dealing with aircraft flight and maintenance operations. "Jug" lives in the western U.S. and is now fully retired.

Lieutenant Gene Griffiths left the army after Vietnam and returned to work with the U.S. State Department. Overseas, Gene had postings in The Netherlands, Australia, the Soviet Union, India, and Canada as well as several stints in Washington, D.C. Gene's last assignment was in the Office of Transportation Policy–International Civil Aviation Office, in Montreal. My hooch mate Gene is now retired, living in the southwestern U.S.

Sergeant First Class Leslie William "Bill" Haley retired from the army as a command sergeant major, the army's highest enlisted rank. Bill passed away in Hawaii in 2002 at the age of 62.

Lieutenant Tom Hargrove left the army after Vietnam and traveled the world assisting other countries in agricultural matters, especially with regard to rice cultivation. Tom passed away in 2011 in his home state of Texas at age 66, due, most believe, to the hardships he endured while he was held as an FARC captive in Colombia.

Warrant Officer One Ralph Howard left the army after his tour in Vietnam and now lives in the western U.S.

Lieutenant Jim Jaegers stayed in the army for several years after Vietnam. After the army, Jim worked for the state of Missouri until his retirement. He now lives in the Midwest.

Lieutenant Travis B. Lee Jr. lives in the memory of his family, his friend Sandra Richardson, those he touched as a Tactical Officer at Engineer OCS, and his soldiers in the 9th Infantry Division. His name is inscribed at Panel W27, Line 101 of the Vietnam Memorial Wall in Washington, D.C. Travis was 23 years old.

Lieutenant Colonel Thomas LeVasseur served in Chuong Thien province for a total of 36 months (12 in 1964–1965 and 24 months as PSA from July 1969 to July 1971). He was a veteran of World War II, Korea, and Vietnam, and retired from the army as a lieutenant colonel. He passed away in Colorado in 2011 at the age of 83.

Captain Howard McCullough got out of the army after his tour in Vietnam and went to work for a food service company in New England. Though he is semi-retired, Howard still watches over the business and remains in the Northeast.

Sergeant First Class Edward G. McGinnis passed away in Hinesville, Georgia, in March 1985 at the age of 46.

Lieutenant Al Miller left the active army after Vietnam and joined the Army Reserve. (I actually bumped into Al while attending the Field Artillery Advanced Course at Fort Sill, Oklahoma, in 1974.) Al passed away in Oklahoma in 2007 at the age of 62.

Lieutenant Dave Nickinovich left the army after Vietnam and

received a Ph.D. from the University of Washington, where he taught for 17 years. Dave later formed a consulting company, which he continues to run. He lives in the Northwest.

Lieutenant Robert "Bob" Noonan stayed in the army and, after a number of overseas and command assignments, ended his 35-year military career in 2003 as a lieutenant general, director of army intelligence. Bob later became an executive vice president at Booz Allen Hamilton. He is now retired, living on the East Coast.

Mr. Norman Olsen was in Vietnam for five years, with two of those years in Chuong Thien province. Norm remained with the U.S. Agency for International Development until his retirement. Accordingly, he had a number of overseas assignments. He now lives on the East Coast.

Staff Sergeant Dave Paulson continued to serve in the army in the intelligence community after Vietnam. Dave was medically retired from the army after he was seriously injured during a surreptitious duty assignment in Germany. Dave now lives in the northwestern U.S.

Lieutenant Frank Perra left the army after Vietnam and pursued a career in ballet. After years with prestigious U.S. and European dance troupes, Frank went to work for several European companies in the information technology and finance fields. Frank is retired and lives in Europe.

William "Bill" Pobanz completed his term in the USAF, after which he lived in southern Illinois, eventually ending up in Missouri. Bill has had an extraordinary career in the aviation industry, accumulating in excess of 20,000 flying hours as a pilot. Bill is now semi-retired living in the Midwest.

Captain Charles Sands returned to the U.S. and entered into the Special Forces following his 18-month stint in Chuong Thien province. However, after eight and one-half years he left the army so he could take care of his family farm. Charlie is now semi-retired and lives in the Southwestern U.S.

Captain George "Buddy" Shieldes left the army after Vietnam and joined the U.S. Army Reserve, where he served in a number of assignments and retired as a lieutenant colonel. He became active in the Catholic Church and served as a deacon. He and his wife reside in the South and share a music ministry in their local community.

Lieutenant Colonel Eugene Smallwood lives in the memory of his family, his friends, and his advisory team teammates. His name is inscribed at Panel W18, Line 59 of the Vietnam Memorial Wall in Washington, D.C. Colonel Smallwood was 42 years old.

Major George Speck served as the forward air controller in Vi Thanh. I have lost all contact with Major Speck.

Captain Howard Taylor remained in the U.S. Air Force and retired as a colonel. His USAF career after Vietnam took him to a number of overseas assignments spent flying and commanding air transport organizations. Howard now lives on the East Coast.

Trung sĩ An Phung Tho remained in Chuong Thien province until it fell to communist forces in April 1975. Being a high-value target for his intelligence work with the Americans, An was able to elude the communist victors and escaped Vietnam in 1977. For his heroic actions in February 1971, An was awarded the United States Bronze Star Medal with "V" device for helping rescue several advisors who found themselves in a VC minefield. An now lives with his family in the Southern U.S.

Sergeant First Class John W. Van Blarcum retired from the army as a master sergeant. He passed away in Arkansas in 2001 at the age of 80.

Sergeant First Class George Edward Walker Jr. lives in the memory of his family, his friends, and his Advisory Team 73 teammates. His name is inscribed at Panel W10, Line 106 of the Vietnam Memorial Wall in Washington, D.C. George was 38 years old.

Captain Harvey Weiner, after Vietnam, completed the remaining months of his service obligation serving as a defense counsel at Fort Dix, New Jersey. After the army, he began a stellar career in law. A partner in a prestigious Northeastern law firm, Harvey has argued cases in courts around the country. Harvey has been very active in his community and in professional, veterans, and faith organizations. He continues to work and has accomplished his goal of seeing a professional baseball game at every one of the major league cities. Harvey resides in the Northeast.

Lieutenant Chauvin Wilkinson left the army after his tour in Chuong Thien province. He returned to his native Louisiana, where he worked in the agricultural field. He later went to law school and became a very successful lawyer. Now fully retired, Chauvin is active in the Catholic Church and lives in the Southern U.S.

Lieutenant Stephen Walter Young lives in the memory of his family, his friends, and his Advisory Team 73 teammates. His name is inscribed at Panel W18, Line 52 of the Vietnam Memorial Wall in Washington, D.C. Steve was 23 years old.

Specialist Fourth Class Mal Zellefrow spent a total of 26 months in Chuong Thien province. Leaving Vietnam and the army in late 1971, Mal went to school, studying to be a civil engineer, but was unable to complete his education due to his growing family. Mal subsequently went to work for a large steel company where he worked for 34 years. He is now retired and lives in the Northeastern U.S.

* * *

As for me, after Vietnam I went to my next assignment at Fort Leonard Wood, Missouri. There, I was promoted to captain in August 1970.

I served as the commander of an engineer advanced individual training company, and there, John, my oldest son, was born. My assignment at Fort Leonard Wood gave me a chance to get reacclimated to life in the U.S. and allowed me time to take evening college classes. In Vietnam, I had made up my mind that I did not wish to stay in the army. However, the army validated my decision when a Pentagon engineer branch assignments officer came to Fort Leonard Wood and recommended I not seek an extension beyond my ETS of August 30.[1]

I returned to Geneseo, and over the next ten years, I resumed working at the Farmall tractor plant; had two more wonderful children, Tom and Jill; completed a degree in accounting from Western Illinois University; tinkered around with farming on the family farm; and joined the Illinois Army National Guard's 2nd Battalion, 123rd Field Artillery. I realized I missed the army and liked it more than I was willing to admit. Over the ensuing years, Sue and I grew apart, and we divorced in 1980.

In the 1980s my life was filled with joys and challenges. On Valentine's Day, 1982, I married Jane, whom I met through our working together at Farmall. Jane was a process engineer while I was a department general foreman (midlevel manager) at the time. Jane and I were blessed with a son, Ryan, in 1983. A month before Ryan was born, my beloved mother passed away at the age of 55. (My father passed away at age 66 in 1990.) Still in the National Guard and by now promoted to major, I attended Command and General Staff College at Fort Leavenworth. Following a lengthy strike in 1979–80 and an economy experiencing interest rates in the high teens, International Harvester divested its agricultural implement manufacturing plants. The Farmall plant, in Rock Island, Illinois, which had been in operation since 1926, had its last tractor roll off the assembly line on May 14, 1985, and officially closed on June 27, 1986. As a result of this corporate tragedy, both Jane and I (with a combined total of 26 years of service) found ourselves unemployed in 1985. This blow was somewhat softened by our having earlier entered the housing market—both flipping houses and buying rental properties.

In 1986 I took a position as an Active Guard Reserve[2] assistant inspector general and our family relocated to Springfield, Illinois. Over the next 13 years on active duty, I received an MBA from the University of Illinois and progressed through a number of positions, including mobilization planner, battalion commander (2/123 field artillery), inspector general for the Illinois National Guard, director of plans, operations and training (G-3), and director of resource management. Included in those 13 years was a one-year Army War College Fellowship at Tufts University in Medford, Massachusetts—a year my family and I truly cherished (though I failed to realize that my Vietnam hooch-mate Harvey Weiner was living within minutes of Tufts). I retired from the army as a colonel with a total of 33 years in uniform. My retirement was just two days short of my 52nd birthday.

Post-army, I worked five and a half years for the Illinois Commerce Commission before I landed the best job in my life—administrative officer for the United States Attorney's Office–Central District of Illinois. I worked at this position for nearly nine years, and finally, at age 66, I became convinced I had worked enough for one lifetime—a total of 48 years. I fully retired in 2014 and have not stopped smiling since. What a blessed life for a poor farm kid from Edford Township!

Glossary

.45 caliber pistol, M-1911A1. The pistol issued to officers and certain enlisted soldiers. It was a single-action, semi-automatic, magazine-fed, recoil-operated pistol chambered for the .45 ACP cartridge. The magazine held seven rounds.[1]

.50 caliber machine gun, M-2. The U.S. Army's heavy machine gun. It fired a one-half-inch-diameter round to a maximum effective range of 1,400 meters (~.9 miles) with a rate of fire of 400–500 rounds per minute.[2]

75-mm recoilless rifle. The 75-mm recoilless rifle, Type 52/56 was a Chinese copy of the U.S. M-20 recoilless rifle. It was fielded by the U.S. in the latter days of World War II as a lightweight infantry anti-tank weapon. It was used extensively during the Korean War (on both sides) and saw use among the ARVN and VC in Vietnam. The Type 52/56 had a maximum range of 6,600 meters, and the VC employed it primarily in an indirect fire mode.[3]

82-mm mortar. A Soviet-bloc weapon with a range of 3,040 meters (1.9 miles). This mortar fired a 6.7-pound shell filled with 12 ounces of high explosives. It had a bursting radius of 35–40 meters.[4]

A-1E Skyraider. A single-seat ground support aircraft accepted into service in 1946 and used in both the Korean and Vietnam conflicts. The Skyraider could carry a massive amount of ordnance and could loiter overhead in support of ground troops for a long time.[5]

Advanced Individual Training. Specialized training following Basic Training that resulted in a soldier receiving a Military Occupational Specialty (MOS). For example, when I graduated from the 10-week Medical Corpsman training at Fort Sam Houston, I received an MOS of 91A10.

AFVN. Armed Forces Vietnam Network. The American radio station run by the military in Vietnam. AFVN provided music and news, with its primary purpose being to improve morale.

"Agency." A slang term for the CIA or CIA personnel.

Agent Orange. The term for the toxic chemicals used to strip vegetation. Also see "Defoliation" in this glossary.

AH-1 "Cobra" helicopter. The "Cobra" entered service in 1967 and was a sleek and fast attack helicopter with a top speed of 141 miles per hour. It had a two-man crew consisting of a pilot and a copilot/gunner and carried a variety of weapons systems internally or on its stub wings. Its weapons included a grenade launcher, mini-gun, rockets, a 20-mm cannon, and later, TOW (Tube-launched, Optically tracked, Wire-guided) missiles. "Cobras" first arrived in Vietnam in late 1967.[6]

Aid station. A place that provided the lowest level of medical care in the field. One or several medical corpsmen operated an aid station.

AIK. Assistance In Kind. A fund used by U.S. personnel for the purchase of certain commodities and/or labor from the Vietnamese. It was funded in piasters.

Airmobile operation. A military operation that involved the helicopter insertion of troops into a pre-established landing zone in search of the enemy.

AK-47 rifle. The Soviet-bloc standard infantryman's automatic weapon, used extensively by the NVA and VC main force units. This very rugged rifle fired a 7.62 × 39-mm round to an effective range of 400 meters at a rate of 600 rounds per minute.[7]

ARVN. Army of the Republic of Vietnam.

ASAP. As soon as possible.

Azimuth. A direction expressed in degrees as determined by using a lensatic compass, or with enough experience, from looking at a map. An azimuth expressed the direction to travel (heading for aircraft) to a specific point, e.g., an enemy location, lone hooch, pickup location, etc.

"Backseater." A slang term for someone riding in the rear seat of an aircraft. In the O-1 aircraft, the backseater most often called for and adjusted artillery fire onto enemy locations.

Ba Mươi Ba. A Vietnamese manufactured rice-based beer. Its name was a translation of "33," the prominent numbers on its label.

Bandolier. A cloth pocketed belt that came with the 5.56-ammo cans and which was used for carrying ammunition. Each ammo can contained six bandoliers of 140 rounds each or 840 rounds. An M-16 bandolier had seven pockets and a cloth sling to allow the bandolier to be carried over one's shoulder.

BAR. Browning automatic rifle, a World War II and Korean War–era squad automatic weapon. The M-60 machine gun replaced the BAR.[8]

Basic Allowance for Quarters. Basic Allowance for Quarters was an allowance prescribed by geographic duty location, pay grade, and dependency status. It provided compensation when government quarters were not provided. In 1969, Basic Allowance for Quarters (for me) was $120.00 per month.

Basic Allowance for Subsistence. Basic Allowance for Subsistence is the amount given to officers and to enlisted soldiers without access to a mess hall. In 1969, Basic Allowance for Subsistence was $47.88 per month.

Basic Training. In 1967, an eight-week course that transitioned new entrants into the army by issuing uniforms, giving required immunizations and teaching the basics of being a soldier. Subjects taught included military traditions; courtesy, code of military justice; drill and ceremony; weapons qualification; first aid; field craft; physical fitness; bayonet drill; nuclear, chemical and biological warfare; and others.

Battalion. A military organization comprised of three or more companies. VC battalions in Chuong Thien province were typically light infantry units and had about 200–300 soldiers. A typical U.S. infantry battalion in Vietnam had about 700 men authorized.

Battlefield zero. A battlefield zero was the procedure through which an M-16 rifle was fired and subsequently adjusted for windage and elevation ("sited-in") on a special 25-meter target. Zeroing a weapon gave a soldier the highest probability of hitting a target at 250 meters.[9]

BDA. Bomb damage assessment.

Beaucoup. A French word meaning "a lot," as in "There are *beaucoup* VC in that village."

Binh nhất. A Vietnamese Army private equivalent to a U.S. Army private, E-3.

Binh nhì. A Vietnamese Army private first class, equivalent to a U.S. Army private, E-2.

Binh sĩ. A Vietnamese word for soldiers or troops.

"Bird Dog." The O-1 "Bird Dog" was a fixed-wing Cessna 305 slightly modified for military use. First produced in 1947, the aircraft was used in the Korean Conflict designated as the L-19. The L-19 was re-designated O-1 in 1962 and carried a pilot and one passenger, normally an artillery spotter. The O-1 had a maximum speed of 115 mph and usually flew at 1,500 feet in Vietnam. It was armed with three or four rocket tubes under each wing which could fire 2.75" high explosives (HE), white phosphorus (WP, also called "Willie Peter"), or smoke rockets.[10]

Blocking position. A position established to prevent enemy troops from escaping converging forces. It was set up on the most likely avenue of enemy exfiltration.

BOQ. Bachelor Officer Quarters.

Bronze Star for Valor. An award that recognized a courageous act(s) during combat operations against the enemy. The Bronze Star with "V" (signifying for valor) ranked just below the Silver Star. (A Bronze Star without a "V" was awarded for meritorious service.)

C-4 explosives. A military high explosive.

C-7 Caribou. A twin-engine U.S. Air Force cargo and troop transport aircraft. Smaller that the C-123, the Caribou was used in Vietnam due to its short takeoff and landing capability and its ability to land on unimproved airfields. It could carry about 12,700 pounds of cargo.[11]

C-123 Provider. A twin-engine U.S. Air Force cargo and troop transport aircraft. It was used extensively in Vietnam due to its short takeoff and landing capability and its ability to land on secondary airfields. A C-123 could carry 24,000 pounds of cargo or 60 passengers.[12]

C-130 Hercules. The C-130 is a four-turboprop engine, primarily cargo aircraft. It entered the U.S. Air Force inventory in 1956, and, with a crew of five, it was designed to carry 92 passengers or 40,000+ pounds of cargo over extended ranges. One of its variants was the AC-130 gunship, call sign "Puff the Magic Dragon."[13]

C&C command and control helicopter. The UH-1 "Huey" helicopter that carried a senior Vietnamese officer and a U.S. advisor. Via radio the Vietnamese officer with the assistance of the U.S. advisor controlled the actions of the ground element during an operation.

Cao Đài. A religion established in southern Vietnam in 1926 that combined Buddhism, Christianity, Taoism, Confucianism, and Islam. *Cao Đàis* often painted the "all seeing eye" on their sampans.[14]

CARE package. The term "CARE package" was taken from the international humanitarian agency whose acronym was CARE. 1950s and 1960s commercials encouraged Americans to donate money so CARE could send foodstuffs to needy countries. In Vietnam, CARE packages came from our families back in the States, since we were the ones in need.

CH-47 Chinook helicopter. A twin-rotor helicopter, the Chinook entered service with the U.S. Army in 1962 and served as a cargo, passenger, and equipment lift helicopter. It had a 3-man crew consisting of a pilot, copilot, and flight engineer. It could transport 33–55 troops or 24,000 pounds of cargo and had a maximum speed of 188 miles per hour.[15]

"Charlie." The nickname for the VC taken from the military phonetic alphabet, where "Victor" stood for the letter "V," and "Charlie" stood for the letter "C." See also "VC" in this glossary.

Checkpoint. A prominent terrain feature used on an operations map as a reference point. Checkpoints were used to track the progress of ground operations.

Chiêu hoi. The *Chiêu hoi* program literally translated as "Open Arms" and was a propaganda program designed to have VC and North Vietnamese soldiers desert and come to the side of the South Vietnamese government. *Chiêu hoi* leaflets were spread throughout the Vietnamese countryside and promised safe contact to anyone carrying the leaflet when surrendering to GVN forces.[16]

Chuẩn ùy. Vietnamese officer cadet (Aspirant).

CIB. Combat Infantryman's Badge.

CIDG. Civilian Irregular Defense Group. A program developed by the U.S. government in the Vietnam War to develop South Vietnamese irregular military units from minority populations.

CIF. Central Issue Facility. A building located on the MACV headquarters complex in Saigon that issued and received military equipment to/from MACV soldiers.

Civil Affairs. A trained assignment within the U.S. Army. A Civil Affairs officer would initiate and assist in nonmilitary actions taken to help the Vietnamese population. These civil efforts included, providing medical care to remote villages, helping to increase crop production, building schools, reimbursements for damages to property, educating the populace on democracy, etc.

"Clacker." See "M-18 Claymore mine" in this glossary.

Claymore. See "M-18 Claymore mine" in this glossary.

Close Air Support (CAS). Close air support was the technical term for engagement of enemy targets in the near vicinity of friendly troops by primarily high-performance aircraft. Any air support, fixed wing or helicopter gunships, could be called close air support.

Cô. The Vietnamese word *Cô* was equivalent to the English word "Miss," meaning a young unmarried woman.

"Cobra." See "AH-1" in this glossary.

Cold LZ. A landing zone in which there is no enemy activity.

Collective training. Training a group of soldiers (crews, teams, squads, platoons, and companies) to do tasks required of a group as a whole.

Combat arms soldiers. Those serving in the armor, field artillery, or infantry branches.

Command group/command element. The command element typically consisted of the operation's ground commander, the RTOs (to enable contact with higher and subordinate organizations), a Vietnamese medic, and the American advisors.

Company. Within the Regional Forces, an infantry company consisted of 123 soldiers (on paper). A company had four platoons armed with predominantly M-16 rifles, with select soldiers carrying M-79 grenade launchers, M-60 machine guns, 60-mm mortars, light anti-tank weapons (M-72) and/or recoilless rifles. In the field, a company had assigned radios, RTOs, and corpsmen to assist them in accomplishing their tactical mission.[17]

Company commander. The officer, normally a *Dai úy* (captain) or *Trung úy* (first lieutenant) responsible for the actions of all men assigned to his company. This responsibility included combat operations, training, logistical support, payroll, and welfare.

CORDS. Civil Operations and Revolutionary Development Support. A joint U.S.-Vietnamese military and civilian program focused on pacification. It emphasized security, centralized planning, and operations against the Viet Cong.

Corpsman. A soldier specially trained to provide basic medical care and treatment.

Counterpart. An advisor term for the Vietnamese soldier or civilian you were advising.

CQ. Charge of quarters. The duty-roster appointed NCO whose responsibility was to answer the phone in the orderly room, report serious incidents to the proper person, wake people up as required, sound the alarm in the event of ground or indirect fire attack and, periodically, check the compound perimeter.

C-rations. Though officially designated Meal, Combat Individual during Vietnam, the term C-rations was a carryover term from World War II and Korea. C-rations could be eaten hot or cold and came in a small rectangular cardboard carton containing a meat-based entrée; a bread item; a dessert; and an accessory pack (containing coffee, salt, pepper, spoon, toilet paper, sugar and creamer). All items except the accessory pack were in tin containers.

Crew chief. The enlisted soldier responsible for the basic maintenance, refueling, and re-arming of an aircraft. On UH-1 "Huey" helicopters, the crew chief had the additional responsibility of loading and unloading materials and passengers as well as operating the M-60 machine gun mounted on the side of the aircraft.

Đại úy. The Vietnamese rank equivalent of a U.S. Army captain.

"Davids." Call sign of the U.S. Air Force forward air controllers.

Defoliation. The process of removing foliage from trees and vegetation through the aerial spraying of toxic chemicals. See also "Agent Orange" in this glossary.

Deputy province senior advisor. The principal assistant to the province senior advisor. This person was normally a civilian assigned to CORDS and focused primarily on the civilian aspects of the advisory effort.

DEROS. Date Estimated Return from Over Seas. This term was associated with the date 365 days from the date one arrived in Vietnam. DEROS was the date a military member was to return to the U.S. Knowing this date fostered the pervasive obsession of counting days until DEROS.

Det cord. The slang term for detonation cord, an explosive in the form of ¼-inch-diameter white explosive-laden plastic rope that was used to connect explosives together. It could also be used as an explosive by itself when wrapped around an object.

Diem regime. Named for Ngo Dinh Diem the President of South Vietnam from 1955 to 1963. Believing him to be corrupt, a group of Vietnamese Army officers deposed and assassinated Diem in November 1963.

District chief. The senior Vietnamese officer assigned to oversee all military operations and civilian programs within the district. The district chief was normally a *Thiếu tá* (major).

District headquarters. The administrative building from which the district staff and district chief operated.

District/subsector. A defined area within a province, similar to a county in the United States. Within Chuong Thien province, there were five districts: Duc Long, Kien Hung, Kien Long, Kien Thien, and Long My.

DMAC. Delta Military Assistance Command. Command element for all U.S. advisory efforts in IV Corps, the Mekong Delta area of South Vietnam. In 1971, this was re-designated MR4, Military Region 4.

Glossary

Dry season. The months of November–April each year. Though it still rained, the dry season saw the absence of the daily heavy monsoon rains.

DSA. District senior advisor. The senior U.S. advisor in a district (sub-sector), whose principal duty was to advise the Vietnamese district chief. The DSA also commanded the assigned 3–6 man district advisory team members. The DSA was normally a U.S. Army captain or Major.

"Dustoff." Medical evacuation helicopters/crews were called "dustoffs." This moniker came from the call sign of the helicopter.

Eagle Flight. An Eagle Flight was a night airmobile operation in which troops were inserted to relieve a besieged outpost; or on other occasions (based on highly reliable intelligence reports) to engage the enemy or interdict his movement.[18]

ETS. Expiration Term of Service. The scheduled discharge date for a soldier.

F-4 Phantom. A two-seat high-performance jet aircraft flown by a pilot and a weapons systems officer. In Vietnam, the F-4 was both an air superiority and close air support platform. In its ground support role, the F-4 could carry a payload of 18,650 pounds consisting of bombs, missiles, and/or napalm.[19]

FAC. Forward air controller. A U.S. Air Force (later Vietnamese) officer flying in an O-1 "Bird Dog" aircraft whose mission was to provide aerial reconnaissance and mark enemy locations for engagement by attack aircraft (A-1Es, F-4s, or helicopter gunships). As required by the tactical situation, the FAC could attack ground targets with their on-board 2.75" rockets.

Family separation allowance. A military allowance given to soldiers with dependents (spouses and/or children) for being away from their home station. In 1969, family separation allowance was $30.00 per month.

Farmall plant. The International Harvester plant located in Rock Island, Illinois, that made agricultural tractors.

"Fast movers." A slang term for jets.

***Field Manual* (FM) 5-34, *Engineer Field Data*.** FM 5-34 was the engineer's bible. It was designed to be easily carried in one's cargo pocket and contained instructions on most every task an engineer soldier could encounter.

Firefight. An exchange of weapons fire between friendly and enemy forces. In this book, a firefight is further defined as an exchange of short duration, generally less than 30 minutes.

"Fire in the hole." A phrase that was shouted three times as a warning that an explosive charge was about to be set off.

First sergeant. The senior enlisted man (Grade E-8) on Advisory Team 73 who was responsible for the welfare of enlisted soldiers and for advising the PSA on enlisted matters/concerns.

Fixed wing aircraft. Aircraft other than helicopters. This included cargo and observation airplanes as well as jets.

Flak jacket. A shoulder-to-waist, vest-like body armor that provided some protection against fragmentation devices (grenades, mines, or shrapnel), but offered limited to no protection against rifle or machine gun rounds. The flak jacket weighed about eight pounds, and despite its limitations, gave one a sense of security.

Force structure. The number and type of soldiers and equipment authorized by an official document. See also "TDA" and "TO&E" in this glossary.

"Fragging." When a disgruntled soldier attempted or succeeded in killing a perceived abusive officer or NCO, often by throwing a fragmentation grenade into their sleeping quarters. Toward the later years of U.S. involvement in the Vietnam War, incidents of "fragging" grew in number.

Free fire zone. An area established by the district and province chief that was determined to be enemy (VC) controlled. Within this area, artillery or aircraft could attack men or material without clearance. A free fire zone was often marked on reconnaissance pilots' maps.

Friendly/friendlies. Nicknames for American or ARVN forces.

"Gook," "slope," "dink." Derisive slang terms for the VC and Vietnamese people used by some Americans.

Government. The term as often used herein to refer to the elected South Vietnamese government. Also called the GVN.

Green Berets. Green Berets is the common name given to U.S. Army Special Forces. They were first formed in 1952 and authorized their trademark Green Beret by President Kennedy in April 1962. With their headquarters at Fort Bragg, North Carolina, the Green Berets serve all over the world. In Vietnam, they operated in remote portions of the country, primarily training indigenous forces to fight the communists.

Grid coordinates. A specific spot on a military map. Grid coordinates had an alphabetic two-letter prefix (in Chuong Thien province, this was WR [Whiskey Romeo]) followed by a six-digit number to identify a point on the ground to the nearest 100 meters. Ground forces used these alphanumeric grid coordinates to identify enemy positions, MEDEVAC pickup sites, LZs, PZs, the location of friendly forces on the ground, etc. All advisors and pilots received training in map reading, which included determining grid coordinates.

Gun section. Within a field artillery battery, a gun section consisted of two howitzers. A *Thiếu úy* (U.S. Army second lieutenant equivalent) or senior Vietnamese sergeant normally commanded a gun section. In Chuong Thien province, the weapons (guns) were mostly 105-mm howitzers.

Gunship. A heavily armed helicopter weapons platform, either a "Huey" or "Cobra" helicopter whose sole purpose was to engage enemy ground targets. Gunship weapons differed but were a mixture of machine guns, mini-guns, rockets, and grenade launchers.

GVN. Government of [South] Vietnam. Also called the Saigon government. See "Government" in this glossary.

HAM radio operator. Amateur radio operators worldwide, but in the context of this book, those within the United States.

H&I (Harassment and Interdiction) fires. Scheduled, intermittent artillery fires on predesignated locations during the evening hours. Target locations were suspected VC movement routes, meeting areas, etc., as identified by the province Intel section. The purpose of H&I fires was to disrupt VC movement and operations.

HE. High explosives. The most common artillery or rocket warhead. These artillery rounds or warheads were commonly loaded with Composition B or C-4.

Heavy contact. A term used to describe an intense battle between friendly and enemy forces.

HES. Hamlet Evaluation System. The province senior advisor was responsible for the preparation of the HES with input provided by district senior advisors, CORDS (Civil Operations and Revolutionary Development Support) personnel, and Vietnamese military and civilian authorities. The monthly HES was a 77-question, multiple-choice statement completed on each hamlet within the province. Then, quarterly, an 88-question multiple-choice statement was prepared for the province. The province senior advisor sent the completed raw data HES assessment up the advisory chain of command for compilation and analysis at headquarters, MACV. The resulting classified HES report was made available to U.S. headquarters, including MACV, the Pentagon, the embassy, in our case DMAC, and the province senior advisor.[20]

Hòa Hảo. An offshoot Buddhist sect. *Hòa Hảo* were strongly anti-communist.

Hồi chánh. *Hồi chánh* were formerly VC or NVA soldiers who rallied to the GVN. They were extensively interrogated for actionable intelligence and to determine their motives/reliability. If deemed to be "genuine," some were integrated in ARVN units. There were instances when the *Hồi chánh* turned out to be double agents.

"Hooch." A slang term for an advisor's room or a remote Vietnamese hut.

Hostile fire pay. Extra pay for being in a designated hostile zone. In 1969, hostile fire pay was $65.00 per month.

Hot LZ. A landing zone in which there was enemy activity—notably enemy fire or movement.

"Huey." See "UH-1" in this glossary.

Hunter-killer team. A hunter-killer team was a Light Observation Helicopter (OH-6) called a Loach (from the abbreviation LOH) or Flying Egg and two helicopter gunships—either UH-1B/C or "Cobras" (AH-1). The Loach would usually fly low in attempt to draw enemy fire. If the enemy fired at the Loach, the Loach pilot would throw a smoke grenade to mark the area from which the fire came and the gunships would swoop in and eliminate the threat. Being the "bait" made life for the Loach pilot very dangerous.[21]

Indirect fire. Indirect fire was engagement on a target by mortar, recoilless rifle, artillery, and rocket fires.

Glossary

Intelligence analyst. A U.S. and/or Vietnamese specialist whose purpose was to review enemy documents, radio intercepts, sightings, and/or interrogations to best determine the enemy's locations and/or likely courses of action. The results of their analysis was passed to the S-3 (Operations section) for action.

IV Corps. The Mekong Delta (southernmost) portion of Vietnam. Vietnam had four corps areas; the north-most portions of South Vietnam were I Corps, the Central Highlands were II Corps, and the provinces around Saigon were III Corps. A Vietnamese lieutenant general commanded each corps area.

JP-4. The fuel used in helicopters.

KBA. Killed by air. Term for enemy killed by gunships, attack aircraft, or O-1 observation aircraft.

KIA. Killed in action.

"Kilo." The slang term for someone killed in action.

Kilometer. A kilometer is 1,000 meters—the standard measurement on military maps. (A kilometer is equal to .621 of a mile.) A grid square was 1,000 x 1,000 meters. Extended distances were expressed in kilometers; shorter distances were expressed in hundreds of meters.

"Klicks." The slang term for kilometers.

LAPE. Low altitude parachute extraction.

Leeches. Black, parasitic worms about 1½" to 3" long living in waterways. They survived by attaching themselves to a host and sucking its blood.

LOH. Called a "Loach" from the abbreviation for Light Observation Helicopter. See "OH-6 Cayuse helicopter" in this glossary.

Loiter. The ability of an aircraft to stay and support friendly ground forces. Most often, this term was associated with an A-1E Skyraider. Loiter time was a function of the aircraft's fuel capacity/usage.

Lựu đạn. The Vietnamese words for hand grenade.

LZ. Landing zone. A predesignated location stated or shown in the operations order where airmobile troops were to land. Not to be confused with a pickup zone; see "PZ," in this glossary.

M-1 carbine. A lightweight World War II and Korean War .30 caliber weapon that was issued to support troops. It saw early use among ARVN troops.[22]

M-1 Garand rifle. A World War II and Korean War vintage standard U.S. infantryman's rifle. The M-14 replaced the Garand in 1958 in the U.S. Army, and in 1965 in the U.S. Marine Corps. For Vietnamese regular troops, the M-16 replaced the Garand.[23]

M-2 60-mm mortar. The 60-mm mortar is a lightweight indirect fire crew served weapon. In Vietnam, it provided the ability to rapidly engage targets out to nearly two kilometers with a number of different projectiles, including high explosive, white phosphorous, and illumination.[24]

Glossary

M-3 "Grease Gun." An inexpensive and crudely made World War II designed submachine gun. The M-3 fired a .45 caliber round at 350–450 rounds per minute. The later version, the M-3A1 was last produced in the early 1950s and was essentially obsolete from the U.S. inventory during the Vietnam War.[25]

M-7 bayonet. The M-7 bayonet was designed for use with the M-16 rifle.

M-16 rifle. The M-16 was the standard issue combat rifle of the Vietnam War, replacing the M-14. The M-16 was 39.5 inches long, weighed 7.18 pounds fully loaded, and fired a 5.56-mm round. Its maximum rate of fire was 650–850 rounds per minute to a maximum effective range of 460 meters.[26]

M-18 Claymore mine. The Claymore was an antipersonnel mine that could be activated by either a trip wire or by using a manual firing device commonly called a "clacker." Upon detonation of its 24 ounces of C-4 explosives, it sent 700 steel balls to an effective range of 50 meters within a 60-degree arc. All components, wire, electric blasting cap, "clacker," and mine, came packaged in a shoulder-carried bag.[27]

M-18 recoilless rifle. The M-18 is a 57-mm shoulder-fired, anti-tank recoilless rifle that was used by the U.S. Army in World War II and the Korean War. It was capable of firing artillery-type shells with greater accuracy almost entirely without recoil. The M-18 was a breech-loaded, single-shot, man-portable, crew-served weapon that could be used in both anti-tank and antipersonnel roles. It had an effective range of 450 meters. In the Vietnam Delta, along with the M-72 LAW (Light Anti-Tank Weapon) it was used primarily as an anti-bunker weapon.[28]

M-26 hand grenade. This grenade was developed during the Korean War and contained 155 grams (about 5.5 ounces) of Composition B explosive. This and its successor, the M-26A1, were used throughout the Vietnam Conflict and had a casualty radius of about 15 meters.[29]

M-60 machine gun. The M-60 fired a 7.62 × 51-mm round to a maximum effective range of 900 meters (~.6 mile) with a cyclic rate of 600 rounds per minute rate of fire. Designed as a squad support weapon, the M-60 entered service in 1957 and weighed a whopping 23 pounds unloaded. This weapon was affectionately called the "Pig" by U.S. troops due to its weight. A variant of the M-60 machine gun was placed on UH-1 helicopters.[30]

M-61 grenade. The M-61 was an improved variant of the M-26A1 grenade. It had a lethal radius of five meters and a casualty-producing radius of 15 meters.[31]

M-72 LAW. Light Anti-Tank Weapon. The LAW was a one-shot, shoulder-fired, disposable rocket launcher that fired a 66-mm high-explosive anti-tank warhead. The LAW had an effective range of 450 meters and was used in Chuong Thien province as a "bunker buster."[32]

M-79 grenade launcher. A 40 mm single-shot weapon. It was loaded by breaking the breech open, loading a round, and slamming the breech shut. The M-79 had an effective range of 350 meters and fired a variety of rounds: high-explosive, buckshot, smoke, and illumination. With its low muzzle velocity, one could easily watch the round in flight. It was an accurate weapon dependent on the firer's ability to judge distance.³³

M-80. A nonmilitary type of fireworks device whose only function is to make a loud bang.

M-706 armored car. An American armored car designed to be amphibious. It was engineered for the army's military police as an armed convoy escort vehicle. It had a crew of four and carried one or more M-60 machine guns.³⁴

MAAG. Military Assistance Advisory Group. The precursor name for the advisory effort in Vietnam before the establishment of Military Assistance Command Vietnam (MACV) in 1964.

MACV. Military Assistance Command Vietnam. The controlling element for all advisors and the advisory effort in Vietnam starting in 1964.

MACV headquarters. MACV headquarters (Pentagon East) was located on Tan Son Nhut airbase, but one had to exit the terminal portion of the airport to get to it.

MACV patch. The shoulder sleeve insignia worn by MACV advisors to show their assignment to the advisory effort. The MACV patch depicted a white sword protruding upward through a yellow wall symbolic of the Great Wall of China, all on a red background. Designed to symbolize U.S. forces stemming the surge of communism emanating from the North. (In Vietnam, we wore the black and green, subdued version of this patch.)

MACV ration card. This card was issued to personnel in Vietnam. Its purpose was to limit the amount of certain commodities such as beer, liquor, tobacco, etc., someone could purchase—ostensibly to deter black market activities.

Magazine. The proper term for a removable, reusable device that held and fed ammunition into a weapon. Civilians often erroneously call the magazine a clip. An M-16 magazine held 20 or 30 rounds. Also, see "Stripper Clip" in this glossary.

Main force battalion. A battalion in which the VC were full-time guerrilla fighters—not the farmer in the day, VC at night type.

Mark 2 grenade. Commonly called the "pineapple" grenade for its appearance, the Mark 2 was used by U.S. forces from 1918 until into the 1960s (although it had been phased out starting in the 1950s with the adoption of the M-26 grenade).³⁵

MARS. Military Auxiliary Radio System. The military/civilian radio system that enabled military personnel stationed overseas to contact persons living in the United States via telephone.

MAT. Mobile advisory team. A MAT consisted of three to five men, officers and enlisted men. MATs served in some of the most remote areas of the province and spent their time training and assisting the Popular Forces (PF).

MATA. Military Assistance Training Advisor's Course. A six-week course at Fort Bragg, North Carolina, designed to train future advisors for duties in Vietnam.

Maximum ordinate. Maximum ordinate (often shortened to max ord) was the highest point, or apex, reached by a projectile while in flight. The max ord was given out so aircraft, if able to, could fly above any rounds.

Mekong Delta. See "IV Corps."

Mess hall. A military facility that prepares and serves soldiers' meals.

MI. Military Intelligence. The branch in the U.S. Army that specialized in collection and analysis of enemy information and threats.

MIA. Missing in action.

"Mike Boat." Nickname for the LCM-9 (Landing Craft Mechanized), a shallow-draft boat with a crew of 4–6. The Mike Boat could haul 54.4 tons of material and was well suited to the tide-affected rivers of the Delta region.[36]

"Mikes." Slang term for minutes.

Mini-gun. Officially the M-134 for the army was a six-barrel, electrically fired machine gun capable of firing the 7.62 x 51-mm NATO round at a rate of 4,000–6,000 rounds per minute. Mini-guns were used in the UH-1C/D gunships, the LOH, and "Cobra" helicopters. The Air Force used a variant of the M-134 in its "Spooky" and "Puff the Magic Dragon" aircraft.[37]

Monsoon season. Also called the wet or rainy season, the monsoon season occurred during the months of May–October. During monsoon afternoons a sudden heavy, though brief, downpour occurred.

MOS. Military Occupational Specialties. The abbreviation for the code assigned to the various specialties/occupations within the military. For example, MOS 91A10 was the code for a medical specialist.

Motor pool. The designated area for parking and performing maintenance on military vehicles/equipment.

MP. Military police.

MPC. Military payment certificate. The currency used to pay military personnel in Vietnam.

NCO. Non-commissioned officer. An enlisted soldier with the rank of sergeant (E-5) or above.

Negative contact. The term indicating there was no contact with the enemy—visual or exchange of fire.

NSC. National Security Council. The U.S. President's principal forum for considering national security and foreign policy matters with senior advisors and cabinet officials. Its prime function is to advise and assist the President and to coordinate matters of national security among government agencies.

NVA. North Vietnamese Army.

O-1 "Bird Dog." See "Bird Dog" in this glossary.

O-6. A military rank just under a brigadier general or rear admiral. In the air force, army, and Marines, O-6 is a colonel; in the navy and Coast Guard, a captain.

Objective. An identifiable point on the ground that is the focus of the military operation. The purpose of a military operation is to seize the objective and/or destroy an enemy force.

OCS. Officer Candidate School.

OH-6 Cayuse helicopter. A two-person helicopter (one pilot and crewman/passenger) designed for personnel transport, escort, attack missions, and observation. Introduced into the army in 1966, the OH-6 had a maximum speed of 150 miles per hour. When armed, the OH-6 was the observation and "bait" component of a hunter-killer team.[38]

OH-58 Kiowa helicopter. An OH-58 was accepted into army service in May 1969 as a Light Observation Helicopter. In Vietnam, the OH-58 was used as an observation, utility, and training helicopter.[39]

Ông. The Vietnamese word for "mister."

On station. Refers to aircraft being overhead to support a ground operation to engage targets identified by the FACs. Usually used when referring to jets or A-1E Skyraiders being present.

Operational commander. The designated officer who is responsible for all aspects of an operation. The operational commander in Chuong Thien province was always a Vietnamese officer, advised by an American of near-equivalent rank.

Operations officer. An officer whose principal duty was to develop an operation based on the key elements of mission, enemy, terrain, troops, and time available. As the S-3 advisor, the operations advisor worked closely with the ARVN S-3 staff and Intel section to develop operations' orders—the essential basis for conducting a combat operation.

Orderly room. The army name for a unit's administrative building.

Pentagon East. See "MACV headquarters" in this glossary.

PF. Popular Forces. A military force that most often operated at the platoon-level. The PF received limited individual training and less unit collective level training. With exceptions, the Popular Forces were marginally effective, though those advised by the MAT performed better in the field. Often, the PF manned the most remote outpost in the province.

Phoenix program. In concert with U.S. and Vietnamese intelligence agencies, the Phoenix program developed information on, and identified VC and VCI targets for capture, if possible, or elimination if necessary.[40]

Phonetic alphabet. The 26 code words that made up the NATO (North Atlantic Treaty Organization) alphabet. These code words correlated to the 26 letters of the English alphabet. For example, Alpha is A, Bravo is B, etc. The phonetic alphabet facilitated the clear transmission of letters and/or words over military communications means.

Piasters. The currency of the South Vietnamese. One U.S. dollar equaled about 125 piasters. American purchases from Vietnamese merchants were in piasters—not MPC. Also called "Pee."

Platoon leader. Often a second lieutenant who is responsible for the actions and mission accomplishment of the 30–40 members assigned to the platoon. The platoon leader answered to the company commander.

"Pop smoke." The verbal command used to activate a colored smoke grenade to mark one's location for aircraft to see. The protocol was to use a smoke grenade to mark our location for "dustoff" or lift helicopters called "slicks." Once thrown, the pilot would identify a color. If he was correct, we would guide them in for a pickup. (On occasion, the VC would throw a smoke grenade in an attempt to entice a pilot to land in the enemy midst. Hence this procedure of identifying smoke color was extremely important.)

POW. Prisoner of war.

PRC-25 radio. Affectionately called the "Prick 25," this was the primary radio carried in the field by both the advisors and Vietnamese. Weighing about 20 pounds, it had a normal operating range of 3–5 miles. Though it could also be mounted in a vehicle, in Vietnam I only used it in a backpack configuration. Moisture in the handset and limited battery life were its shortcomings.[41]

PRC-77 radio. Though exact in outward appearance to a PRC-25 that it replaced, the PRC-77 operated with transistors rather than vacuum tubes.

Private. The lowest level within the army's enlisted ranks. Privates were usually soldiers who had just entered the army and were pay grade E-1 and E-2.

Private first class. An enlisted soldier within the army at pay grade E-3.

Province. Smaller in size than a U.S. state, a Vietnamese province can be viewed as a political subdivision roughly equivalent to a county within a U.S. state. It did not have a legislative body.

Province engineer advisor. An officer commissioned in the Engineer Corps whose role was to assist Vietnamese military engineers and the civilian Public Works Chief as well as to carry out other assigned engineer duties.

Province Intel Center. The facility in Vi Thanh manned by the Vietnamese and their American advisor counterparts. The Intel center received raw intelligence from multiple sources and analyzed it to assess the enemy's location, disposition, and intentions.

Province reconnaissance company. The Regional Force company that was better trained, equipped, and led than the other RF companies in the province. In Chuong Thien province, this was the 113th RF company. The primary mission of the province recon company was to locate and engage enemy forces.

Province RF/PF advisor. Nominally an army captain, the RF/PF advisor worked under the direction of the S-3 advisor, and his principal duties were to advise and assist in the training of all RF/PF units in the province. Often, the RF/PF advisor accompanied units on combat operations.

PRU. Provincial Reconnaissance Unit. The PRU was an irregular (nonmilitary) force whose primary mission was to capture or eliminate VC and VCI targets identified through the Phoenix program.

PSA. Province senior advisor. The senior American advisor within a province. This person could be either civilian or military, though the majority were military and most were U.S. Army lieutenant colonels. The PSA was responsible for all U.S. advisory efforts in the province, while providing advice and assistance to the Vietnamese province chief.

PSP. Pierced (or perforated) steel planking. PSP is officially called Marston Mat since it was first used near Marston, North Carolina. The airfield at Vi Thanh was not PSP, but rather M8A1 steel matting, which did not have holes but had ribs.[42]

PSYOPS. Psychological operations. (also called psychological warfare). The military application of psychology, especially propaganda, to influence the morale of the enemy in time of war.

PTSD. Post-traumatic stress disorder. A mental health condition in some soldiers (and others) resulting from exposure to terrifying events. PTSD can be triggered by experiencing or witnessing a traumatic or tragic event.

"Puff the Magic Dragon." "Puff" was an AC-130 (a four-engine Hercules airframe) that was armed with mini-guns, 20-mm and 40-mm cannons and a full complement of flares.[43]

***Pun ji* stakes.** Considered "booby traps," *pun ji* stakes were sharpened bamboo stakes designed to inflict casualties. The VC used *pun ji* stakes in pits or moats to impale enemy soldiers; the ARVN sometimes used them as a barrier around ARVN outposts to slow or deter ground assault.

PX. Post exchange.

PZ. Pickup zone. The pickup location for ground troops, normally by helicopter. A smoke grenade marked the PZ.

Quad Cities. The Quad Cities consist of the city of Davenport, Iowa, and the Illinois cities of East Moline, Moline, and Rock Island, all of which are located on the banks of the Mississippi River. For me, Geneseo was close enough to these cities to be included in this catch-all term.

RA. Regular Army. West Point and select ROTC Officers received an RA commission. Others were Reserve Officers. Reserve Officers could request RA commissions, though this was a very selective process.

Radio call sign. A keyword and a number assigned by the Signal Operating Instruction (SOI) to a specific position. The person occupying that position used this designation as their radio call sign when communicating via radio. Radio call signs were used to deceive the enemy (if they were listening) as to the identity of the person(s) talking, and were changed each month unless they were earlier compromised. As example, "Schooner 86" *could* be a call sign.

Radio net. The radio frequency assigned by the SOI. The Operations Order specified the radio frequency to be used by friendly units. Units on the same frequency were on the same radio net.

R&R. Rest and relaxation. R&R gave military personnel a short reprieve from the war. In Vietnam, the military offered both in-country and out-of-country R&Rs.

RC-292 antenna. A man-portable antenna system that was used to increase the range of incoming and outgoing radio transmissions. It took two people to set up the antenna.

"Recon." Slang term for reconnaissance.

Recon by fire. Reconning by fire was a tactic wherein the assaulting forces fire their individual and crew-served weapons at suspected enemy positions for the purpose of keeping the enemy pinned down as the force closes in on them.

RF. Regional Forces. A provincial-level force organized into infantry companies. Better trained than PF forces, the mission of the RF was to take the fight to the enemy.[44]

ROTC. Reserve Officer Training Corps. ROTC was a way a student attending college could receive a commission in a branch of the service by taking special, military-oriented courses and attending summer training.

Rotor wash. The downdraft from a helicopter that blew rice paddy water, rice straw, or other debris into the air.

"Round-eyed women." Slang for non–Asian women.

Route of approach. The assigned direction a unit uses to reach an assigned checkpoint or objective. The operations order map overlay designated the route of approach that guided the direction of friendly units.

RPG. Rocket-propelled grenade. The RPG2 (called a B-40 by the VC) was a Soviet-designed, shoulder-fire, single-shot weapon similar to the American bazooka from World War II and Korea. Though primarily an anti-tank weapon—it carried a 82-mm warhead to a maximum effective range of 100 meters—it was also used against vehicles, bunkers, and personnel. At its optimal range it could penetrate 180 millimeters of armor. In Vietnam's Delta, we faced the RPG2, since the more powerful RPG-7, which had arrived in Vietnam in 1967, had not made its way south yet.[45]

RPM. Revolutions per minute.

RTO. Radio telephone operator.

"Ruff Puffs." A derisive slang term for the RF and PF.

S-1. Personnel. The S-1 was responsible for administrative matters.

S-2. Intelligence. The S-2 collected and analyzed intelligence.

S-3. Operations and Training. The S-3 planned for the conduct of combat operations and training for units.

S-4. Logistics. The S-4 ensured all classes of supplies from beans to bullets to barbed wire were available.

S-5. Civil Affairs. The S-5 planned for and supported civil affairs missions.

Sampan. Small Vietnamese wooden boat propelled by either a person standing in the back of the boat and rowing two oars from an elevated oarlock, or what looked like an oversized lawn mower engine attached to the rear of the boat. This engine was attached to a shaft about 10 feet long, at the end of which was the propeller.

Scrip. Another term for MPC, or the paper money used to U.S. military personnel in Vietnam.

SDO. Staff duty officer.

SEAL. Navy Special Operations forces. The acronym SEAL stands for "SEa, Air, and Land." The SEALs in Chuong Thien province worked primarily with the Provincial Reconnaissance Unit and the Phoenix program to eliminate VC and VCI.

Sergeant. A junior-level U.S. Army noncommissioned officer at pay grade E-5.

Sergeant first class. A career senior U.S. Army noncommissioned officer at pay grade E-7.

Servicemen's Group Life Insurance (SGLI). An insurance program that during my time in Vietnam paid a death benefit of $10,000. It was an optional program that had a monthly premium of $2.00.

"Shotguns." The call sign of U.S. Army aviators who flew the O-1 "Bird Dog" airplane. Their mission was primarily performing reconnaissance and radio relay, directing artillery fires using a Field Artillery Forward Observer flying in the back seat, engaging enemy targets with onboard 2.75" rockets, and air-dropping messages.

Siesta time. Vietnamese soldiers and civilians took a rest of about an hour and a half to two hours after eating lunch, even in the field.

Silver Star. The Silver Star is the third highest U.S. combat award for valor.

SITREP. Situation report. SITREPs enabled the TOC to track the progress of an operation. Each advisor was required to periodically report to the TOC. These reports allowed the TOC to follow and understand the situation on the ground and to quickly marshal resources in the event of trouble. Elements of the SITREP included ground unit location with reference to landing in an LZ, a checkpoint, or objective; enemy contact; friendly casualties—WIAs (called "Whiskeys" from the military phonetic alphabet) or KIAs (called "Kilos" from the military phonetic alphabet); need for MEDEVAC; completion of the operation; and often, safe pickup and departure from the PZ.

SKS Rifle. The SKS (*Samozaryadnyj Karabin sistemy Simonova*) was developed in the Soviet Union as an infantry assault rifle, chambered the same round as the AK-47, and was its precursor in the Soviet-bloc nations. Many communist countries manufactured the SKS as well as the AK-47.[46]

"Slicks." A slang term for a troop transport UH-1 "Huey" helicopter.

Smoke grenade. Officially designated the M-18 smoke grenade, it weighed 19 ounces. Once activated ("popped"), the M-18 was a signaling device to help locate and identify troops on the ground. The grenade, shaped similarly to a soda can, was painted olive drab, and when activated, emitted red, green, yellow, or violet smoke.[47]

SOI. Signal operating instructions. The SOI assigned the frequencies a unit was to use and a call sign for each necessary unit positions. It also provided challenge and passwords and shackle codes for encoding grid coordinates.

SOP. Standing operating procedure. SOPs were established military procedures known and followed by those assigned to the unit or organization.

Specialist five. A U.S. Army non–NCO enlisted rank assigned to a technical specialist, pay grade E-5.

Specialist four. The U.S. Army's lowest level of technical specialist, pay grade E-4.

"Spooky." The call sign of a U.S. Air Force AC-47, which was an armed version of a C-47 (a militarized DC-3). It mounted GAU-2. A 7.62-mm mini-guns and carried flares.[48]

Squad leader. The noncommissioned officer (staff sergeant or sergeant) in charge of leading a squad of about 8–10 men. The squad leader was accountable to the platoon sergeant and platoon leader.

Staff sergeant. A mid-level U.S. Army noncommissioned officer, pay grade E-6.

"Steel pot." A slang term for a steel helmet.

"Straphangers." A derisive slang term used to identify individuals who accompanied a more senior officer to observe an action, often one in which they had little input or effort.

Stripper clip. A disposal metal strip that contained 10 (M-16) rounds. Received from the ammunition manufacturer in a bandolier, there were two clips to a cardboard box, and seven cardboard boxes to a bandolier (140 rounds). See also "Magazine" in this glossary.

Strobe light. An intense hand-held blinking light designed to attract attention during hours of darkness from overhead aircraft. A strobe light helped locate and identify friendly ground troops.

"Swing ship." A helicopter that provided daily transportation for administrative and logistical support within the province. It took personnel, supplies, mail or whatever to the district advisory teams and, occasionally, to the MATs. The helicopter usually started and ended at Vi Thanh with stops at the five distant district team locations.

TA-312. A tactical telephone used by the army in field locations. The TA-312 connected directly to a switchboard or another phone by WD-1 (commo wire) and operated on two D-cell batteries.

TAC. Tactical officer. The acronym TAC stands for "Train, Advise, and Counsel." TACs were ever present during my 23 weeks in OCS.

Tangle foot barriers. Extensive barbed wire barriers strung low to the ground whose purpose was to slow and disrupt ground access to an ARVN installation or outpost.

TDA. Table of distribution and allowances. The document that authorizes positions, ranks, and equipment to nontactical (these were generally *ad hoc*–type) units.[49]

Tet. Vietnamese New Year, the most important celebration in Vietnamese culture. The word is a shortened form of *Tết Nguyên Đán,* which is Sino-Vietnamese for "Feast of the First Morning of the First Day."

Thiếu tá. Vietnamese Army officer rank equivalent to a U.S. Army major.

Thiếu úy. Vietnamese Army officer rank equivalent to a U.S. Army second lieutenant.

Thompson .45. A .45 caliber World WII and Korean War submachine gun that was issued to squad leaders, patrol leaders, and certain officers to provide more firepower for a combat platoon. By the time I arrived in Vietnam, the gun was no longer in use, so I never saw a Thompson.[50]

TO&E. Table of organization and equipment. The document that authorizes positions, ranks, and equipment in tactical units.[51]

TOC. Tactical operations center. The TOC followed all combat operations and monitored activities within the province. Within the TOC there was extensive 24-hour-a-day coordination between the Vietnamese and U.S. assets in, or passing through, the province.

TOC NCO. The noncommissioned Officer(s) whose principal duty was to staff the tactical operations center during the day.

Tracer. A bullet that when fired leaves a luminous trail that can be followed by the eye. The purpose of the tracer was to see the trajectory of the bullet with reference to the target. Friendly weapons (U.S. and ARVN) fired red tracers; Soviet-bloc weapons fired green tracers.

Travis Air Force Base, California. One of two Pacific Coast airbases (the other was McCord AFB, Washington). At Travis AFB individual replacements departed for and returned from Vietnam.

Trinh Sát. Literally translated as "reconnaissance." Members of this RF unit were better, trained, better led, and more aggressive than those of most other RF companies.

Trung sĩ. The Vietnamese noncommissioned officer rank equivalent to a U.S. Army sergeant.

Trung sĩ nhất. The Vietnamese noncommissioned officer rank equivalent to a U.S. Army sergeant first class.

Trung úy. The Vietnamese Army officer rank equivalent to a U.S. Army first lieutenant.

UH-1. The workhorse helicopter of the Vietnam War, the "Huey" entered service in 1960 and served as a transport, gunship, command and control, and medical evacuation helicopter. As a transport (lift) helicopter, with its crew of four, it could carry about 10–12 Vietnamese troops and had a maximum speed of 135 miles per hour.[52]

USAID. United States Agency for International Development.

VC. Viet Cong. Communist insurgents whose purpose was to subvert democracy in South Vietnam through military actions and civilian indoctrination. Their goal was a socialist country. Also called Victory "Charlie" or just "Charlie."

VCI. Viet Cong infrastructure. Communist political leaders whose primary functions were to propagandize, recruit, tax, and administer villages and hamlets under VC control.

Viet Minh. A nationalist movement which originated to force the French to leave Vietnam (North and South). Hijacked by the communists after 1954, the Viet Minh morphed into the VC.[53]

Vietnamization. The Nixon administration plan to end U.S. involvement in the Vietnam War through a policy of "enlarging, equipping and training the forces of US ally South Vietnam to fight the forces of Communist North Vietnam. At the same time, the policy continuously reduced the number of US troops in Vietnam."[54]

VNAF. Vietnamese Air Force.

"Walk in the sun." A slang term for an operation that encountered no enemy activities. The phrase was coined from the only successful activity of the day, exercise and enjoying the weather.

Warrant officer. Specialized military officers—most often pilots, though warrant officers performed duties in supply, administration, and many other areas requiring highly technical skills.

WD-1. Communications ("commo") wire.

"Whiskey." Slang term for a soldier wounded in action (WIA).

WIA. Wounded in action.

Winning the hearts and minds. A phrase coined by President Lyndon Johnson, who declared that "ultimate victory [in Vietnam] will depend upon the hearts and the minds of the [Vietnamese] people who actually live out there." This philosophy guided civilian and military advisors who understood that improving socio-economic and political conditions in Vietnam was equally as important in defeating communism as winning the war on the battlefields in Vietnam.[55]

"The World." A slang term that referred to being back in the United States.

WP. White phosphorus. Also called Willie Pete or Willie Pee. An explosive projectile (artillery, grenade, or rocket) that produces flames and heat in temperatures up to 5,000 degrees. Used primarily as an agent for marking targets.[56]

Chapter Notes

Chapter 1

1. OCS is a program the army used (and continues to use) to commission eligible enlisted soldiers to become second lieutenants. In 1968 Engineer OCS was a rigorous 23 weeks of physical, mental, and academic challenges with an attrition rate of around 40 percent. OCS was one of the three most commonly used commissioning methods, the others being ROTC (Reserve Officer Training Corps) and West Point. For me, I began OCS on March 11, 1968, and was commissioned on August 30, 1968.

2. The acronym TAC stands for "train, advise, and counsel." During OCS, I thought it meant "taunt, abuse, and crush," or the actions of someone whose purpose was to scream at and make life miserable for all officer candidates.

3. Verbiage taken from author's DA Form 71.

4. Technically, the Quad Cities consisted of the city of Davenport, Iowa, and the Illinois cities of East Moline, Moline, and Rock Island, all of which are located on the banks of the Mississippi River. For me, Geneseo was close enough to these cities to be included in the catch-all term.

5. Since a young age, I listened nearly nonstop to a radio. From "How Much Is That Doggie in the Window?" to the Beatles, I appreciated music.

6. Lieutenant Lee was killed in action (KIA) in Vietnam on April 17, 1969, while serving as an infantry platoon leader with the 9th Infantry Division. He was posthumously awarded the Silver Star, Bronze Star with Valor device, Purple Heart, and the Combat Infantryman's Badge.

7. Actually, I was a pretty good shot, having hunted on the farm most of my younger years. I qualified as an expert with the M-14 and attribute my poor performance with the .45 to using a pistol that had probably first seen service in World War I.

8. Due to the prioritization of troops to Vietnam and Germany at the time, my platoon and company had only about 60 percent of their authorized manpower levels.

9. Military Occupational Specialty Code 2162.

10. Note, this acronym typically connotes regular force soldiers and units. I use it generically to mean any South Vietnamese military members.

11. It was certainly a lot heavier than the one that Vic Morrow (who played Sergeant Saunders on the TV show *Combat*) seemed to wield so easily.

Chapter 2

1. I was worried that the flight attendant had approached me to tell me that the airlines had discovered the Colt .25 automatic pistol I had buried deep within my duffel bag. Thankfully, this was not the case.

2. I believe most Vietnam veterans will remember their first and lingering smells of Vietnam.

3. MACV Headquarters (Pentagon East) was actually located on Tan Son Nhut airbase, but one had to exit the terminal portion of the airport to get to it.

4. Advisory Team 73 (August 1968 to March 1973) was the successor to Advisor Team 58 (May 1964 to August 1968),

which descended from MAAG (Military Assistance Advisory Group). MAAG was replaced by MACV in 1964.

5. Chuong Thien is pronounced "Chewung Tin".

6. Medical evacuation helicopters/crews were called "dustoffs." This moniker came from the call sign of the helicopters, for example, "Dustoff 82," which was the call sign of the MEDEVAC helicopter flown by CW2 Robert W. Aberle from Peoria, Illinois. Throughout this book, I use the terms "MEDEVAC" and "dustoff" interchangeably to describe the medical evacuation helicopter/crew/process.

7. Vi Thanh is pronounced "Vee Tahn."

Chapter 3

1. Pierced steel planking is most commonly called PSP. Officially, it is called Marston Mat, because it was first used near Marston, North Carolina. The airfield at Vi Thanh was not PSP, but rather M8A1 steel matting, which did not have holes but ribs. For ease and clarity, I will call all airfield steel matting PSP. "Marston Mat." Updated 10 June 2021. en.wikipedia.org/wiki/Marston_Mat. Accessed 21 August 2021.

2. An orderly room is the Army name for a company's administrative buildings.

3. The U-Minh was also called the Forest of Darkness.

4. There was no real border between these two provinces, just a line on a map that bisected the U-Minh Forest.

5. Lieutenant James N. Rowe was captured by the VC and spent most of his five-plus years as an American POW in the U-Minh forest. He was rescued in late December 1968, and initially debriefed in Ca Mau in neighboring An Xuyen province. Olson, James S., ed. *In Country: The Illustrated Encyclopedia of the Vietnam War*. Sources: James H. Rowe, *Five Years to Freedom*. 1971; and Contemporary Authors, 1st rev., vols. 37–40, 1979, pp. 469–471; *U.S. Veteran Dispatch*, 1985. Metro Books. 2008. p. 501.

6. Smaller in size than a U.S. state, a Vietnamese province can be viewed as a political subdivision roughly equivalent to a county within a U.S. state. It did not have a legislative body.

7. The Viet Cong and NVA resented and never accepted the legitimacy of Chuong Thien province. With the fall of Saigon and thus South Vietnam in April 1975, the victors immediately renamed Chuong Thien to Hau Giang province. It has been subsequently further divided between Can Tho and Hau Giang provinces.

8. The province senior advisor was responsible for the preparation of the HES with input provided by district senior advisors, CORDS (Civil Operations and Revolutionary Development Support) personnel, and Vietnamese military and civilian authorities. The monthly HES was a 77-question, multiple-choice statement completed on each hamlet within the province. Then, quarterly, an 88-question multiple-choice statement was prepared for the province. The province senior advisor sent the completed raw data HES assessment up the advisory chain of command for compilation and analysis at headquarters, MACV. The resulting classified HES report was made available to U.S. headquarters, including MACV, the Pentagon, the embassy, in our case DMAC, and the province Senior Advisor. "Hamlet Evaluation System." *Civil Operations and Rural Development Support Research and Analysis Directorate*. MACV Document Number DAR R70–79, CM-018 Command Manual. 1 September 1971. National Archives. archives.gov/files/research/military/vietnam-war/rg-472-hes-command-manual.pdf. Accessed 20 August 2021.

9. Demographic, economic, topographic, climatic, agricultural, and statistical information for Chuong Thien province in this chapter was gleaned from an unattributed and undated report written at the direction of the province senior advisor in late 1971. "Chuong Thien Province-IV Corps-Briefing." Texas Tech University's The Vietnam Center and Sam Johnson Vietnam Archive. Updated 4 September 2018. Document Number 1071717011, in the Glenn Helm Collection. wa.vietnam.ttu.edu/images.php?img=/images/107/1071717011.pdf. Accessed 5 August 2021.

10. The term "government" used herein means the elected South Vietnamese government. Also called GVN.

11. Called VCI or VC Infrastructure.
12. Within the province and distinct from Advisory Team 73 was a small element from Advisory Team 51. The approximate half dozen advisors from Team 51 were assigned as tactical advisors to the 2nd Battalion, 31st Regiment of the ARVN 21st Division located in Vi Thanh. For the most part, these advisors lived with their Vietnamese counterparts, though on occasion, they would eat in our mess hall.
13. Vi Thanh sat on the banks of the *Kinh Xa Nõ* canal, which emptied into the *Sông Cai Tu Long* river.
14. Made of PSP but without the fancy terminal as at Vi Thanh.
15. Midway through my tour, the army promoted Harvey to captain.
16. Reserve Officer Training Corps, ROTC, was a way a student attending college could receive a commission in a branch of the service by taking special military-oriented courses and attending summer training.
17. After his delayed commissioning due to his attendance at law school, Lieutenant Weiner attended the U.S. Army Infantry School at Fort Benning, Georgia, and later the Military Intelligence School at Fort Holabird, Maryland. Officers wishing to be "branched" in military intelligence were required to attend a combat arms basic course before receiving their training in the MI branch. This requirement was either recognition of the attrition rate in the MI course, or, perhaps, an incentive to do well in the MI course.
18. Every MI officer I met in Vietnam wore something other than MI insignia on their collar. MI officers presented a lucrative target for kidnapping and exploitation or elimination by the VC. Therefore, MI officers attempted to conceal their true purpose in Vietnam.
19. The *Chiêu hoi* ("Open Arms") program and was a propaganda program designed to have VC and North Vietnamese soldiers desert and come to the side of South Vietnam. *Chiêu hoi* leaflets were spread throughout the Vietnamese countryside and promised safe conduct to anyone carrying the leaflet when surrendering to GVN forces. Olson, James S., ed. *In Country: The Illustrated Encyclopedia of the Vietnam War*. Sources: Frances FitzGerald, *Fire in the Lake*: The *Vietnamese and the Americans in Vietnam*. Little, Brown.1972; Tran Dinh Tho, *Pacification*. 1979; and Andrew Krepinevich, Jr. *The Army and Vietnam*. 1986. Metro Books. 2008. p. 125.
20. Army lieutenant colonels were often just called colonels in the same sense first and second lieutenants were just called lieutenants and enlisted grades E-5 to E-9 were referred to as sergeants.
21. During his first tour in Vietnam, Colonel LeVasseur was the S-3 Advisor on Advisory Team 58 (the predecessor to Advisory Team 73) stationed in Vi Thanh.
22. In Chuong Thien province indirect fire was mostly mortar and recoilless rifles rounds, but later it also included 122-mm rockets.
23. I have a picture of me standing on my hooch doorsteps where the unpainted repair job from this recoilless rifle round is visible. On this repair, I drew a skull and crossbones with the intent to ward others away.
24. The military called these events "hale and farewell."
25. The likely cause of this was Advisory Team 73 was at the far end of the supply chain, and the better main entrées didn't make it that far down the supply channels.
26. On one occasion, several Vietnamese children (12 years or younger) placed and lit some leftover artillery propellant charges near the compound chain-link fence. These charges did not explode, but rather burned intensely. The guards chased off those children.
27. Date Estimated Return from Over Seas. This term was associated with the date 365 days from the time one arrived in Vietnam. DEROS was the date a military member was to return to the U.S. Knowing this date fostered the pervasive obsession of counting days until DEROS.
28. The CORDS compound was where the civilian advisors, mostly United States Agency for International Development (USAID) personnel, lived. It was right across the street from the southwest corner of the MACV compound.

Chapter 4

1. As I consider this thought about taking a camera to Vietnam, I realize the

first part of this statement was only partially true. Forty-plus years after my time in Vietnam, former teammates were gracious enough to share some of their pictures with me.

2. This may have been a common remedy for an ingrown toenail, but it was one I had never heard of before. Nonetheless, I was impressed with SFC Ramirez's empathy and the simple solution.

3. Ironically, Harvey Weiner told me that intelligence reports in 1970 indicated a high incidence of North Vietnamese Army (NVA) troops in the province contracting malaria.

4. The M-16 was the standard-issue combat rifle of the Vietnam War, replacing the M-14. The M-16 was 39.5 inches long, weighed 7.18 pounds fully loaded, and fired a 5.56-mm round. Its maximum rate of fire was 650–850 rounds per minute to a maximum effective range of 460 meters. Owen, J.I. H., ed., *Brassey's Infantry Weapons of the World*; compiled by: Gerald Wyndham, Stanley Parr, James Dowdall, and John Marriott; Advisory eds., Major S.R. Elliott CD and R.H. F. Cox TD; Bonanza Books; 1978; New York. pp. 77–78.

5. This was despite M-16 "qualification" orders I received at Fort Bliss. I had seen a demonstration of the M-16 in OCS, but before Vietnam I had only qualified with the M-14 rifle, both in basic training and OCS. My issue weapon at Fort Hood while in the engineer company was a .45 caliber pistol.

6. Obtaining a battlefield zero was the procedure through which an M-16 rifle was fired and subsequently adjusted for windage and elevation ("sited-in") on a special 25-meter target. Zeroing a weapon gave a soldier the highest probability of hitting a target at 250 meters. Department of the Army. *Field Manual 23–9, M-16A1 Rifle Marksmanship*. June 1974.

7. "History of Tables of Distribution and Allowances (TDA) Units." *U.S. Army Center of Military History*. Prepared by DAMH-FPO. 30 May 1995. history.army.mil/html/forcestruc/tda-ip.html. Accessed 21 August 2021.

8. The staff positions of S-1 to S-4 are first found at the battalion-level. The S-1 was responsible for administrative matters. The S-2 collected and analyzed intelligence. The S-3 planned for the conduct of combat operations and training for units. The S-4 ensured that all classes of supplies from beans to bullets to barbed wire were available. The S-5 planned for and supported civil affairs missions.

9. Combat arms soldiers were those serving in the armor, field artillery, or infantry branches.

10. During my time in Chuong Thien, all MACV personnel killed in action there were members of a MAT. MAT 54 lost three of our four teammates KIA during my 10½ month tour of duty.

11. The O-1 was a fixed-wing Cessna 305 slightly modified for military use. The aircraft was often referred to as a "Bird Dog." First produced in 1947, the aircraft was used in the Korean conflict designated as the L-19. The L-19 was re-designated O-1 in 1962 and carried a pilot and one passenger, normally an artillery spotter. The O-1 had a maximum speed of 115 mph, and usually flew at 1500 feet in Vietnam. It was armed with three or four rocket tubes under each wing that could fire 2.75 inches high explosives (HE), white phosphorus (WP also called Willie Peter), or smoke rockets. In Chuong Thien, O-1 pilots often provided invaluable tactical assessment, field artillery adjustment, and radio relay capability. "Cessna O-1 Bird Dog." Updated 8 July 2021. en.wikipedia.org/wiki/Cessna_O-1_Bird_Dog. Accessed 20 August 2021. Armament information from George "Jug" Eastman.

12. One of the compound's Cambodian security guards was nicknamed "*Beaucoup* Kilo," owing to his extra-large stature.

13. The TOC was on a Vietnamese compound about three blocks from the MACV compound and was the nerve center for the province. The TOC followed all combat operations and monitored activities within the province. Within the TOC there was extensive 24-hour-a-day coordination between the Vietnamese and U.S. assets in or passing through the province.

Chapter 5

1. Regular army as opposed to reserve commissioned officer. West Point and

select ROTC Officers received an RA commission. Others, such as myself, were reserve officers. Reserve officers could request RA commissions, though this was a very selective process.

2. Most of us wore a much better-looking Vietnam-produced baseball cap.

3. "Pop smoke" was the command to activate a colored smoke grenade to mark one's location for aircraft to see. The protocol was to use a smoke grenade to mark our location for "dustoff" or lift helicopters called "slicks." Once the grenade was thrown, the pilot would identify a color. If he was correct, we would guide them in for a pickup. (On occasion, the VC would throw a smoke grenade in an attempt to entice a pilot to land in the enemy midst. Hence this procedure of identifying smoke color was extremely important.)

4. Advisor Team 73 worked with combat forces consisting of Regional Forces (RF) and Popular Forces (PF). While both the RF and PF were assets of the province chief (the senior Vietnamese officer in the province, usually the equivalent of a U.S. Army colonel), the RF were better manned, trained, and equipped. RF and PF were sometimes derisively called "Ruff-Puffs," a term I personally despised and never used.

5. The role of the S-5, in concert with Vietnamese local governmental officials, was to initiate and coordinate projects beneficial to civilian, private, and public agencies in the province. These activities included building/repairing schools, providing assistance to orphanages, and ensuring the populace heard of the good things their government was doing for them.

6. I called this siesta time. Siestas, to me, were a troubling practice in Vietnam. Vietnamese soldiers and civilians took about an hour-and-a-half to two-hour rest after eating lunch, even when in the field.

7. The PRU was an irregular (nonmilitary) force whose primary mission was to capture or eliminate VC and VCI targets identified through the Phoenix Program.

Chapter 6

1. While the Mekong Delta region was flat, atmospheric conditions often affected radio communications; hence the need for a radio relay This radio relay was especially necessary if the "Shotguns" or FACs were not in the air and/or the operation was a great distance from the TOC.

2. A café only in the most rudimentary sense of the word. It was a hooch with several chairs and a small table that had an overhead thatched roof and sunshade.

3. The RC-292 antenna was a man-portable antenna system that was used to increase the range of incoming and outgoing radio transmissions. It took two people to set up the antenna. The PRC-25 radio, affectionately called the "Prick 25," was the primary radio carried in the field by both the advisors and Vietnamese. Weighing about 20 pounds, it had a normal operating range of 3–5 miles. Though it could also be mounted in a vehicle, in Vietnam I only used it in a backpack configuration. Moisture in the handset and limited battery life were its shortcomings. "AN/PRC-25 and AN/PRC-77 Backpack Radio." *Olive-Drab*. n.d. olive-drab.com/od_electronics_anprc25.php. Accessed 20 August 2021.

4. The RPG2 (called a B-40 by the VC) was a Soviet-designed, shoulder-fired, single-shot weapon similar to the American bazooka from World War II and Korea. Though primarily an anti-tank weapon, it carried an 82-mm warhead to a maximum effective range of 100 meters and was also used against vehicles, bunkers, and personnel. At its optimal range it could penetrate 180 millimeters of armor. In Vietnam's Delta, we faced the RPG2, since the more powerful RPG-7, which arrived in Vietnam 1967, had not made its way south yet. Owen, J.I. H., ed., *Brassey's Infantry Weapons of the World*; compiled by: Gerald Wyndham, Stanley Parr, James Dowdall, and John Marriott; advisory eds., Major S.R. Elliott CD and R.H. F. Cox TD; Bonanza Books; 1978; New York. pp. 175–76.

5. Craig Breedlove was born in 1937. In 1965, he established a land speed record of 600.6 miles per hour in his specially designed *Spirit of America–Sonic I*. Wilkinson, Sylvia. "Breedlove, Craig." *World Book Encyclopedia*. World Book Inc. 1991. p. 603.

6. FM 5–34 was the engineers' bible. It was designed to be easily carried in one's

cargo pocket and contained instructions on most every task an engineer soldier could encounter. It was extensively used/taught during OCS.

7. The "swing ship" was a helicopter that provided daily transportation for administrative and logistical support within the province. It took personnel, supplies, mail, or whatever to the district advisory teams and, occasionally, to the MATs. The helicopter usually started and ended at Vi Thanh with stops at the five distant district team locations.

8. "Battle of Kien Long." *Wikipedia*. Updated 4 July 2021. en.wikipedia.org/wiki/Battle_of_Kien_Long. Accessed 20 August 2021.

9. The U.S. WIA were mostly aircrews supporting the ARVN.

10. During my time in Chuong Thien province, I visited all district teams. The facilities of the other district teams were similar to those at Kien Long. I was especially impressed with the liquefied petroleum (LP) refrigerators at the team houses, as I had never seen these before.

11. I noticed the Vietnamese practiced that age-old male game of drinking alcohol with a stranger (aka an American advisor) for the purpose of seeing who got sick or drunk first.

Chapter 7

1. The command element typically consisted of the operation's ground commander, the RTOs (to enable contact with higher and subordinate organizations), a Vietnamese medic, and the American advisors.

2. As standard practice, the American advisors accompanying a Vietnamese unit *always* had immediate access to their own radio set to a separate advisor channel.

3. Accompanying gunships would fire rockets, mini guns, machine guns, or grenade launchers (whatever configuration they possessed) into the tree lines surrounding the rice paddies where we landed. The purpose was to kill or suppress any enemy hiding therein, and was a routine, or in military parlance, standing operating procedure (SOP).

4. Reconning by fire was a tactic wherein the assaulting forces fire their individual and crew-served weapons at suspected enemy positions for the purpose of keeping the enemy pinned down as the force closes in on them.

5. Vietnamese sampans were either propelled by a person standing in the back of the boat and rowing two oars from an elevated oarlock or by what looked like an oversized lawn mower engine attached to the rear of the boat. This engine was attached to a shaft about 10 feet long, at the end of which was the propeller. Either propulsion method was interesting to watch.

6. On operations, we always carried several smoke grenades affixed to the straps of the PRC-25 radio.

7. The Vietnamese rank of *Trung úy* was two brass "pips" roughly resembling two rose pedals.

8. Unless compromised earlier, each month the team was issued a new signal operating instruction (SOI). The SOI assigned the frequencies the team was to use and a call sign to each of the advisory team positions. It also provided challenge and passwords and shackle codes for encoding grid coordinates.

9. Leeches were black parasitic worms about 1½" to 3" long living in waterways. They survived by attaching themselves to a host and sucking its blood.

Chapter 8

1. For example, an Intel assessment of A-1 meant the information came from an American source and was highly reliable. The lower a numeric value, the less reliable the information.

2. Olson, James S., ed. *In Country: The Illustrated Encyclopedia of the Vietnam War.* Sources: David Halberstam, *Ho.* 1971; Charles Fenn, *Ho Chi Minh: A Biographical Introduction.* 1973; Stanley Karnow, *Vietnam: A History*, 1983; and William J, Duiker, *Ho, A Biography*, 2002. Metro Books 2008. pp. 256–57.

3. This was my first exposure to the siren and an incoming mortar attack. You can actually hear the "thuunk" of mortar rounds leaving the mortar tube due to their relative short range. The max range of an 82-mm mortar was about 3,000 meters. With its high arch-like trajectory,

an 82-mm mortar round can take 25–40 seconds to reach its target. The 82-mm mortar was of Soviet design and was used throughout Vietnam. The 82-mm mortar fired a round which contained about 6.5 pounds of high explosives to a range of around 3,000 meters. Owen, J.I. H., ed., *Brassey's Infantry Weapons of the World*; compiled by: Gerald Wyndham, Stanley Parr, James Dowdall, and John Marriott; advisory eds., Major S.R. Elliott CD and R.H.F. Cox TD; Bonanza Books; 1978; New York. pp. 132–33.

4. I always tied my bandolier around the M-16 barrel each evening.

5. It was team policy that there be two Americans accompanying the ARVN. This was in the event that if something happened to one of them, then the other could manage the situation.

6. The military occupational specialty (MOS) for a trained infantryman was 11B10.

7. A blocking position was established to prevent enemy troops from escaping converging forces. It was set up on the most likely avenue of enemy exfiltration.

8. Assigned to the Duc Long district team.

9. "Klicks" was the slang word used to denote kilometers. A kilometer was 1,000 meters (1,093.6 yards) or .62 miles, and all U.S. military map distances during the Vietnam conflict were measured using the metric system.

10. As taught by Captain McCullough, when I air-assaulted into an LZ, I always carried the radio until the time there appeared to be no imminent enemy threat.

11. SITREPs enabled the TOC to track the progress of an operation. Each advisor was required to periodically report to the TOC. These reports allowed the TOC to follow and understand the situation on the ground and to quickly marshal resources in the event of trouble. Elements of the SITREP included ground unit location with reference to landing in an LZ; a checkpoint, or objective; enemy contact; friendly casualties—WIAs or KIAs (called "Whiskeys" or "Kilos," respectively, from the military phonetic alphabet); need for MEDEVAC; completion of the operation; and, often, safe pickup and departure from the PZ.

12. Olson, James S., ed. *In Country:* *The Illustrated Encyclopedia of the Vietnam War*. Source: Nguyen Dinh Tho Nam. *Hoa Hao Buddhism in the Course of Vietnamese History*. 2004. Metro Books. 2008. pp. 253–54.

13. This was a Dexedrine tablet, an amphetamine derivative. This was the first and only time I used these tablets.

14. I called this siesta time. Siestas, to me, were a troubling practice in Vietnam. Vietnamese soldiers and civilians took a rest after eating lunch of an hour and a half or two hours, even in the field.

15. Pilots (army and USAF) were restricted on the number of flying hours they could accumulate in a day. On occasions when the unit(s) they were supporting were under heavy contact, these restrictions were conveniently worked around.

16. When communicating time in Vietnam, minutes were called "Mikes," from the military phonetic alphabet,

17. On this mission, I did not confirm coordinates with the pilot since the C&C had established the LZ. I really didn't know where we were to be inserted, only that I was to "charge to the sound of the distant guns."

18. The AK-47 was the Soviet-bloc standard infantryman's automatic weapon used extensively by the NVA and VC Main Force units. This very rugged rifle fired a 7.62 x 39-mm round to an effective range of 400 meters at a rate of 600 rounds per minute. Owen, op. cit., pp. 69–70.

19. I later learned that a VC sniper repeatedly shot at Lieutenant Carlile throughout the day, hitting him numerous times.

20. A main force battalion was one where the VC were full-time guerrilla fighters—not the farmer by day, VC by night type.

21. To me these enemy casualty numbers were pure fiction. The VC waited until the ARVN were totally exposed in the rice paddies about 200–300 meters from their well-constructed bunkers to open fire. It was hard for me to believe there were any enemy casualties inflicted by the ground forces. I believe any VC casualties could have only resulted from the large number of artillery rounds fired, close air support, and rocket fire from the

observation aircraft. Though the reinforced ground forces later occupied the VC positions and saw blood trails, they found no bodies.

22. It was a common practice for the VC to target radios and RTOs. Radio antennae indicated the location of the unit commander and advisor. The VC's correct logic was that if they eliminated radio communications, they could prevent air or artillery support, and degrade a commander's ability to effectively maneuver his unit.

23. These 7.62 x 39-mm bullets were fired from the AK-47 and SKS rifles as well as the RPD light machine gun.

Chapter 9

1. Actually, each province had an AIK fund to manage, although the funding amounts may have been different.

2. "Income in 1969 of Families and Persons in the United States, Report Number P60–75." *U.S. Census Bureau*, December 14, 1970, Revised April 9, 2018. census.gov/library/publications/1970/demo/p60–75.html#:~:text=The%20median%20income%20of%20all,median%20income%20of%20about%20%248%2C600. Accessed 16 August 2021.

3. If I ate every meal in the mess hall, it would have consumed my basic allowance for subsistence. I never had more than two meals a day in the mess hall.

4. Their cigarettes had a picture of a tiger on the pack, so we called them Tiger cigarettes. They were strong, similar to U.S. Camel cigarettes.

5. The official exchange rate was that $1.00 equaled about 125 piasters. Therefore, the 200 piasters I paid for laundry and cleaning services amounted to about $1.60 per week.

6. The Vietnamese word *Cô* was equivalent to the English word "Miss," meaning a young unmarried woman.

7. The term CARE package was taken from the international humanitarian agency whose acronym was CARE. 1950s/1960s commercials encouraged Americans to donate money so CARE could send foodstuffs to needy countries. Our CARE packages came from our families back in the States, since in Vietnam we were the ones in need.

8. One advantage of being in Vietnam was that we did not have to use postage stamps on our letters. We simply wrote "free" in the upper right corner of our letter. Also, regarding mail, it took on average 10 days for a letter to travel from Vietnam to the U.S., or vice versa.

9. "Round eyed women" meant non-Asian women and was never meant as a pejorative term.

10. I was surprised that the inside pages of *Time* and *Newsweek* magazines were printed on heavy newspaper stock; not the smooth shiny paper we were used to in the U.S.

11. "Eugene Fenton Smallwood, Lieutenant Colonel, United States Army." *Arlington National Cemetery.* Updated 30 July 30, 2006. arlingtoncemetery.net/efsmallwood.htm. Accessed 20 August 2021.

12. The song "San Francisco" was another tearjerker, since San Francisco and specifically nearby Travis Air Force Base was a common departure and return point for many personnel going to or returning from Vietnam.

13. Yes, we adopted this siesta practice on the MACV compound because our counterparts were unavailable.

14. George Hamilton (b. 1939) was a popular movie star of the late 1950s and beyond. His nickname was "Tan Man" due to his deep year-round tan. "George Hamilton (actor)." *Wikipedia:.* Updated 12 August 2021. en.wikipedia.org/wiki/George_Hamilton_(actor). Accessed 21 August 2021.

15. "Charlie" was the shortened name for the VC. This was taken from the military phonetic alphabet where Victor stood for the letter "V," and Charlie stood for the letter "C."

16. Maximum ordinate (often shortened to max ord) was the highest point (apogee) reached by the projectile while in flight. Said differently, max ord was the apex of the round's trajectory and was given out so aircraft, if able, could fly above any rounds.

17. These moats were excavated during the construction process to provide material for the outpost walls.

18. The maximum range for the

Vietnamese artillery with their M-101A1, 105-mm howitzer was 11,000 meters (11 kilometers). Most outposts were built within range of a supporting artillery unit. Stanton, Shelby L., Captain U.S. Army, Retired; *Vietnam Order of Battle A Complete Illustrated Reference to U.S. Combat and Support Forces in Vietnam 1961–1973;* Foreword by General William C. Westmoreland, U.S. Army, Retired; Stackpole Books; 2003; Mechanicsburg, PA; p. 278.

19. "Spooky" was the call sign of a U.S. Air Force AC-47, which was an armed version of a C-47 (a militarized DC-3). It mounted GAU-2.A 7.62-mm mini-guns and carried flares. Another USAF gunship was "Puff the Magic Dragon." "Puff" was an AC-130 (a four-engine Hercules airframe) that was armed with mini-guns, 20-mm and 40-mm cannons, and a complement of flares. Olson, James S., ed. *In Country: The Illustrated Encyclopedia of the Vietnam War.* Sources: Jack S. Ballard. *The United States Air Force in Southeast Asia: Development and Employment of Fixed Wing Gunships 1962–1972.* 1982 and Kevin J. Fitzpatrick, *Flying Gunships.* 2000. Metro Books. 2008 pp. 18–20.

20. I say making an appearance since there was nothing in my training or background that prepared me for public works activities. Plus, Mr. Son was a well-educated and competent engineer.

21. Although during the Tet 1968 Offensive (January–April 1968) the VC occupied portions of Saigon. The offensive included occupying portions of the city and carrying out a brazen attack on the U.S. embassy. Olson. op. cit., Sources: Don Oberdorfer, *Tet! The Turning Point.* 1983; Robert Pisor, *The End of the, Line: The Siege of the Khe Sanh.* 1982; and Pham Van Son and Le Van Duong, eds., *The Viet Cong Tet Offensive 1968.* 1969. Metro Books. 2008. pp. 556–58.

Chapter 10

1. The Mauser was not a weapon issued to Vietnamese militia organizations through U.S. sources. Most were believed to be those captured by the Russians from the Germans during World War II and later supplied to communist insurgents. Throughout my tour, we often found pictures on detained individuals, on dead VC, or inside hooches of VC posing with Soviet-bloc weapons. In the same way we Americans would have a picture taken of us standing in front of our cars, the VC had pictures of themselves holding weapons.

2. These "taxed"/confiscated items were used to feed and supply local VC in the area.

3. I do not know what the acronym RPAC stands for; this is just what we called them.

4. The CH-47 had a cruising speed of about 150 mph. Olson, James S., ed. *In Country: The Illustrated Encyclopedia of the Vietnam War.* Source: *Jane's All the World's Aircraft, 1963–64.* 1964. Metro Books. 2008 pp. 119–20.

5. Det cord was the slang term for detonation cord, an explosive in the form of ¼-inch-diameter white explosive-laden plastic rope that was used to connect explosives together. It could also be used as an explosive by itself when wrapped around an object.

6. Abbreviated from "communication wire."

7. This was a tributary of the *Sông Cai Lớn* river.

8. This "clacker" produced an electrical surge that detonated the blasting cap, which in turn detonated the explosives. I had to use a "clacker," since I did not have an electric detonator. I later learned I could use a PRC-25 battery for this purpose.

9. This was the same road I used when we launched the September 6 operation, and it was within several hundred meters of where the artillery was set up that day.

10. As with U.S. NCOs, unless specified, I will refer to all Vietnamese grades of sergeant as *Trung sĩ*.

11. *Sea Hunt* was a popular TV program during the late 1950s and early 1960s starring Lloyd Bridges.

12. During our demolition class in OCS, we were instructed to yell "Fire in the hole" three times as a warning that we were about to set off an explosive charge. Before I set off a charge, I either yelled this verbal warning or fired a weapon three times to get everyone's attention.

13. I would take a Claymore mine as my source for an explosive chain. Within the device's canvas bag were its necessary components: the mine, with its internal C-4 explosives (which I would access by removing the front cover and prying out the explosive); 100 feet of wire; blasting cap; and "clacker."

14. The unexploded mortar round was on the far side of the canal that separated the MACV compound from the Vietnamese province headquarters building. The round was nearly completely buried in the Vi Thanh to Duc Long road, with only its fins showing. It was less than 100 meters from the MACV compound main gate.

Chapter 11

1. "Fragging" was when a disgruntled soldier attempted or succeeded in killing a perceived abusive officer or NCO, often by throwing a fragmentation grenade into their sleeping quarters. Toward the later years of U.S. involvement in the Vietnam War, incidents of "fragging" grew in number.

2. Yes, there were female Vietnamese soldiers, but they served primarily in administrative and medical roles or in those specialties with extensive public contact.

3. Later in my tour, the soldiers replaced the recoilless rifle with the M-72 LAW (Light Anti-tank Weapon).

4. Not quite, since the rifles were about 48 inches long, but it was still humorous. However, the Civilian Irregular Defense Group (CIDG), a village militia organization, still possessed these weapons and often had younger, sometime preteen boys and women in its ranks.

5. Defoliation was used to kill vegetation in presumed VC areas to prevent its use as cover by the enemy. The Vietnamese identified the areas for spraying with defoliant and initiated defoliation requests. These requests went through both Vietnamese and U.S. channels; the latter required the translated version. If approved, the U.S. Air Force would fly the actual missions under the operational name of "Ranch Hand." Post-Vietnam, the U.S. government determined Agent Orange was a carcinogen and human exposure to Agent Orange could result in death and/or serious health issues, including birth defects. Olson, James S., ed. *In Country: The Illustrated Encyclopedia of the Vietnam War.* Sources: J. B Neilands, *Harvest of Death: Chemical Warfare in Vietnam and Cambodia*, 1972; William A. Buckingham, Jr., *Operation Ranch Hand: The United States Air Force and Herbicides in Southeast Asia, 1967–1971*, 1982; Fred A. Wilcox, *Waiting for an Army to Die: The Tragedy of Agent Orange*, 1983; and Philip James Griffith, *Agent Orange: Collateral Damage in Vietnam*, 2003. Metro Books. 2008. pp. 162–63.

6. Since the vast majority of Vietnamese did not have the ability to refrigerate anything due to lack or limited availability of electricity, beer was served with ice.

7. The members of this unit wore a tab embroidered *Trinh Sát* (similar in shape, but not qualifications, to an Army Ranger tab) on their shoulder. This tab and their burgundy-colored, yellow-fringed scarf set them off from other soldiers.

8. Pilots always wanted to know if it was a "hot" (receiving enemy fire) PZ. If it was a hot PZ, I would give them the type of fire we were encountering and a compass approach heading so they could avoid flying over the enemy.

9. "Dustoff" pilots carried a calling card that was very much like a modern-day business card. I took their use of these cards to be evidence of their pride in accomplishing their dangerous mission.

Chapter 12

1. Most often the C&C was a UH-1 helicopter that had an added radio console. The advisor and Vietnamese controller used these radios to communicate with their respective advisor/unit and the TOC.

2. We would give our location relative to checkpoints or objectives which were designated on all operations map overlays. When giving a grid coordinate location, we always assumed the enemy was listening. For MEDEVACs, or LZ pickups we either encoded our location or gave a four-digit (grid square) coordinate since by popping smoke; the helicopter crew could easily spot us from the air.

3. From the SOI, signal operating instructions.
4. "Lima" was the phonetic alphabet word for the letter "L"; "Charlie" was the phonetic alphabet word for the letter "C." In our parlance "Lima Charlie" meant loud and clear.
5. A wing waggle was when a pilot rocked his wings repeatedly up and down, almost like waving to a person.

Chapter 13

1. The AH-1 "Cobra" was a sleek and fast helicopter designed solely as an attack helicopter. It was armed with a 40-mm grenade launcher, a mini-gun, and rockets (later TOW anti-tank missiles). It had a two-man crew, a pilot and gunner. "Cobras" first arrived in Vietnam in late 1967. Meeks, Tom. "AH-1G "Cobra" Gunship." *Centaurs in Vietnam.* n.d. centaursinvietnam.org/History/ihistoryEqAir5.html. Accessed 21 August 2021.
2. To stand down meant to cease all offensive operations. Here I should mention that irrespective of the day of the week, we on Advisory Team 73 performed all assigned and required duties: TOC, operations, recon flights, etc.

Chapter 14

1. A mechanical ambush was constructed by taking Claymore mines and/or expedient items: Hand grenades, tin cans, clothespins, batteries, plastic spoons, blasting caps, trip wires, etc., and configuring them in a way to explode and inflict enemy casualties. Once constructed, the device was placed primarily around ARVN outposts, thereby fortifying the barrier around the outpost.
2. Dependent on the travel time to the selected R&R destination.
3. The military had regular R&R flights to Hawaii; Sidney, Australia; Hong Kong; Bangkok, Thailand; Kuala Lumpur, Malaysia; Manila, Philippines; Singapore; Taipei, Taiwan; and Tokyo, Japan.
4. Not being the adventurous type and preferring to save money, I only took one R&R.
5. Bar girls frequented places where GIs went during their off-duty hours and were often just called B-girls. They would solicit Americans to buy them overpriced and often alcohol-free drinks that they called "Wikkey Coke." This term was a bastardization of the term "whiskey Coke."
6. Soviet-bloc weapons, which the VC possessed, used green tracers while American weapons fired red tracers.
7. Cholon was a large commercial district within Saigon that was mostly inhabited by ethnic Chinese. Cho Lon was the site of the Thu Pho Racetrack-the site of an extended battle during Tet in 1968.
8. In Vietnam, most Americans referred to being back in the "world" as being back in the USA.
9. Sadly, within a year after getting home from Vietnam, I outgrew all of this well-made wardrobe.

Chapter 15

1. I later learned this well-built bunker took a direct hit from a 122-mm rocket in May 1971 with no serious damage to the structure or those inside.
2. Breaking down the payroll meant dividing the amount received from the Finance Office into the exact amount to be paid to each soldier. All soldiers were paid in military payment certificates, or MPCs. Needless to say, there was no room for error as the Class A agent had to show the soldier their pay voucher entitlement and count out the amount being paid in front of the soldier.

Chapter 16

1. After SFC Bill Haley left at the end of his tour, there was no "regular" NCO available to go on operations. As such, NCOs were assigned to accompany me on operations. This was the case on this day when Staff Sergeant Tolson, the riverboat advisor, went on this land operation. The bad part of this policy was I established no rapport with and had no idea of the tactical competence of the NCO I was given.
2. Rube Goldberg (1883–1970) was a cartoonist best known for the inventions of his main character, which solved a simple task in the most overcomplicated, inefficient, and inane way possible. "Who

Was Rube Goldberg?" *Rube Goldberg: The World of Hilarious Invention.* https://www.rubegoldberg.com/rube-the-artist/. Accessed August 25, 2021.

3. Jesse Owens was a sprinter and gold medal winner in the 1936 Berlin Olympics. Ronkov, Richard. "Owens, Jesse (1913–1980)." *World Book Encyclopedia.* World Book Inc. 1991. pp. 890–91.

4. Throughout my tour, the majority of VC casualties I encountered were KBAs.

5. "Close air support" was the technical term for engagement of enemy targets in the vicinity of friendly troops primarily by high-performance aircraft. It could be argued that *any* air support, whether fixed wing or helicopter gunships, could be called close air support.

6. In 1970, with the preponderance of U.S. troops north of the Delta, high-performance aircraft seldom loitered in our area. The aircraft were stationed in Saigon or Binh Long, and, at the quickest, they were a half an hour away.

7. On an occasion or two, we had "Cobras," AH-1s.

8. Since all operations were planned by the ARVN, the province chief approved the LZ location as being in enemy-occupied areas. As such, movement in and around the LZ was considered hostile and gunships were free to engage.

9. Officially designated the M-5 armament subsystem, this weapon was affectionately called "Frog" by its crew due to its appearance on the nose of the "Huey."

10. The U.S. called them .51 caliber machine guns. The Soviets, who also manufactured these weapons, called them a 12.7 x 108-mm DShK 38/46 heavy machine gun. The .51 caliber machine gun had a rate of fire of 540–600 rounds per minute and an effective anti-aircraft range of 1,000 meters. It was a formidable weapon that, in the hands of a skilled gunner, could easily shoot down a helicopter. Owen, J.I. H., ed., *Brassey's Infantry Weapons of the World*; compiled by: Gerald Wyndham, Stanley Parr, James Dowdall, and John Marriott; advisory eds., Major S.R. Elliott CD and R.H. F. Cox TD; Bonanza Books; 1978; New York. pp. 116–17.

11. I never took a siesta in the field but had gotten quite used to taking one while I was on the compound.

12. My concern was that a crew chief manning a machine gun or the accompanying gunships might mistake him for a VC or just use him for target practice.

13. An OH-58 was accepted into army service in May 1969 as a light observation helicopter. in Vietnam, the OH-58 was used as an observation, utility, and training helicopter. "Bell OH-58 Kiowa." *Vietnam Combat Aviation Resource Guide.* Warbirds Resource Group. n.d. vietnam. warbirdsresourcegroup.org/oh58kiowa.html. Accessed 21 August 2021.

14. John Paul Vann, a retired army lieutenant colonel, was the deputy for Civil Operations and Rural Development Support CORDS IV and commander of all civilian and military advisors in the Delta Military Assistance Command. This was a general officer equivalent command. Vann served in his capacity in IV Corps from November 1968 to May 1971. He was killed in a helicopter (OH-58) crash in Kon Tum province, II Corps Tactical Zone on June 9, 1972. Olson, James S., ed. *In Country: The Illustrated Encyclopedia of the Vietnam War.* Neil Sheehan. *A Bright and Shining Lie: John Paul Vann and America in Vietnam.* 1988. Metro Books. 2008. pp. 590–91.

Chapter 17

1. *Hồi chánh*s were extensively interrogated by the GVN for actionable intelligence and to determine their motives/reliability. If deemed to be "genuine," some were integrated in ARVN units. There were instances when the *Hồi chánh*s turned out to be double agents.

2. It is possible the weapons cache was a ruse to get ARVN and U.S. personnel to travel this particular route with the mine there in waiting.

Chapter 18

1. The VC were notorious for setting up *pun ji* pits.

2. "Monthly Summary January 1970." *Texas Tech University's The Vietnam Center and Sam Johnson Vietnam Archive.* MACV Office of Information. Document Number 7390206001 in the John M. Shaw Collection. Updated 23 February 2005.

vva.vietnam.ttu.edu/images.php?img=/ images/739/7390206001a.pdf. Accessed 22 August 2021.

3. A popular Peter, Paul and Mary song released in 1963.

4. A hunter-killer team was a light observation helicopter (OH-6), called a "Loach" (from the abbreviation for LOH) or Flying Egg, and two helicopter gunships—either UH-1B/C or "Cobras" (AH-1). The Loach would usually fly low in attempt to draw enemy fire. If the enemy fired at the Loach, the Loach pilot would throw a smoke grenade to mark the area from which the fire came, and the gunships would swoop in and eliminate the threat. Being the "bait" made life for the Loach pilot very dangerous. Porter, Donald. "In Vietnam, These Helicopter Scouts Saw Combat Up Close." *Air Space Magazine*, September 2017. www.airspacemag.com/military-aviation/snakes-loaches-180964341/. Accessed 21 August 2021.

5. In fact, the Vietnamese often sank their sampans, filling them with water when not in use. This was to prevent them from floating away and kept the wood from drying out.

Chapter 19

1. These were rats who foraged in the rice paddies—not garbage or urban rats. In fact, rats tasted good, similar to the squirrels I had hunted and eaten as a teen.

2. I did not like snake because it was too tough and did not have much taste.

3. Fish were often obtained by throwing a hand grenade into the canal or river, and soldiers jumping in and grabbing the stunned fish by hand. This method sure beat the impatience I felt with a fishing pole in my younger years.

4. We shared canteens among the advisors and the Vietnamese as necessary.

5. In Vietnam, when your host or a senior person placed something in your rice bowl, it was impolite not to eat it.

6. Harry Blackstone Sr. (1885–1965) was a magician and USO entertainer. His son, Harry Blackstone, Jr. (1934–1997), was also an accomplished magician. "Harry Blackstone Sr." *Wikipedia..*

Updated 2 July 2021. en.wikipedia.org/wiki/Harry_Blackstone_Sr. Accessed August 21, 2021.

7. At a team reunion many years later, I learned the barber was a VC agent.

8. Through the 1970s, Fort Leonard Wood was the home of the Army's Engineer School for enlisted soldiers and was located near Waynesville, Missouri.

Chapter 20

1. In Vi Thanh the CQ was a duty-roster appointed NCO whose responsibility was to answer the phone in the orderly room, report serious incidents to the proper person, wake people up as required, sound the alarm in the event of ground or indirect fire attack, and, periodically, check the compound perimeter.

2. An Eagle Flight was a night airmobile operation that inserted troops to relieve a besieged outpost; or on other occasions (based on highly reliable intelligence reports) to engage the enemy or interdict his movement. Olson, James S., ed. *In Country: The Illustrated Encyclopedia of the Vietnam War*. Sources: John S. Bowman, ed., *The Vietnam War Almanac*. 1985; and Shelby L. Stanton, *The Green Berets at War*. 1985. Metro Books. 2008. p. 176.

3. This operation showed the effectiveness and elusiveness of the VC. On that particular day, they made a successful attack, overran an outpost, took prisoners, weapons, and equipment, and then seemed to vanish into thin air.

4. This was formerly the 29th Evacuation Hospital, where Lieutenant Carlile was initially taken. The army redesignated it as the 3rd Surgical Hospital in October 1969. Stanton, Shelby L., Captain U.S. Army, Retired; *Vietnam Order of Battle: A Complete Illustrated Reference to U.S. Combat and Support Forces in Vietnam 1961–1973;* Foreword by General William C. Westmoreland, U.S. Army, Retired; Stackpole Books; 2003; Mechanicsburg, PA; pp. 214–15.

5. In fairness, I will surmise the hospital staff was trying to determine what treatment(s) I needed.

6. Bill lived on a farm a quarter of a mile from me, and we had been best

friends as far back as I could remember. We attended church together, hung around together, and I worked for both his grandfather and father as a teenager.

Chapter 21

1. A C-130 is a four-turboprop engine, primarily cargo aircraft. It entered the U.S. Air Force inventory in 1956 and, with a crew of five, it was designed to carry 92 passengers or 40,000+ pounds of cargo over extended ranges. One of its variants was the AC-130 gunship-call sign "Puff the Magic Dragon." "C-130 Hercules." *U.S. Air Force.* 20 June 2018. af.mil/About-Us/Fact-Sheets/Display/Article/1555054/c-130-hercules/. Accessed 19 August 2021.
2. This method was technically called LAPE, for low-altitude parachute extraction.
3. I think Bob Noonan and Harvey Weiner may have been there as well.
4. The senior enlisted man (Grade E-8) on Advisory Team 73 who was responsible for the welfare of enlisted soldiers and for advising the PSA on enlisted matters/concerns.
5. The SKS (*Samozaryadnyj Karabin sistemy Simonova, 1945*) was developed in the Soviet Union as an infantry assault rifle, chambered the same round as the AK-47, and was its precursor in the Soviet-bloc nations. Many communist countries manufactured the SKS as well as the AK-47. *Trung úy* An got this weapon from a friend of his after the Cambodian invasion and gave it to me. The weapon was in pristine condition and was still packed in Cosmoline. I intended to register this weapon and legally bring this home with me. As it turned out, I was unable to complete the process before my departure. Owen, J.I. H., ed., *Brassey's Infantry Weapons of the World*; compiled by: Gerald Wyndham, Stanley Parr, James Dowdall, and John Marriott; advisory eds., Major S.R. Elliott CD and R.H. F. Cox TD; Bonanza Books; 1978; New York. p. 69.
6. Calls were scheduled with the knowledge that a 5:00 p.m. call in Vietnam was 5:00 a.m. CST (the same day) in the Midwest.
7. I would always think of Lily Tomlin's character Ernestine on the then-popular TV program *Laugh-In.*

Chapter 22

1. The M-79 was a 40-mm single-shot weapon. It was loaded by breaking the breech open, loading a round, and slamming the breech shut. The M-79 had an effective range of 350 meters and fired a variety of rounds: High explosive, buckshot, smoke, and illumination. With its low muzzle velocity, one could easily watch the round in flight. It was an accurate weapon dependent on the firer's ability to judge distance. Owen, J.I. H., ed., *Brassey's Infantry Weapons of the World*; compiled by: Gerald Wyndham, Stanley Parr, James Dowdall, and John Marriott; advisory eds., Major S.R. Elliott CD and R.H. F. Cox TD; Bonanza Books; 1978; New York. p. 236.
2. The NVA had a different and distinctive dialect. The language difference between the North and South Vietnamese was similar to, for example, someone speaking with a Boston accent being distinguishable from someone speaking with a deep Southern accent.
3. We considered the NVA more disciplined and better equipped and trained than their VC cousins. VC, perhaps, still held a slight edge in motivation, and certainly in terrain/area familiarization.
4. Lieutenant Nickinovich ended his tour of duty with a Silver Star, two Bronze Stars for Valor, and the Vietnamese Cross of Gallantry. To the best of my knowledge, only one other member of Team 73 received higher recognition for bravery. Sergeant First Class Edward McGinnis was awarded the Army Distinguished Service Cross, the nation's second highest award for bravery, for his actions in Kien Hung District on February 10–11, 1969.

Chapter 23

1. I later learned my five-year-old brother, Don, had been playing with the .22 caliber pistol I left in my home for protection. He accidentally shot my nephew,

Davie, in the chest and his condition was serious. Given the nature of this event, the police were conducting an investigation that amplified everyone's fears. As it turned out, Davie, after a lengthy hospital stay, made a full recovery and the incident was ruled an accident.

2. Due to the suddenness of my departure, I only brought home a few pictures of VC and their activities, a Ho Chi Minh mourning patch, two authentic VC flags (one of which was made from a sack that had the faded image of the "shaking hands" from a U.S. Aid shipment of rice. It had been dyed red and blue), the silk picture of Ho Chi Minh that *Trung úy* An had given me, and some French and VC money.

Epilogue

1. This may be something as simple as someone walking up behind me and beginning to talk or my hearing a sharp noise.

2. I mean this in the sense that as a child I was afraid of the dark or afraid of my father's wrath when I had not completed all my chores or misbehaved. This to me was fear, and I felt none of this in Vietnam.

3. O'Neill, John E. and Jerome R. Corsi. *Unfit for Duty: Swift Boat Veterans Speak Out Against John Kerry*. Regnery Publishing. 2004.

4. U.S. Congress, Senate, "Mr. John Kerry Testimony at Hearings before the Committee on Foreign Relations," *United States Senate, 92nd Cong.*, 1st sess., 22 April 1971, Washington, DC: Government Printing Office, 1971. lschs.org/cfhttp.cfm?script=extensions/includes/resource/resourcecontent.cfm&pageid=608&rid=271. Accessed 23 August 2021.

5. Officers were ineligible for award of the Good Conduct Medal-only enlisted soldiers.

6. LT is the proper army abbreviation for "lieutenant."

7. Tom Hargrove was a graduate of Texas A&M and was the Agricultural Advisor in Chuong Thien province during the same time I was there. He was instrumental in the introduction of IR8 rice into the province. Tom spent a career in rice production and later ended up in Colombia, where he was captured in 1994 by the FARC (Revolutionary Armed Forces of Colombia) and held captive for 11 months. His capture was the basis of the 2000 movie *Proof of Life*.

8. In his book, Tom wrote about my Long My to Vi Thanh sniper incident, though he misspelled my name.

Those in This Book

1. Many other captains received the same recommendation not to seek such extensions. As the Vietnam War was winding down, the army was downsizing, shedding officers and junior enlisted men. Essentially, those officers without a college degree, often commissioned through OCS, were among the first invited to leave the army or relinquish their commission and continue serving in an enlisted status.

2. Active Guard Reserve is a program begun in the late 1970s and is where a National Guard or reservist soldier works full-time for his component service while serving on active duty. This is under Title 32 USC for the Army and Air National Guard, which means the soldier is subject to the orders of the state adjutant general, but must meet all active duty educational and physical fitness standards.

Glossary

1. Owen, J.I. H., ed., *Brassey's Infantry Weapons of the World*; compiled by: Gerald Wyndham, Stanley Parr, James Dowdall, and John Marriott; advisory eds., Major S.R. Elliott CD and R.H. F. Cox TD; Bonanza Books; 1978; New York. pp. 20–21.

2. Owen, op. cit., pp. 117–18.

3. Owen, op. cit., p. 153.

4. Owen, op. cit., pp. 132–33.

5. "A1-E Skyraider." *Wikipedia*. Updated 19 August 2021. en.wikipedia.org/wiki/Douglas_A-1_Skyraider. Accessed 23 August 2021.

6. Meeks, Tom. "AH-1G "Cobra" Gunship." *Centaurs in Vietnam*. n.d. centaursinvietnam.org/History/ihistoryEqAir5.html. Accessed 21 August 2021.

7. Owen, op. cit., pp. 69–70.
8. Owen, op. cit., pp. 73–74.
9. Department of the Army. *Field Manual 23-9, M-16A1 Rifle Marksmanship.* June 1974.
10. "Cessna O-1 Bird Dog." *Wikipedia.* 8 July 2021. en.wikipedia.org/wiki/Cessna _O-1_Bird_Dog. Accessed 20 August 2021.
11. "deHavilland C-7 Caribou." *Vietnam Combat Aviation Resource Guide. Warbirds Resource Group.* n.d. vietnam. warbirdsresourcegroup.org/c7caribou-specifcations.html. Accessed 21 August 2021.
12. Hildreth, Tom. "C-123 Provider." *The Aviation Zone.* n.d. theaviationzone. com/factsheets/c123_specs.asp. Accessed 21 August 2021.
13. "C-130 Hercules." *U.S. Air Force.* 20 June 2018. af.mil/About-Us/Fact-Sheets/Display/Article/1555054/c-130-hercules/. Accessed 19 August 2021.
14. Olson, James S., ed. *In Country: The Illustrated Encyclopedia of the Vietnam War.* Sources: Victor L. Oliver, *Cao Dai Spiritualism: A Study of Religion in Vietnamese Society,* 1976; Denis Warner, *The Last Confucian,* 1963; and Bernard Fall, *The Political Religious Sects of Vietnam, Pacific Affairs,* 28 (1965):235–253; caodai.org/pages/?pageID=1. Metro Books. 2008. pp. 112–13.
15. "Boeing CH-47 Chinook." *Wikipedia.* Updated 24 August 2021, en.wikipedia.org/wiki/Boeing_CH-47_Chinook. Accessed 24 August 2021.
16. Olson, James S., ed. *In Country: The Illustrated Encyclopedia of the Vietnam War.* Sources: Frances FitzGerald, *Fire in the Lake: The Vietnamese and the Americans in Vietnam.* 1972: Tran Dinh Tho, *Pacification.* 1979; Andrew Krepinevich, Jr. *The Army and Vietnam.* 1986. Metro Books. 2008. p 125.
17. "Civil Guard (Regional Forces)." GlobalSecurity.org. n.d. globalsecurity. org/military/world/vietnam/rvn-civil-guard.htm. Accessed 21 August 2021.
18. Olson, James S., ed. *In Country: The Illustrated Encyclopedia of the Vietnam War.* Sources: John S. Bowman, ed., *The Vietnam War Almanac.* 1985; and Shelby L. Stanton, *The Green Berets at War.* 1985. Metro Books. 2008. p. 176.
19. "McDonnell Douglas F-4 Phantom II." *Vietnam Combat Aviation Resource Guide. Warbirds Resource Group.* n.d. vietnam.warbirdsresourcegroup.org/ f4phantom-specifcations.html. Accessed 21 August 2021.
20. "Hamlet Evaluation System." *Civil Operations and Rural Development Support Research and Analysis Directorate.* MACV Document Number DAR R70–79, CM-018 Command Manual. 1 September 1971. National Archives. archives.gov/ files/research/military/vietnam-war/rg-472-hes-command-manual.pdf. Accessed 20 August 2021.
21. Porter, Donald. "In Vietnam, These Helicopter Scouts Saw Combat Up Close." *Air Space Magazine,* September 2017. <https://www.airspacemag.com/military-aviation/snakes-loaches-180964341/>. Accessed August 21, 2021.
22. Owen, op. cit., pp. 75–76.
23. Owen, op. cit., p. 74.
24. Owen, op. cit., pp. 137–38.
25. Owen, op. cit., p. 44.
26. Owen, op. cit., pp. 77–78.
27. "M18 Claymore mine." *Wikipedia.* Updated 14 August 2021. en.wikipedia. org/wiki/M18_Claymore_mine. Accessed 25 August 2021.
28. Owen, op. cit., p. 185.
29. Owen, op. cit., p. 227.
30. Owen, op. cit., pp. 111–12.
31. "M-61 Fragmentation Grenade." *U.S. Grenades WW II and After.* 12 April 2021. inert-ord.net/usa03a/usa3/m61/ index.html. Accessed 23 August 2021.
32. Owen, op. cit., pp. 186–87.
33. Owen, op. cit. p. 236.
34. Stanton, Shelby L., Captain U.S. Army, Retired; *Vietnam Order of Battle A Complete Illustrated Reference to U.S. Combat and Support Forces in Vietnam 1961–1973;* Foreword by General William C. Westmoreland, U.S. Army, Retired; Stackpole Books. 2003. Mechanicsburg, PA; p. 224–15.
35. "Mk 2 Grenade." *Wikipedia.* Updated 31 July 2021. en.wikipedia.org/ wiki/Mk_2_grenade. Accessed 21 August 2021.
36. "LCM-8." *Wikipedia.* Updated 2 August 2021. en.wikipedia.org/wiki/ LCM-8#:~:text=The%20LCM%2D8%20 (%22Mike,Vietnam%20War%20 and%20subsequent%20operations.&text=The%20acronym%20stands%20for%20

%22Landing,%22Lima%20Charlie%20 Mike%22. Accessed 21 August 2021.
37. "M134 GAU-17 Gatling Gun." Military.com. n.d. military.com/equipment/m134-gau-17-gatling-gun. Accessed 21 August 2021.
38. "Hughes OH-6 Cayuse." *Wikipedia*. Updated 23 August 2021. en.wikipedia.org/wiki/Hughes_OH-6_Cayuse. Accessed 23 August 2021.
39. "Bell OH-58 Kiowa." *Vietnam Combat Aviation Resource Guide*. Warbirds Resource Group. n.d. vietnam.warbirdsresourcegroup.org/oh58kiowa.html. Accessed 21 August 2021.
40. Olson, James S., ed. *In Country: The Illustrated Encyclopedia of the Vietnam War*. Sources: John Prados, *Presidents' Secret Wars: CIA and Pentagon Covert Operations Since World War II*, 1986; Douglas Valentine, *The Phoenix Program*, 2000; John L. Cook, *The Advisor: The Phoenix Program in Vietnam*, 2000; and Stuart Herrington, *Stalking the Viet Cong. Inside Operation Phoenix: A Personal Account*, 2004. www.thememoryhole.org/phoenix/. Metro Books. 2008. pp. 461–62.
41. "AN/PRC-25 and AN/PRC-77 Backpack Radio." *Olive-Drab*. n.d. olive-drab.com/od_electronics_anprc25.php. Accessed 20 August 2021.
42. "Marston Mat." *Wikipedia*. Updated 10 June 2021. en.wikipedia.org/wiki/Marston_Mat. Accessed 21 August 2021.
43. Olson, James S., ed. *In Country: The Illustrated Encyclopedia of the Vietnam War*. Sources: Jack S. Ballard. *The United States Air Force in Southeast Asia: Development and Employment of Fixed Wing Gunships 1962-1972*. 1982 and Kevin J. Fitzpatrick, *Flying Gunships*. 2000. Metro Books. 2008 pp. 18–20.
44. "Civil Guard (Regional Forces)." *GlobalSecurity.org*. n.d. globalsecurity.org/military/world/vietnam/rvn-civil-guard.htm. Accessed 21 August 2021.
45. Owen, op. cit., pp. 175–76.

46. Owen, op. cit., p. 69.
47. "M18 smoke grenade." *Wikipedia*. Updated 26 July 2021. en.wikipedia.org/wiki/M18_smoke_grenade. Accessed 25 August 2021.
48. Olson, James S., ed. *In Country: The Illustrated Encyclopedia of the Vietnam War*. Sources: Jack S. Ballard. *The United States Air Force in Southeast Asia: Development and Employment of Fixed Wing Gunships 1962-1972*. 1982 and Kevin J. Fitzpatrick, *Flying Gunships*. 2000. Metro Books. 2008. pp. 18–20.
49. "History of Tables of Distribution and Allowances (TDA) Units." *U.S. Army Center of Military History*. Prepared by DAMH-FPO. 30 May 1995. history.army.mil/html/forcestruc/tda-ip.html. Accessed 21 August 2021.
50. Owen, op. cit., pp. 43–44.
51. U.S. Army Center of Military History. op. cit.
52. Olson, James S., ed. *In Country: The Illustrated Encyclopedia of the Vietnam War*. Source: *Jane's All the World's Aircraft, 1970-1971*, 1971; *Jane's All the World's Aircraft, 1985-1986*, 1986. Metro Books. 2008. pp. 284–86.
53. Olson, James S., ed. *In Country: The Illustrated Encyclopedia of the Vietnam War*. Source: William J. Duiker. *The Communist Road to Power in Vietnam*, 1981. Metro Books. 2008. p. 596.
54. Dunham, Will. "Ex-Pentagon Chief Laird Dies, Advocated 'Vietnamization' Policy." 16 November 2016. reuters.com/article/us-people-melvinlaird/ex-pentagon-chief-laird-dies-advocated-vietnamization-policy-idUSKBN13B2YU. Accessed 25 August 2021.
55. "Hearts and Minds." *Wikipedia*. Updated 28 July 2021. en.wikipedia.org/wiki/Hearts_and_Minds_(Vietnam_War). Accessed 21 August 2021.
56. "White Phosphorus Munitions." *Wikipedia*. Updated 15 July 2021. en.wikipedia.org/wiki/White_phosphorus_munitions. Accessed 21 August 2021.

Works Cited

"A1-E Skyraider." *Wikipedia.* Updated 19 August 2021. en.wikipedia.org/wiki/Douglas_A-1_Skyraider. Accessed 23 August 2021.
"AN/PRC-25 and AN/PRC-77 Backpack Radio." *Olive-Drab.* n. d. olive-drab.com/od_electronics_anprc25.php. Accessed 20 August 2021.
"Battle of Kien Long." *Wikipedia.* Updated 4 July 2021. en.wikipedia.org/wiki/Battle_of_Kien_Long. Accessed 20 August 2021.
"Bell OH-58 Kiowa." *Vietnam Combat Aviation Resource Guide.* Warbirds Resource Group. n.d. vietnam.warbirdsresourcegroup.org/oh58kiowa.html. Accessed 21 August 2021.
"Boeing CH-47 Chinook." *Wikipedia.* Updated 24 August 2021, en.wikipedia.org/wiki/Boeing_CH-47_Chinook. Accessed 24 August 2021.
"C-130 Hercules." *US Air Force.* 20 June 20, 2018. af.mil/About-Us/Fact-Sheets/Display/Article/1555054/c-130-hercules/. Accessed 19 August 2021.
"Cessna O-1 Bird Dog." *Wikipedia.* Updated 8 July 2021. en.wikipedia.org/wiki/Cessna_O-1_Bird_Dog. Accessed 20 August 2021.
"Chuong Thien Province-IV Corps-Briefing." Texas Tech University's The Vietnam Center and Sam Johnson Vietnam Archive. Updated 4 September 2018. Document Number 1071717011, in the Glenn Helm Collection. wa.vietnam.ttu.edu/images.php?img=/images/107/1071717011.pdf. Accessed 5 August 2021.
"Civil Guard (Regional Forces)." GlobalSecurity.org. n.d. globalsecurity.org/military/world/vietnam/rvn-civil-guard.htm. Accessed 21 August 2021.
"deHavilland C-7 Caribou." *Vietnam Combat Aviation Resource Guide.* Warbirds Resource Group. n.d. vietnam.warbirdsresourcegroup.org/c7caribou-specifcations.html. Accessed 21 August 2021.
Department of the Army. *Field Manual 23–9, M-16A1 Rifle Marksmanship.* June 1974.
Dunham, Will. "Ex-Pentagon Chief Laird Dies, Advocated "Vietnamization' Policy." 16 November 2016. reuters.com/article/us-people-melvinlaird/ex-pentagon-chief-laird-dies-advocated-vietnamization-policy-idUSKBN13B2YU. Accessed 25 August 2021.
"Eugene Fenton Smallwood, Lieutenant Colonel, United States Army." Arlington National Cemetery. Updated 30 July 2006. arlingtoncemetery.net/efsmallwood.htm. Accessed 20 August 2021.
"George Hamilton (actor)." *Wikipedia.* Updated 12 August 2021. en.wikipedia.org/wiki/George_Hamilton_(actor). Accessed 21 August 2021.
"Hamlet Evaluation System." *Civil Operations and Rural Development Support Research and Analysis Directorate.* MACV Document Number DAR R70–79, CM-018 Command Manual. 1 September 1971. National Archives. archives.gov/files/research/military/vietnam-war/rg-472-hes-command-manual.pdf. Accessed 20 August 2021.
"Harry Blackstone, Sr." *Wikipedia.* Updated 2 July 2021; en.wikipedia.org/wiki/Harry_Blackstone_Sr. Accessed 21 August 2021.
"Hearts and Minds." *Wikipedia.* Updated 28 July 2021. en.wikipedia.org/wiki/Hearts_and_Minds_(Vietnam_War). Accessed 21 August 2021.

Works Cited

Hildreth, Tom. "Fairchild C-123 Provider." *The Aviation Zone.* n.d. theaviationzone.com/factsheets/c123_specs.asp. Accessed 21 August 2021.

"History of Tables of Distribution and Allowances (TDA) Units." *US Army Center of Military History.* Prepared by DAMH-FPO. 30 May 1995. history.army.mil/html/forcestruc/tda-ip.html. Accessed 21 August 2021.

"Hughes OH-6 Cayuse." *Wikipedia.* Updated 23 August 2021. en.wikipedia.org/wiki/Hughes_OH-6_Cayuse. Accessed 23 August 2021.

"Income in 1969 of Families and Persons in the United States, Report Number P60–75." *US Census Bureau.* December 14, 1970, Revised 9 April 2018. census.gov/library/publications/1970/demo/p60-75.html#:~:text=The%20median%20income%20of%20all,median%20income%20of%20about%20%248%2C600. Accessed 16 August 2021.

"LCM-8." *Wikipedia.* Updated 2 August 2021. en.wikipedia.org/wiki/LCM-8#:~:text=The%20LCM%2D8%20(%22Mike, Vietnam%20War%20and%20subsequent%20operations.&text=The%20acronym%20stands%20for%20%22Landing,%22Lima%20Charlie%20Mike%22. Accessed 21 August 2021.

"M-61 Fragmentation Grenade." *US Grenades WW II and After.* 21 April 2021. inert-ord.net/usa03a/usa3/m61/index.html. Accessed 23 August 2021.

"Marston Mat." *Wikipedia.* Updated 10 June 2021. en.wikipedia.org/wiki/Marston_Mat. Accessed 21 August 2021.

"McDonnell Douglas F-4 Phantom II." *Vietnam Combat Aviation Resource Guide.* Warbirds Resource Group. n.d. vietnam.warbirdsresourcegroup.org/f4phantom-specifcations.html. Accessed 21 August 2021.

Meeks, Tom. "AH-1G "Cobra" Gunship." *Centaurs in Vietnam.* n.d. centaursinvietnam.org/History/ihistoryEqAir5.html. Accessed 21 August 2021.

"M18 Claymore mine." *Wikipedia.* Updated 14 August 2021. en.wikipedia.org/wiki/M18_Claymore_mine. Accessed 25 August 2021.

"M18 smoke grenade." *Wikipedia.* Updated 26 July 2021. en.wikipedia.org/wiki/M18_smoke_grenade. Accessed 25 August 2021.

"M134 GAU-17 Gatling Gun." *Military.com.* n.d. military.com/equipment/m134-gau-17-gatling-gun. Accessed 21 August 2021.

"Mk 2 Grenade." *Wikipedia.* Updated 31 July 2021. en.wikipedia.org/wiki/Mk_2_grenade. Accessed 21 August 2021.

"Monthly Summary January 1970." Texas Tech University's The Vietnam Center and Sam Johnson Vietnam Archive. MACV Office of Information. Document Number 7390206001 in the John M. Shaw Collection. Updated 23 February 2005. vva.vietnam.ttu.edu/images.php?img=/images/739/7390206001a.pdf. Accessed 22 August 2021.

Olson, James S., ed. *In Country: The Illustrated Encyclopedia of the Vietnam War.* Metro Books. 2008.

O'Neill, John E., and Jerome R. Corsi. *Unfit for Duty: Swift Boat Veterans Speak Out Against John Kerry.* Regnery Publishing. 2004.

Owen, J. I. H., ed. *Brassey's Infantry Weapons of the World*; compiled by: Gerald Wyndham, Stanley Parr, James Dowdall, and John Marriott; Advisory eds., Major S. R. Elliott CD and R. H. F. Cox TD; Bonanza Books; 1978; New York.

Porter, Donald. "In Vietnam, These Helicopter Scouts Saw Combat Up Close." *Air Space Magazine,* September 2017. airspacemag.com/military-aviation/snakes-loaches-180964341/. Accessed 21 August 2021.

Ronkov, Richard. "Owens, Jesse (1913–1980)." *World Book Encyclopedia.* World Book Inc. 1991. pp. 890–91.

Stanton, Shelby L., Captain US Army, Retired. *Vietnam Order of Battle: A Complete Illustrated Reference to US Combat and Support Forces in Vietnam 1961–1973;* Foreword by General William C. Westmoreland, US Army, Retired. Stackpole Books. 2003.

US Congress, Senate, "Mr. John Kerry Testimony at Hearings before the Committee on Foreign Relations," *United States Senate, 92nd Cong.,* 1st sess., 22 April 1971. Government Printing Office, 1971. lschs.org/cfhttp.cfm?script=extensions/includes/resource/resourcecontent.cfm&pageid=608&rid=271. Accessed 23 August 2021.

Works Cited

"White Phosphorus Munitions." *Wikipedia*. Updated 15 July 2021. en.wikipedia.org/wiki/White_phosphorus_munitions. Accessed 21 August 2021.

"Who Was Rube Goldberg?" *Rube Goldberg: The World of Hilarious Invention*. n.d. https://www.rubegoldberg.com/rube-the-artist/. Accessed August 25, 2021.

Wilkinson, Silvia. "Breedlove, Craig." *World Book Encyclopedia*. World Book Inc. 1991. p. 603.

Index

"ABC" (song) 126
Aberle, CWO 2 Robert 177, 208
Abraham Lincoln Presidential Museum 1
ace of spades 118, 127
Active Guard Reserve 182, 221
adjutant general 221
adjutant general corps branch 37
administrative officer 182
Advisory Team 51 209
Advisory Team 58 32, 174, 207, 209
Advisory Team 73 15, 19, 24, 26, 29, 31, 36, 40, 56, 67, 104, 122–123, 155–159, 171, 174, 177–178, 181, 191, 207, 211, 217, 220
Advisory Teams 54 and 55 149
AFVN (Armed Forces Vietnam Network) 74, 108, 155, 185
"Agency" *see* CIA
Agent Orange 22, 97, 114, 157, 185, 190, 216
Aid Station 28, 29, 186
AIK (Assistance in Kind) 68, 81–83, 111–112, 144–145, 148, 150, 157, 186, 214
Air America 124, 148
Air Defense Artillery branch 37
Air Medal 173
aircraft: A-1E Skyraiders 38, 119–120, 185, 191, 194, 198; B-17 Flying Fortress 122; C-7 Caribou 19, 126, 188; C-123 Provider 17, 187; C-130 Hercules 133, 147–148, 188, 220; Cessna 305 187, 210; F-4 Phantom 191, 198–199; L-19 52, 187; O-1/"Birddog" 33–34, 38, 41–43, 45, 51, 64–65, 94, 105, 186–187, 191, 194, 197, 202, 210; Pan Am 727 124; PC-6 Porter 124; "Puff the Magic Dragon"/AC-130 133, 188, 197, 200, 215, 220; "Spooky"/ AC-47/C-47 Dakota 80, 133, 197, 203, 215; Stukas 119
AIT (advanced individual training) 6, 139, 182, 185
Allan, Lt. Virgil 144
Americans 15, 17, 23, 25, 32–34, 43, 46, 49–50, 56–59, 63–64, 66, 73–74, 78, 81–82, 86, 88, 91, 96–97, 103–104, 124–125, 128, 130–132, 134, 137, 145, 150, 153–154, 161–162, 165, 169–170, 172–174, 177, 181, 185, 189, 192, 196, 198–201, 211– 213, 215, 217

ammo bunker 29, 88, 90–91
An, Phung Tho Trung sĩ 36, 181
An, Trung úy 98, 109–110, 121, 130, 153–155, 157, 167, 171, 177, 220, 223
An Xuyen Province 22, 208
Anchorage, AK 162
Andrews, Capt. Dave 37, 69
Animals (music group) 74
áo dài (Vietnamese dress) 82
Apollo 11 (NASA moon landing) 12
Ard, Sgt. 1C Howard 47, 99, 138, 177
Arkansas 181
armor branch 26, 38, 153, 189, 210
army nurse 1, 143
army officer's register 174
Army Ranger 216
Army Reserves 178–180
Army Times (magazine) 74
Army War College 182
ARVN (Army of the Republic of Vietnam) 11, 14, 17, 22–24, 45–46, 52–53, 61, 66, 78, 82, 84, 86, 95, 128, 131, 144, 155–157, 160, 165, 170–171, 177, 185–186, 192–194, 198, 200, 204, 209, 212–213, 217–218
assistant inspector general 182
Australia 179
AWOL (Absent Without Leave) 125, 144
Ayers, Bill 170

B-girls 111, 217
Ba Mười Ba (33) Beer 30, 52, 70, 90, 99, 110, 175, 186, 216
Ba Xuyen Province 22, 86
Bac Lieu Province 86–87, 151
Bắc Việt (derisive term for NVA soldiers) 155
bananas 21
Bangkok, Thailand 217
base pay 70
basic allowance for quarters 70, 186
basic allowance for subsistence 70, 186, 214
basic training 6, 15, 32, 81, 138, 186, 210
battalion commander 121, 182
Battle of Ap Bac 45
Battle of Kien Long 212

229

Index

Battle of the Bulge 22, 139
battlefield zero 32, 77, 187, 210
BDA (bomb damage assessment) 187
Beatles (English band) 207
betel nut 135
Bien Hoa Airport, South Vietnam 161–162
Biggs Field, TX 12
Binh Long, South Vietnam 218
Binh nhất (Vietnamese private first class) 99, 187
Binh nhì (Vietnamese private) 46, 160, 187
Binh Thuy, South Vietnam 79, 143, 160
Bish, Staff Sergeant 10, 90
Black Label Beer 70, 90
Black Market 76, 196
Blackstone, Harry 135, 219
blasting caps 88, 91–93, 216–217
Booz Allen Hamilton 180
BOQ (bachelor officer quarters) 15–16, 18, 29, 81–83, 111, 150, 161, 187
"Born to Be Wild" (song) 8
Boston, MA 25, 220
Bowie knife 48
"A Boy Named Sue" (song) 112
branch assignments' officer 11, 182
Breedlove, Craig 44, 211
Bridges, Lloyd 215
Bronze Star 30, 41, 173–174, 177, 181, 187, 207, 220
Bryson, Lt. Rob 91, 93
Buddhism (religion) 23, 58, 85, 314, 188, 193, 213
Bugansky, Capt. Jim 42, 53, 177
Bundons, Capt. Al 46, 177
bunker (US) 27–29, 46–47, 56, 75–76, 88, 90–91, 143, 147–148, 201, 211
Burg, Lt. Rick 29–30
Burns, Ken 1
Burr, Raymond 75

C-4 87–92, 188, 193, 195, 216
C-rations 45, 48, 52, 101, 130–131, 140, 189–190
Ca Mau 208
cà phê sua nong (Vietnamese coffee) 109
Cam Ranh Bay 144
Camaro 8, 10–12, 70, 163
Cambodia 20, 23, 34, 78, 99, 120, 155, 171–172, 210, 220
Can Tho, South Vietnam 17–18, 24, 63, 66–68, 79, 91, 106–107, 112, 116, 126, 142–145, 151 159–161, 208; Airfield 17, 112, 144, 160
Canada 167, 169, 179
Cao Đài (religion) 23, 188
CARE Package 71, 72, 188, 214
Carlile, Lt. Rick 41, 57–63, 66–68, 81, 101, 113, 161, 177, 213, 219
CAS (close air support) 118–119, 153, 189, 191, 213, 218

Cash, Johnny (singer) 112
Cassidy, Maj. Gen. Patrick F. 5, 178
Catch 22 (novel) 150
Catholic (religion) 10, 23, 97, 108, 138, 180–181
champagne 13, 152, 163
"Charlie" (VC) 77, 127, 156, 188, 205, 214
Chicago, IL 12–13, 138, 163
chicken 86, 101, 135–136, 150
chicory coffee 8
chief of army personnel operations 1
Chiêu hoi ("Open Arms" program) 25, 99, 188, 209
Childress, Capt. Richard 37–38, 67, 123, 152, 178
China 23, 27, 84–85, 123, 185, 196, 217
Cho Lon, South Vietnam 36, 112, 217
chopsticks 101, 136
Christianity (religion) 188
Christmas 47, 107–108, 123
Chuẩn úy (Vietnamese Officer Cadet (Aspirant)) 58, 60, 62, 188
CIA 34, 40, 52, 124, 185
CIB (Combat Infantryman's Badge) 5, 30, 107, 127, 173–174, 188, 207
CIDG (Civilian Irregular Defense Group) 188, 216
CIF (central issue facility) 15, 32, 81, 112, 159, 188
Civil War 5
"clacker" 88–89, 189, 195, 215–216
Clark Air Force Base, Philippines 14, 124
Class A agent 115–116, 217
Class 516-A 7
Cô Yen 71
Coco Palms Hotel 110
coconuts 21, 54, 135
cognac 80
Coke 111, 217
Colombia, South America 179, 221
Colorado 179
Colt Firearms Company 117
Columbia Law School 25
Combat (TV show) 5, 207
combat arms 33, 107, 131, 189, 209–210
Command and General Staff College 182
commo section 91
Communications/Command bunker 29, 114, 218
communications security advisor 33
Company C, 16th Engineer Battalion 9–10
Confucianism (religion) 188
Constitution of the United States 7
Continental Hotel 82
CORDS (Civil Operations and Revolutionary Development Support) 30, 33–34, 38, 189–190, 193, 208, 218
CQ (charge of quarters) 140, 148, 158–159, 189, 219
Cronkite, Walter 112

Index

cryptosporidiosis (disease) 143
Cuba 159

DA Form 71 207
DA Form 1594 Staff Duty Officer's Journal 77, 79, 106
Da Lat, South Vietnam 97
Đại úy (Vietnamese captain) 62–63, 189–190
danseur 41
Dao, Brig. Gen. Le Minh 171, 178
Datsun 125
Davenport, IA 200, 207
"Davids" 34, 39, 190
Delaware 51
Democrat 69
Denver, CO 175
Department of Defense 6
Department of the Army 115
Deputy CORDS for IV Corps 122
deputy district senior advisor 32, 34
det cord 87–88, 91–92, 190, 215
Dexedrine tablet/anti-drowsiness tablets/pep pills 59, 63, 213
Diamond Head 125
Diaz, Lt. Ralph 8–9, 178
Diem, Pres. Ngo Dinh 22, 58, 190
Dietze, Lt. Knute 8, 178
"Different Drum" (song) 10
director of Asian Affairs 178
director of plans, operations and training (G-3) 182
director of resource management 182
Distinguished Flying Cross 105
Distinguished Service Cross 220
district team 24, 29, 38, 44, 68, 78, 80, 87, 115, 123, 144, 157, 203, 212
DMAC (Delta military assistance command) 17, 190, 193, 208, 218
Donaway, Lt. Robert 41, 57, 99, 138, 178
Dorhn, Bernadine 170
DPSA (deputy province senior advisor) 47, 50, 190
A Dragon Lives Forever (book) 174
DSA (district senior advisor) 33, 38, 46, 123, 152, 191, 193
Duc Long 17, 24, 38, 40–41, 44, 90, 110, 123, 127, 132, 156, 190, 213, 216
ducks 86, 101, 135
"dustoff"/MEDEVAC 3, 17, 33, 51, 62–63, 78–79, 81, 101–105, 111, 124, 128–129, 143, 159–160, 172–173, 191–192, 199, 202, 204–205, 208, 211, 213, 216
Dykes, Lt. Roger 153

Eagle Flight 140, 142–143, 191, 219
Eakin Compound 18
East Coast (USA) 180–181
East Moline, IL 158, 162, 200, 207
Easter Bunny 29

Eastman, Lt. George "Jug" vi, 28, 38–39, 60, 64–65, 67, 73, 112, 134, 152, 178, 208
Edford Township 12, 145, 183
eel 135
18th ARVN Division 171
82nd Airborne Division 12
82nd Medical Detachment (Air Ambulance) 79, 129
Eisenhower, Pres. Dwight 12
Emerald Isle 40
Engineer Equipment Officer Course 8
Engineer School (US Army) 8, 219
English 55, 71, 80, 82, 97–98, 141, 189, 198, 214
ETS (expiration term of service) 115
Europe 150, 180
"Eve of Destruction" (song) 9
explosive ordnance disposal (EOD) 40, 62

FAC (forward air controller) 34, 38–39, 41, 45, 51, 53, 56, 65, 105, 112, 118–120, 172–173, 180, 190–191, 198, 211
Facebook 174
family farm 12, 19, 22–23, 61, 65, 87, 106, 108, 129, 138, 145, 166, 180, 182–183, 207, 213, 219, 221
family separation allowance 70, 191
FARC (*Fuerzas Armadas Revolucionarias de Colombia*, Marxist-Leninist guerrilla group) 179, 221
Fayetteville, NC 12–13
FBI 170
ferry 87–90
field artillery branch 37, 39, 42, 179, 189, 192, 202, 210
Fifth U.S. Army 178
50th Regiment, 25th ARVN Division 74
52nd Signal Battalion/detachment 29, 33, 36, 76, 114, 149, 151, 159
Finance Office 215, 217
First Armored Division 9
fish 37, 47, 84, 101, 135, 219
501st Replacement Company 9
flak jacket 56, 91, 154, 192
Flying Wallendas 146
FM 5-34 *Engineer Field Data* 45, 88, 191, 211
Fold3.com 174
Fonda, Jane 169
foosball 109
Fort Belvoir, VA 5–8, 172, 178
Fort Benning, GA 40–41, 209
Fort Bliss, TX 11–12, 48, 74, 172, 210
Fort Bragg, NC 11–12, 15, 21, 51, 74, 80, 135, 137, 172, 192, 196
Fort Campbell, KY 6, 15
Fort DeRussy, HI 125–126
Fort Dix, NJ 181
Fort Holabird, MD 40, 209
Fort Hood, TX 8–11, 36, 90, 144, 172, 210
Fort Leavenworth, KS 182
Fort Leonard Wood, MO 138–139, 181–182, 219

Fort Sam Houston 6, 9, 185
Fort Sill, OK 39, 179
4CV Renault (taxi) 81
416th RF company 140, 142
Fourth Army NCO Academy 9, 172
4th Corps (NVA) 171
Fourth of July 87, 123
free fire zone 94, 122, 192
French 20, 29, 58, 80, 109, 171, 187, 205, 221
French poodle 77
French Quarter 8

Garden Plot 10
general foreman 182
Geneseo, IL 8, 10, 12, 120, 139, 182, 200, 207
Geneseo Republic (newspaper) 72–73 144
Geneva Convention card 15
Gere, Lt. Tim 55
German Sheppard 76
Germany 178, 180, 207, 215
Gideon's (Bible society) 138
Gillis, Frank 34, 38, 142, 145
GIs 111, 116, 124, 147, 217
God 7, 11, 142, 161–162, 165, 173
Goldberg, Rube 117, 217
Golden Gate Bridge 13
Golden Nugget Casino 25, 27
Good Conduct Medal 173, 221
Good Humor man 149
Google 174
Great Wall of China 196
Green Berets/Special Forces 11, 117, 171, 180, 192
grenades: hand 14, 27, 29, 54, 76, 118, 127, 147, 192, 194–196, 216–217, 219; M-26 195; M-61 54, 195; Mark-2 48, 196; smoke 29, 48, 60, 102, 104, 128, 155, 193, 199–200, 202–203, 211–212, 219
Griffiths, Lt. Gene vi, 40–41, 54, 69, 72, 74, 76, 91–93, 50, 124, 147–149, 153, 159, 179
Gulf of Thailand 149
GVN (Government of Vietnam) 77, 84, 108, 130, 137, 171, 177, 188, 192–193, 208–209, 218

H&I (harassment and interdiction) 63–64, 77–79, 106, 132, 193
Haley, SFC William "Wild Bill" 40, 52–53, 57, 84, 152, 172, 179, 217
HAM radio/operators 150–151, 193
Hamilton, George 76, 214
Hanoi, North Vietnam 56, 169
Hargrove, Lt. Tom 174, 179, 221
"Harper Valley PTA" (song) 8
Hau Giang Province 208
Hawaii 110–111, 124–125, 179, 218
heavy weapons' advisor 33
helicopters: AH-1 "Cobra" 106–107, 185–186, 189, 192, 197, 217–219; C&C (Command and Control) 37, 50–51 58, 103–105, 122, 142, 159, 187, 204, 213, 216; CH-47 Chinook 86–87, 107, 130, 188, 215; crews 29, 48, 64–65, 94, 102, 120–121, 157, 159, 190, 208, 217–218; gunship (UH-1C) 50–51, 59, 91, 94, 100, 102, 104–105, 118, 120–121, 141, 153, 157–159, 172, 187, 189, 191–195, 197, 204, 212, 218–219; OH-6/LOH/"Loach" 134, 193, 197–198, 219; OH-58 Kiowa 122, 198, 218; "swing ship" 45, 47, 115, 203, 212; UH-1/"Huey"/"slicks" 48–49, 105, 120–121, 140–141, 156, 190, 192–193, 199, 202, 204–205, 211, 216, 218
Heller, Joseph 150
Henderson, Sgt. Lewis 62–66
Henry County, IL 12
HES (Hamlet Evaluation System) 22, 193, 208
Hickey, Larry vi, 125
Hinesville, GA 179
Hòa Hảo (religion) 23, 58, 99, 158, 193
*hồi chánh*s (VC ralliers to GVN) 23, 124, 193, 218
Holiday Inn 126
"Homeward Bound" (song) 74
Hong Kong 112, 217
Honolulu, HI 14, 125–126
Hope, Bob 82
hostile fire pay 70, 149, 193
"How Much Is That Doggie in the Window" (song) 207
Howard, WO1 Ralph 41–42, 53, 60, 121–122, 149, 179
Hurricane (alcoholic drink) 8
Hussey, Olivia 73

I Corps 16, 194
ice cream 71, 82
II Corps 194, 218
III Corps Headquarters (Fort Hood) 9
III Corps (Vietnam) 194
Illinois 19, 71, 139, 177, 180, 200
Illinois Commerce Commission 183
Illinois National Guard 177, 192, 221
Illinois State Militia 149
India 179
Indy 500 116
infantry branch 15, 25, 30, 36, 40–41, 39, 42, 52, 55, 61–64, 107, 127, 155, 172, 185–186, 189–187, 207, 209–210
inspector general 182
Intel 25, 36, 47, 85, 133–134, 141, 193–194, 198–199
International Harvester/Farmall 6, 108, 181, 191
Interstate 10 9
Islam (religion) 188
IV Corps 17–18, 22, 33, 62, 106, 122, 155, 190, 194, 197, 208, 218
Ivy League 69

Jackson Five (musical group) 126
Jaegers, Lt. Jim 29–30, 53, 179

Index

Jane (Raschke) vi, 167, 182
Japan 29, 58, 67, 162
Jell-O 5
Jessel, George E. 75
Jiffy Pop 71
Johnson, Capt. Ken 55
Johnson, Pres. Lyndon 205
Juarez, Mexico 12
Judaism (religion) 25, 30

Kansas 177
Kauai 110, 125–126
KBA (killed by air) 118–119, 156, 194, 218
Kennedy, Pres. John F. 69, 192
Kent State University 155
Kerry, John 169–170, 221
KIA (killed in action; /"kilos") 41, 45, 64–66, 85, 118, 157, 161, 194, 202, 207, 210, 213
Kien Giang Province 22, 27, 148
Kien Hung 17, 24, 38, 87, 124, 128, 130, 142, 152, 190, 220
Kien Long 17, 24–25, 30, 45–47, 68, 80, 132, 190, 212
Kien Thien 17, 24, 48, 94, 106, 140, 142, 190
Kinh Xa Nõ Canal 24, 209
Kissinger, Secretary of State Henry 157
Kon Tum Province 218
Korea 145
Korean War 11, 22, 48, 74, 119, 139, 148, 179, 185–186, 189, 194–195, 201, 204, 210–211
Kuala Lampur, Malaysia 217

Lackland Air Force Base, TX 144
Lambretta 81
Lancers (wine) 82
Las Vegas, NV 175
Laugh-In (TV show) 8, 220
"Leaving on a Jet Plane" (song) 74
Lee, Lt. Travis 8, 144, 179, 207
leeches 54, 101, 147, 194, 212
Lehigh University 40
LeVasseur, Lt. Col. Thomas 26, 32, 36, 45–46, 55–56, 67–70, 107, 114–115, 123, 127, 133, 147–148, 153–155, 158–159, 179, 209; *see also* province senior advisor
light weapons' advisor 33
Long My 17, 24, 30, 43–45, 87, 115, 190, 221
Louisiana 181
Louisiana State University 153
Lutheranism (religion) 138
LZ (landing zone) 49–51, 55, 57–58, 61–62, 64, 67, 86–87, 99–100, 102, 105, 117, 120, 131, 141, 186, 189, 192–194, 202, 213, 216, 218

M&M Enterprises 150
M-7 bayonet 54, 135, 194
M-8A1 steel matting 208
M-80s (fireworks) 87, 190
M-706 Armored Car 78, 196

MAAG (Military Assistance Advisory Group) 32, 196, 208
MACV Headquarters (Pentagon East) 15–16, 69, 81, 111, 124, 150, 161, 188, 193, 196, 198, 207–208
MACV ration card 15, 196
mail 15, 29, 71, 114, 203
malaria 31–32, 210
mangrove 21–22
Manila, Philippines 217
MARS (military auxiliary radio system) 150–151, 196
Marston Mat 200, 208
Marston, NC 200, 208
Martinson, Maj. James 36–37, 58–60, 86–87, 103, 140, 147–148, 154–155
MAT (mobile advisory team) 29, 33, 41, 47, 56–57, 68, 78–79, 90, 115–116, 144, 156, 196, 198, 203, 210, 212
MATA (Military Assistance Training Advisor's Course) 11–12, 25, 121, 196
Mateus (wine) 82
MBA (master of business administration) 182
McCord Air Force Base, WA 204
McCullough, Capt. Howard 37, 48, 49–52, 55, 57, 60, 100, 152, 167, 172, 179, 213
McGinnis, SFC Edward 179, 220
McGuire, Barry 9
McKenzie, Scott 74
McNamara, Secretary of Defense Robert 22, 85
Medford, MA 182
medical advisor 33
medical specialist/medic/corpsman 6, 31, 40, 47, 62, 79, 102, 143, 156, 160, 185–186, 189, 196–197
Mekong Delta 15, 17–18, 20–22, 29, 54, 57, 90, 103–104, 122, 141, 197, 201, 211, 218
Merritt, Bernie 30, 34, 40
mess hall 15, 18–19, 21, 27–29, 31, 33, 36, 56, 66, 70–71, 77, 82, 106, 111, 114, 161, 186, 197, 209, 213–214
mess officer 10
mess sergeant 28, 108
MIA (missing in action) 45, 178, 197
Mickey's Ears 34–35, 106, 140
Midwest (USA) 5, 65, 115, 138, 179–180, 220
"Mike" boats 130, 197
military driver's license 15
military intelligence (MI) 25, 33, 40, 197, 209
military liaison NCO 13
Miller, Lt. Al 30, 46, 179
Minderbinder, Milo 150
Minh, Pres. Ho Chi 39, 56, 121, 155, 212, 221, 223
Minh, *Trung sĩ* 97–98, 109, 177
Mississippi River 207
Missouri 30, 179–180
mobilization planner 182

Moline, IL 3, 7, 12, 163, 200, 207
"monkey bridge" 146
Montreal, Canada 179
Mormon (religion) 41
Morrow, Vic (TV character "SGT Saunders") on *Combat*) 207
mortar attack 45–46, 56, 73, 79, 90, 132–133, 143, 148, 212, 219
motor officer 10
movement specialist 158, 160
MP (military police) 81–82, 111–112, 124, 162, 197
MPC (military payment certificates) 15, 71, 75–76, 124, 150, 197, 199, 202, 217
MR4 (Military Region 4) 190

napalm 119, 191
National Security Council (NSC) 178, 197
Netherlands 179
New England 56, 179
New Orleans, LA 8–9, 178
New Testament 138
New Year's 108, 123
Newsweek (magazine) 74, 214
next of kin notification 15
Nickinovich, Lt. Dave vi, 38, 41, 123, 153–154, 156–157, 179, 220
987th RF Company 54, 55, 96–101, 110, 130, 153, 157, 171
1936 Berlin Olympics 218
1968 Summer Olympics 8
9th Infantry Division 179, 207
nipa palm 21
Nixon, Pres. Richard M. 9; administration 155, 157, 205
Noonan, Lt. Robert "Bob" vi, 38, 40–41, 99, 106–107, 123, 127, 152–154, 156–157, 179, 220
North Carolina 11, 40, 329
Northeast (USA) 40, 69, 179, 181
Northwest (USA) 180
Notre Dame 40
nước mắm (fish sauce) 101, 123, 135–136, 142
NVA (North Vietnamese Army) 22, 56, 108, 132, 155–156, 169, 171–172, 186, 188, 193, 197, 205, 208–210, 213, 221

Oahu 125
"Ode to Billy Joe" (song) 8
OER (officer efficiency report) 37–38, 174
Office of Transportation Policy-International Civil Aviation 179
Officer Candidate School (OCS) 3, 5–9, 39–42, 87–88, 138–139, 143–144, 172, 179, 198, 203, 207, 210, 212, 215, 221
officer of the day 10
O'Hare Airport 5
Ohio 155
OIC (officer in charge) 33, 47, 91
Oklahoma 179
Old Glory 109

Olderson, Capt. Robert "Bob" 39–40, 84, 107, 127, 140–142, 172
Olsen, Norman "Norm" 32–34, 174, 180
113th RF province reconnaissance (recon) company 96–101, 117–118, 171, 199
120th RF company 57–62, 84
120th Transportation company 144
Operation *Cửu Long* (Mekong) 155
operations/intelligence advisor 33
operations' officer 11, 198
operation's order 55
orderly room 19, 21, 29, 108, 140, 151, 158–159, 161, 189, 198, 208, 219
Owens, Jesse 117, 218
Ozark Airlines 12, 163

PA&E (Pacific Architects and Engineers) 29, 56
Pacific Ocean 13, 126
palm trees 21, 135–136, 146
Pat O'Brien's 8
Paulson, SSgt. Dave 36, 180
Pentagon 11, 182, 193, 208
Peoria, IL 208
Perra, Lt. Frank vi, 41, 97, 129–130, 158, 180
personnel specialist 6, 15, 19, 161
Peter Paul and Mary (music group) 74, 219
Pham, *Binh nhất* (bodyguard) 99–100
Philippines 14, 29, 38
Phoenix Program 25, 40, 46, 52, 327, 329, 198, 200, 202, 211; advisor 30, 33, 40, 1 27
Phuong Dinh Province 22
piasters 68, 71, 83, 186, 199, 213–214
Pierre 77
pigs/pork 86, 123, 195
Pima County, AZ 178
pineapples 21, 126, 135
plague shot 12
platoon leader 9, 86, 199, 203, 207
platoon sergeant 10, 90, 147, 203
Playboy (magazine) 73–74, 112, 156
Pobanz, Bill 144–145, 180
Poipu Beach 110
Popular Forces (PF) 26, 39–40, 47, 51–52, 79, 87–89, 91, 93, 95–96, 101, 106–107, 128–130, 140–142, 156–157, 174, 196, 198–199, 201, 211
post-traumatic stress disorder (PTSD) 166, 200
PRC-25 radio 43, 91, 100, 104, 199, 211, 215
PRC-77 radio 104, 199, 211
prisoner of war (POW) 22, 112, 141–142, 178, 199, 208, 219
process engineer 182
Proof of Life (movie) 221
prostitution 111
Protestant chaplain 138,
province agriculture advisor 33, 153, 221
province assistant Phoenix program advisor 25

province assistant RF/PF advisor 39, 107, 127, 153
province engineer advisor 26, 30, 33, 86, 174, 199
province Phoenix program advisor 25
province senior operations'/training advisor 37
province reconnaissance company *see* 113th RF Company
PRU (provincial reconnaissance unit) 40, 52, 98, 200, 202, 211
PSA (province senior advisor) 20, 26, 28, 34, 41, 47, 50, 77, 154, 179, 190, 193, 200, 208, 220; *see also* Lt. Col. LeVasseur, Thomas
PSP (perforated steel planking) 27, 45–46, 56, 65, 114, 129, 148, 158, 200, 208
pun ji stakes 79, 85, 129, 200, 218
Purple Heart 67, 177, 207
PX (post exchange) 21, 28–29, 36, 70–71, 112, 200
PZ (pick-up zone) 51, 60, 87, 121, 186, 192, 194, 200, 202, 213, 216

Quad Cities 7, 200, 207
Quartermaster Corps branch 153, 200

R&R (rest and relaxation) 110–111, 124- 127, 200, 217
Rach Gia, South Vietnam 148
Rach Giao Du River 106
Rach Nuoc Trong River 140
radio relay 43–45, 91, 104, 210–211
Rameriz, SFC Ruffino 31, 142, 210
Raschke, Betty (mother) 7, 8, 72, 115, 308
Raschke, Don (brother) 220
Raschke, Ed (brother) 12
Raschke, Edward (grandfather) 10, 138
Raschke, Goldie (grandmother) 10, 72, 108, 138
Raschke, Jill (daughter) 182
Raschke, John (son) 174, 182
Raschke, Lt. John 8, 54, 69, 73, 92, 155, 174
Raschke, Marvin (father) 7–8, 149, 163, 182, 221
Raschke, Ryan (son) 182
Raschke, Tom (son) 182
Ratdog 76, 133
RC-292 antenna 45, 201, 211
Reagan, Pres. Ronald 178
Recondo Teams 117
Red Cross 101, 129, 158–160
Regional Forces (RF) 26, 39–40, 47, 51–52, 59–60, 62, 79, 84, 86–87, 91–93, 95, 100–101, 104, 106, 118, 120, 125, 130, 140–142, 153, 160–161, 174, 189, 199, 201, 204, 211; advisor 33, 174, 178, 199
Regular Army 37, 200, 211
Republicans 69
Rhesus monkey (Bridgette) 123, 138
Rhode Island 22

rice whiskey 47, 80
river boat advisor 33, 117, 217
roast beef 28
Rock Island, IL 6, 182, 191, 200, 207
rocket pod 91–94, 187, 210
Romeo and Juliet (movie) 73
ROTC (Reserve Officer Training Corps) 25, 37, 41, 153, 201, 207, 209, 211
"round eyed" 73, 75, 143, 201, 214
Rowe, Lt. James N. 208
RPAC 86, 215
RTO (radio telephone operator) 33, 78, 128, 131, 141, 152, 189, 200–201, 212, 214
Russia 215

S-1 7, 32, 66, 201, 210
S-2 25, 32, 36, 55, 149, 201, 210
S-3 32, 36, 55, 150, 194, 201, 210; advisor 77, 198–199, 209
S-4 32, 66, 201, 210
S-5 Civil Affairs 32, 37, 40, 188, 201, 210–211
Saigon, South Vietnam 14, 22–23, 32, 36, 8, 27, 30, 41, 45, 55, 68, 71, 81, 83–84, 107, 111–112, 124, 144–145, 150–151, 158–161, 163, 188, 192, 194, 208, 215, 217–218
St. John's Lutheran Church 107
St. Louis, MO 175
Saint Malachy's Catholic Church 10
Salem cigarettes/cigarettes 54, 70, 96, 100, 110, 112, 117, 150, 214
Sampans 47, 51, 58, 122, 134, 137, 146, 188, 202, 212, 219
San Antonio, TX 6, 144,
"San Francisco" (song) 74, 214
San Francisco, CA 13, 137, 162–163
Sands, Capt. Charles "Charlie" 66, 116, 180
Sands of Iwo Jima (movie) 147
Scandinavia 40
SDO (staff duty officer) 77–79, 331
Sea Hunt (TV show) 88, 215
seasons: dry 22, 91, 93, 97, 104, 110, 114, 116–117, 128, 135, 137, 167, 191, 197; rainy/monsoons 14, 19, 22, 27, 30, 51, 63, 71, 104, 137, 191, 197
Second Armored Division 9
2nd Battalion 123rd Field Artillery 182
2nd Battalion 31st Infantry, 21st ARVN Division 80, 86, 155, 209
Secretary of State/State Department 34, 38, 40, 170, 178–179
Senate Foreign Relations Committee 221
"Sergeant Striker" (movie character in *Sands of Iwo Jima*) 147
Servicemen's Group Life Insurance (SGLI) 15, 70, 202
7-Up (soda) 70, 110, 113 123, 202–203
Sherman, Gen. William Tecumseh 119
Shieldes, Capt. George "Buddy" 38, 152, 180
"shitters" 137, 143

236　Index

"Shotgun" 33–34, 38, 41–42, 51, 56, 76, 105, 118, 149, 172–173, 202, 211
Shrapnel 27, 46, 56, 192
shrimp 110, 142
Sidney, Australia 217
siesta 60, 76, 121, 136, 142, 202, 211, 213–214, 218
Signal Corps branch 36
Silver Star 40–41, 15, 61, 63, 67, 109, 154, 157, 187, 202, 207, 220
Simon and Garfunkel (musical duo) 74
Singapore 217
SITREP (situation report) 58, 100, 105, 142, 202, 213
Smallwood, Lt. Col. Eugene 74, 180, 214
snake 135, 219
Snake River 34, 57, 59–60, 67, 84, 158
Soaring Sixties 108
Soc Trang, South Vietnam 140
SOI (signal operating instructions) 54, 107, 201, 203, 212, 216
Son, Ông 80, 133, 157, 177, 215
Song, Trung sĩ 97, 114
Sông Cai Lớn River 24, 128, 215
Sông Cai Tu River 24, 87, 209
SOP (standing operating procedures) 93, 200–201, 203, 212
South (USA) 178, 180–181
South China Sea 162
Southeast (USA) 178
Southeast Asia 155, 178
Southwest (USA) 179–180
Soviet Union 121, 169, 179, 186, 201–202, 204, 211–213, 215, 217–220
Speck, Maj. George 53, 180
"The Spider and the Fly" 111
Spirit of America (Craig Breedlove's car) 211
Springfield, IL 175, 182
Springfield, MA 40
squad leader 9, 203
squid 43, 110
squirrels 219
Stars and Stripes (newspaper) 74
steaks 71, 82, 150
"steel pot" (helmet) 48, 54, 56, 75, 82, 84, 98, 148, 203
Stone Poneys (musical group) 10
Students for a Democratic Society 170
subsector (district) 23–24
Sue (Raschke) 10, 72, 125, 163, 182
Sunday School 138, 163
Susi (dog) 76–77

TA-312 telephone 25, 27, 151, 203
Table of Distribution and Allowances (TDA) 32–34, 192, 204, 210
Table of Organization and Equipment (TO&E/) 46, 191, 204
TAC officer 6, 8, 179, 203, 207
Taipei, Taiwan 217

Tan Son Nhut Airport 14–15, 17, 19, 81, 83, 106, 111, 124, 126, 161, 196, 207
Tang 71
Taoism (religion) 186
Taylor, Capt. Howard 38–39, 67, 73, 112–113, 134, 180–181
tennis 21, 29, 76, 98, 149
Tet 123–124, 204
Tet 1968 112, 215, 217
Texas 11, 178–179
Texas A&M 38, 221
Thanksgiving 106
Thiếu tá (Vietnamese major) 150, 190, 204
Thiếu úy (Vietnamese second lieutenant) 99, 192, 204
3rd Surgical Hospital 142–144, 160, 219
303rd VC Main Force Battalion 55, 66
Thu Pho Racetrack 217
Tiger cigarettes 214
Time (magazine) 74, 214, 156
Title 32, United States Code 221
TOC (tactical operation center) 34, 36, 43–44, 58, 62–64, 66, 77–80, 86–87, 89–91, 93, 101–106, 122, 128, 131, 138, 142, 151–152, 156, 159, 202, 204, 210–211, 213, 216–217
Tokyo, Japan 217
Tolson, Staff Sergeant 117, 217
Tomlin, Lily (TV character "Ernestine" on *Laugh-In*) 220
Top of the Mart Restaurant 8
top secret 11, 133
tracers 112, 120–122, 133, 141, 204, 217
Travis Air Force Base, CA 12–13, 162–163, 204, 214
Trinh Sàt (reconnaissance) 204, 216
Trung sĩ (Vietnamese sergeant) 88–89, 110, 204, 215
Trung sĩ nhất (Vietnamese sergeant first class) 97, 204
Trung úy (Vietnamese first lieutenant) 54, 189, 204, 212
Tucson, AZ 175
Tufts University 182–183
29th Evacuation Hospital 66–67, 219
20-ton crane 89–90
2½-ton trucks 19, 116
273rd VC Regiment 132
2001 A Space Odyssey (movie) 12
221st Reconnaissance Airplane company 33, 41

U-Haul 10
U-Minh 21–22, 25, 34, 45, 132, 208
United States 14, 22, 27, 29, 51, 55–56, 67–68, 70, 76, 78, 80, 108, 110, 112, 114, 123, 126, 133, 135, 143, 145, 150, 155–156, 159–160, 167–168, 170, 172, 176, 178–183, 186–190, 194–196, 197–200, 202, 204–205, 208–210, 213, 215–218
United States Agency for International Development (USAID) 180, 205, 209, 223

Index 237

US Air Force (USAF) 18, 34, 38–40, 42, 45, 56, 65, 80, 113, 119, 139, 144, 147, 162, 178, 180, 188, 190, 197–198, 213, 215–216, 220
US Army 3, 6–7, 9–10, 18, 22, 28–29, 31–33, 36, 38–41, 45–46, 54–56, 58–59, 69, 71, 74, 77, 90, 95, 97–100, 105, 108, 115, 120, 123, 138, 170–171, 174, 177–178, 180, 182, 186–188, 190, 194–198, 204, 207–210, 213, 217–218, 220
US Army Engineers 7–10, 18, 22, 45, 69, 86, 89–90, 107, 114, 130, 150, 172–173, 178, 182, 191, 199
United States Attorney's Office 183
US Coast Guard 198
US Embassy 112, 193, 208, 215
US Marine Corps 29, 40, 132, 173, 194, 198
US Navy: 132, 149, 170, 198; Riverine forces 18, 149; Seabees 27; SEALs 18, 34, 40, 52, 117, 202; swift boat 169
US Senate 169–170, 223
University of Illinois 182
University of Rhode Island 41
University of Vermont 37
University of Washington 180
USO (United Service Organization) 28, 75, 82, 219
Utah 41

vacation Bible school 138
Van Blarcum, SFC John W. 56–58, 60–61, 63–65, 181
Van Buren Street Military Induction Station 138
Vann, John Paul 122, 218
vector control officer 10
Vi Thanh: airfield 19–20, 24, 32, 34, 43, 45, 48, 64–66, 77, 83, 86, 89, 91, 94, 122, 134, 140–141, 147–148, 151, 158–160, 208; compound 18–19, 21, 24–26, 29–30, 31, 33, 36, 40–41, 44, 47, 53, 56, 66, 68, 70–71, 73, 76–77, 87, 91, 94, 110, 114–115, 117, 122, 132–133, 138, 144–145, 148–151, 153, 158, 159–160, 165, 173, 190, 209–210, 214, 216, 218; downtown 50, 108–109, 231; hospital 79, 120, 128, 143, 145, 159
Victoria, TX 178
Viet Cong (VC): assassin 16, 161; attacks 79–80, 87–88, 140, 280; barber 138, 219; bunker/fighting position 67, 118–120, 147, 193, 213; casualties 45, 60, 64, 66, 85–86, 118, 132, 153, 156, 213, 215, 218; "dam" 86–87; documents 25; double agent 47; flag 44, 86, 133, 150, 223; governance 23–24; infrastructure 24–25, 40, 52, 198, 200, 202, 205, 209, 211; main force battalion 55, 86, 157, 196, 213; mine/minefield 84, 101, 121, 124, 156, 165, 181, 192, 218; money 223; propaganda 25; sappers 79, 133; sniper 44–45, 67, 119, 133, 165, 213, 221; tactics 112, 197; unit 57, 60, 84, 86, 94, 117, 141, 153; weapons 117–118

Viet Minh 21, 58, 205
Vietnam: service 167–168; war protester 1
Vietnam Memorial Wall 106, 177–181
Vietnam Veterans' Against the War 156, 169
Vietnam War Memorial Statue 82
Vietnam: artillery 22, 65, 51, 57, 60–61, 64, 77–78, 80, 103, 119, 153, 157, 215; backseater/artillery spotter 38, 41–42, 51, 60, 186–187, 202, 210; "boat person" 1; bunker/fighting position 23, 63–64, 79; civilian driver 14, 161; civilians 14, 23, 46, 62–64, 68, 78, 88, 93, 109, 112, 124, 131, 137, 177, 213–214; command group/command element 48, 58, 62–64, 103–104, 117–118, 121, 189, 212, 214; cooks 28, 108; culture 11, 66, 137, 170, 172–173; district chief 45, 190–192; engineers 86–87; history 11, 15, 19, 171, 173; instructors 12, 170; interpreter 36, 46, 48, 57, 59, 61, 86–89, 96–98, 100–101, 130–131, 141, 158; language 12, 160; language training 11–12, 37, 172; Marines 132, 171; medic 62, 101, 71, 159, 189, 212; National Police 24, 112, 150; outpost 79–80, 106–107, 116, 128–131, 140–142, 157, 191, 198, 200, 204, 214–215, 217, 219; peasant farmers 23–24, 58, 63, 74, 78, 84–85, 121, 135, 196; province chief 90, 124, 148, 171, 192, 200, 211, 218; province headquarters 24, 56, 90–91, 156, 216; Public Works 29, 38, 80, 133, 157, 199; rangers 171; restaurant 81–82, 109–110, 126, 175, 211; security guard 14, 122, 128, 210; special forces 171; vendors 24, 46, 66, 68, 71, 80, 82, 84, 112, 199
Vietnamese Advisor's and Vietnamese Language School 3, 74
Vietnamese Air Force (VNAF) 38, 119, 156, 205
Vietnamese Cross of Gallantry 173, 220
Vietnamization 24, 34, 78, 120, 142, 156, 205
volleyball 21, 114

Waikiki Beach 125
"walk in the sun" 56, 94, 101, 105, 132, 155, 165, 167, 205
Walker, SFC George 138, 156–157, 181
Wallace Theater 5, 7
Warrant Officer Candidate Program 41
Washington, Pres. George 51
Washington, DC 7–8, 177, 174–175, 177–181
Washington National Airport 7–8
watermelons 21, 135
Wayne, John 5
Waynesville, MO 219
"We Gotta Get Out of this Place" (song) 74
weapons NCO advisor 33
weapons: AK-47 61, 102, 117, 186, 202, 213–214; B-40 201, 211; BAR/Browning automatic rifle 11, 96, 186; Claymore M-18 antipersonnel mine 88–91, 129–130, 189, 195, 216–217; Colt .25 automatic 16, 31,

Index

54, 64, 159, 207; .50 caliber machinegun, M-2 11, 130, 185; .51 caliber (12.7-mm DShK 38/46/ heavy) machinegun 120, 218; 57-mm recoilless rifle, M-8 11, 51, 95–96, 195; German Mauser 84, 215; 60-mm mortar, M-2 11, 96, 189, 195; 75-mm recoilless rifle, Type 52/56 27, 185; 82-mm mortar 46, 90, 185, 212–213; 40-mm cannon 200, 215; 40-mm grenade launcher (M-5 armament subsystem) 120–121, 192, 212, 217; .45 caliber pistol 9, 52, 98, 149, 154, 185, 195, 204, 207; M-1 Carbine 11, 29, 85, 194; M-1 Garand 11, 47, 96, 194; M-3 "Grease" gun 11, 98, 195; M-14 194, 207, 210; M-16 29, 32, 45, 47–49, 51, 53–54, 56, 61, 64, 70, 75, 77, 80, 93, 96, 112, 117, 122, 131–132, 140, 142, 150, 154, 186–187, 189, 194, 196, 210, 213; M-20 recoilless rifle 185; M-60 machinegun 48, 102, 120, 186, 189–190, 195–196; M-72 LAW 189, 195, 216; M-79 Grenade Launcher 154, 189, 195, 220; mini-gun 80, 120, 133–134, 186, 192, 197, 200, 203, 212, 215, 217; 105-mm howitzer 51, 57, 60, 132, 192, 214; 122-mm rocket 194, 209, 217; 155-mm howitzer 132; RDP 7.62x39-mm light machinegun 100, 214; RPG (rocket propelled grenade) 44, 201, 211; SKS 50, 85, 155, 202, 214, 220; .30 caliber machinegun 11, 82; Thompson sub-machinegun 11, 204; TOW (tube-launched, optically tracked, wired guided) missile 186, 217; 20-mm cannon 119, 186, 200; 2.75" rocket 42, 60, 65, 91, 94, 122, 187, 191, 202, 210

Weather Underground 170
Weiner, Capt. Harvey vi, 25- 27, 30–31, 40–41, 44, 47, 52, 54, 66–67, 69, 72, 74, 76, 81–83, 110, 112, 124, 125, 220, 153, 181–182, 209–210, 220
West Point (United States Military Academy) 14, 66, 200
Western (USA) 179
Western Illinois University 182
whiskey 111
White House 178
White Pages.com 174
Whiting, Leonard 73
WIA (wounded in action; "whiskeys") 45, 60, 62–64, 66, 85, 96, 98, 101, 104, 160, 178, 202, 205, 212–213
"Wikkey" Coke 111, 217
Wilkinson, Lt. Chauvin vi, 152–153, 181
World War I 207
World War II 11, 22, 46, 48, 22, 119, 149, 179, 181, 185–186, 189, 194–195, 201, 204, 211, 214–215

x-ray technician 6
Xuan Loc, South Vietnam 171

Year of the Dog 123
Yippies 170
Young, Lt. Stephen 41, 57–60, 66, 81, 112, 138, 157, 161, 181

Zellefrow, S4C Mal vi, 20- 21, 36, 181

www.ingramcontent.com/pod-product-compliance
Ingram Content Group UK Ltd.
Pitfield, Milton Keynes, MK11 3LW, UK
UKHW041940140426
5217IPUK00014B/586